REMEDIOS

Also by Aurora Levins Morales: *Getting Home Alive* (with Rosario Morales)

REMEDIOS

Stories of Earth and Iron from the History of Puertorriqueñas

Aurora Levins Morales

Beacon Press Boston

Beacon Press
25 Beacon Street
Boston, Massachusetts 02108-2892
www.beacon.org

Beacon Press books
are published under the auspices of
the Unitarian Universalist Association of Congregations.

03 02 01 00 99 98   8 7 6 5 4 3 2 1

This book is printed on recycled acid-free paper that contains
at least 20 percent postconsumer waste and meets the uncoated paper
ANSI/NISO specifications for permanence of paper as revised in 1992.

Text design by Julia Sedykh
Composition by Wilsted & Taylor Publishing Services

LIBRARY OF CONGRESS CATALOGING-IN-PUBLICATION DATA
Levins Morales, Aurora, 1954–
    Remedios : stories of earth and iron from the history of Puertorriqueñas /
Aurora Levins Morales.
        p.   cm.
    Includes bibliographical references.
    ISBN 0-8070-6516-1 (cloth)
        1. Women—Literary collections.   2. Puerto Rican women—
Literary collections.   3. Women, Crimes against.   I. Title.
    PN6071.W7M67   1998
    808.8'99287—DC21   98-17498

✤ DEDICATORIA

TO LAS MUJERES OF MI FAMILIA.

Aurora "Lola" Moure Diaz
1910–1993

Trying to understand her life got me started on this project. For her laughter and bitterness, melodrama and vulgarity, perfumed soaps and sharp tongue, her self-pity and self-mockery, for the way she screamed with pleasure when we arrived on a visit, and always called me her santa nieta, and for the education she never got. Here, abuela, I kept my promise.

Rosario Morales

For my mother, who taught me to speak truth in my own voice.

If I had not known how to read with the intense pleasure
I copied from you
devouring story and delicious language with equal delight . . .
If you had not given me the alphabet early
so that I had already claimed the page and the teller's voice for my own . . .
If you had not been such a persistent digger for the roots of things
so that I always wanted to know the history and workings
of whatever happened to me . . .

If you had not taught me that life, however horrible,
was always interesting . . .
If you were not so stubborn about getting things right . . .
If you had not taught me the simple and permanent pleasure of color,
pointed out pine against sky, the rich brown on cream of snail shells,
particular bits of the sunset sky to be admired, taught me
the names of your paints and how to mix them,
given me the sixty-four color box of crayons including magenta
I would not be alive today.

If you had not by your outrage, taught me the meaning of solidarity
and fighting against odds,
I would not be here.

I was captured by the enemy,
in secret, without your knowledge,
against your will.
You were not able to prevent it
any more than the mothers with their photographs
carried everywhere on picket signs.
But tell yourself this:
if I had not been your daughter
I would not have survived.

Alicia Raquel Otis Levins

whose birth inspired me to undertake this task, who endured years of waiting for Mami to do just a few more pages before she could play, and who en-
thusiastically cheered me on anyway, requested stories from history on the
way to school, has memorized numerous pieces from Remedios and tells
everyone, including strangers in grocery stores, how proud she is of me.
Also, for Dori, climbing trees, peering into smoky kitchens, listening to

stories, worrying about the outcomes of history, refusing to knuckle under to conquistadores and for Iris Cruz Agostini, companion of my childhood, with whom I made gardens of wild plants, ate stolen tangerines, and told stories.

I thank the Spirit who gave me life and made me a storyteller in times of danger, courage, and possibility.

CONTENTS

ABUELAS

DISCOVERY

HURACÁN: 1492–1600

JENJIBRE: 1600–1699

PARTERAS: 1700–1798

LAZOS: 1798–1898

AGUACERO: 1899–1929

DERRUMBE: 1930–1954

AGRADECIMIENTOS

Researching and writing a book like *Remedios* is something that happens only in community. As I labored to make the work of Puerto Rican women visible, to unearth the names of women deemed unimportant by the writers of official histories, to reveal relationships that have been ignored or denied, I have thought about all those who have contributed in various ways to my own work. Many people supported and inspired me through the process of making this book. Some are people whose names I will never know, whose faces in a crowd responded to my stories and reminded me they were necessary. Some are long dead women and men who left some fragment of accomplishment, courage, or yearning behind them for me to find just when I needed it. Others are central people in my life whose contributions to this and every other project I undertake are far too deep, wide, rich, and complex to fully acknowledge in a few sentences.

I thank everyone who has believed in me, challenged me, given me scraps of stories, names, books, told me to keep going, reminded me how difficult and rewarding my work is, found paid work that helped support me, fed me, cheered every small milestone, run errands for me, and loved me unstintingly throughout the last seven years. I thank the following people in particular:

My mother, Rosario, is the best imaginable writer's companion. She knows when to be bracing and when to oooh and aaah, asks the right questions, and cries at all the good parts. I called her hundreds of times during this process, to share a tentative new idea or exciting discovery, for encouragement and help in figuring out what was wrong when I got stuck. Gracias, Mami. I thank my father, Richard, for making me fall in love with history and story-telling, for being so smart about complexity and so generous and respectful about people, for being willing to hear all the gory details of the abuse I suffered as a child and ask intelligent questions about it, and for his profound trust in humanity's capacity to figure things out; my brother Ricardo for gossiping about the last several thousand years with me, sending me irresistible historical tidbits about ancient alliances, uprisings, and common sense and getting me hooked on the history of food, for being available to talk shop as another artist activist, and for asking if he could illustrate *Remedios*; my brother Jandro for believing in my projects and never doubting that I could finance them, for letting me know exactly how important I am to him, and for his skillful and meticulous practical help in administering my complex life.

My daughter Alicia Raquel, who gives me the thumbs up at readings, boasts about me to the world at large, has been giving me encouraging notes and drawings for years, and is an impassioned artist, writer, singer, and person of conscience. My former husband, Jim Otis, co-parent, and compañero of many years, who supported me through hard times and sleepless nights with love and cash and cups of tea, carnations and little notes on the computer, who continues to support and cherish me in many ways.

My beloved husband, Barry, for eighteen years of friendship flowering into passion, delight, and abiding love, for compañerismo, seven-day kisses, deep listening, integrity, shabbat candles, and other sacredness. For the return of joy.

Lori Kandels, witness and advisor on the long journey home from abuse. In her rooms I moved back and forth between my own nightmares and revelations and the web of history, retying broken threads and weaving myself back into wholeness. For her trust in my self-knowledge, the sacred space she held for me so I could do my work, her gentleness, respect, and humor, I hold her name in blessing.

Minnie Bruce Pratt, the dream dissertation advisor, mentor, and ally, for keeping me true to myself, reminding me to trust my writer's process, and laughing at my perfectionist worries. Time after time she reminded me what it was I was doing and that there were people waiting for my work. To Nola Hadley for talking history with me for hours, insisting that I deserve only the best treatment, and for crying all the way through every single time I read the draft aloud to her. Ann Filemyr, her partner Essie Hynes, and their Granny for their home in Ohio and for the stories around the fire, and Ann for her encouraging e-mails. Sandra Harding for guidance, bibliographies, and stimulating correspondence. Yamila Azize for writing the first book on Puerto Rican women's history that I ever read and for numerous resources during the research process. These women formed my doctoral committee at the Union Institute where I researched and wrote *Remedios* as part of my doctoral dissertation.

Becky Logan, for hours and hours and hours of the best talk, for excursions into cemeteries and used bookstores searching for sources, for understanding what I meant at two in the morning and always being fascinated, for asking great questions, always letting me know that being interested in everything is completely reasonable, and not letting me feel alone with the vastness of history. Deb Shultz for shop talk, validation, visits, mutual support around disability, and humor when it was urgently needed. Liza Fiol Matta for her excitement, opportunities to read work in progress to her students at Hunter College, and a place to stay in the Village. Rina Benmayor for enthusiasm, recipes, contacts, and friendship. Gabriel Melendez for his support and comradeship as my undergraduate advisor, for encouraging me to go to graduate school, and for the phrase a literary distillation of history. Isabel

Velez for long talks, food, and laughter. Jack Delano for documenting the lives of Puerto Rican women and giving me faces to look at while I wrote. To Nelida Perez and the library archives staff at the Center for Puerto Rican Studies.

My aunt Hilda and uncle Cayo for their stories about the family and for sending me the seeds of cilantro and ají. My aunt Lydia and my cousin Sonia for their warmth and pasteles and talk about Spirit. Luisa Teish for the song to Yemayá that I sang through months of long journeys. Las mujeres of the Latina Feminist Scholars group for sabiduría and tales of survival: Luz del Alba Acevedo, Norma Alarcon, Celia Alvarez, Ruth Behar, Rina Benmayor, Norma Cantu, Daisy Coco de Filipis, Gloria Cuadraz, Liza Fiol Matta, Yvette Flores, Inez Hernandez, Iris Lopez, Myrtha Quintanales, Eliana Rivero, Caridad Souza, Pat Zavella.

To Paula Buel, Alison Ehara Brown, Gail Mandella, Miki Kashtan, Nicky Gonzalez Yuen, Victor Lewis, Julie Saxe, Michael Taller, Jenny Ambramson-Helbrun, and to the Re-evaluation Counseling communities as a whole for high quality support and vision.

Tara Kelly and the Client Choice Project staff at the Center for Independent Living in Berkeley. When I lost the use of my hands to Repetitive Stress Injury part way into the writing phase, they obtained a voice-activated computer system for me, on which *Remedios* was written.

Savy Vann Phorn and Thong Soun Phorn who cared for my daughter and cleaned my house so I could read hundreds of books and write this one. Although their grandmothers lived on the other side of the world from mine, this is their story, too.

Ruth Mahaney, Nina Jo Smith, Paul Kivel, Diana Lion, Jill Nagle, Alina Ever, Shakti Butler, Shannon Nelson, my parents and many others who helped me through a major financial and health crisis as I was nearing the end of this project. Jean Caiani at Speak Out! for keeping me somewhat employed on the lecture circuit and coming over to wash dishes when my hands hurt too much. The Davis Putter Fund for helping fund my research for this book during graduate school.

Remedios has grown over many years. I now realize how many earlier projects helped bring this one to fruition. My appreciation to those who worked with me. To Becca Harber and other members of the Chicago Womens Liberation Union in 1970–71, with whom I began thinking about women's history, and with whom I helped produce a local women's radio show. To the Puerto Rican Socialist Party women's study group of 1976–77, with whom I began work on a play about our history: Laura Brainin Rodriguez, Myrtha Chabrán, Myrna Flores, Aixa Gannon, and Cristina Medina. To Helene Lorenz and Kathleen Vickery, with whom I wrote scripts for multimedia theatrical productions about Latin American history that were a seedbed for *Remedios*; to the other members of La Peña Cultural Productions Group and to all those who built and have contributed to La Peña Cultural Center in Berkeley, where this work was done. Thanks also to Max Dashu, whose remarkable slide shows of recaptured women's history from around the world excited me years ago.

✒ PREFACE: YERBA BRUJA

✒ **YERBA BRUJA** (Bryophylum pinnatum, fam. Crasulaceas). **Nombre vulgar: bruja, yerba bruja, life plant.**

Este yerbajo, típico de las regiones cafetaleras sobrevive casi todos los tratamientos eradicación, desde el desyerbo a mano hasta concentraciones altas del yerbicida 2,4-D. El nombre vulgar de bruja hace referencia a su resistencia a los tratos mas crueles que puedan dársele. El tallo carnoso retoña con facilidad; y cada ondulación o mella de las hojas también carnosas, es una region potencial para el desarrollo de una matita, aún guardadas en libros o suspendidas en clavos, las hojas suelen retoñar.

This plant, typical of the coffee regions, survives almost all efforts at eradication, from hand weeding to high concentrations of the herbicide 2,4-D. Its common name, "witch," refers to its resistance to even the most cruel treatment that can be inflicted on it. The fleshy stalk sprouts easily; and every indentation or notch in the leaf, which is also fleshy, is a potential site for the development of a seedling. Even when kept pressed between the pages of books or hung on a nail, the leaves will sprout.

from PLANTAS TROPICALES *by Ismael Vélez*

Bruja. It grew lush and inextinguishable all over the farm, in among the acres of impatiens and coleus, which we called alegría and vergüenza, joy and shame. It grew wild and flourishing in the shade of the coffee forest; in the grassy, weedy clearings blazing with full tropical sun, everywhere. The flowers hung pale and creamy, blushed with purple, long puffy bags filled with air that we kids would pop between our fingers. The thick fleshy leaves we would pin down with a rock or bit of dirt and watch for the "daughters" to spring up from the notched edges of the "mother." Like a coven gathered around their wounded elder, the seedlings always grew in a circle, marking the place where the long decayed leaf had lain.

How the shapes we grow into mark long gone places, residues of ash or blood or iron, broken shards, the print of a foot, a kernel of corn, a fragment of rope. This story is about reading the residues of two intertwining histories. One is the vast web of women's stories spinning out in time and space from the small island of Puerto Rico and encompassing some of the worst disasters to befall humanity: the Crusades; the Inquisition; the African slave trade; the witch persecutions; the European invasions of America, Africa, Asia, and the Pacific; and the enclosure of common lands in Europe itself, that sent a land-starved and dispossessed peasantry out rampaging in the wake of greedy aristocrats, merchants, and generals across the world—and all the plagues, tortures, rapes, famines, and killings that accompanied these events. It is also the story of endless resourcefulness, courage, hard work, defiance, friendship, risk-taking solidarity, and the stubborn refusal to be extinguished.

The second story is exactly the same: invasion, torture, rape, death, courage, solidarity, resistance. It is a much smaller history. It does not sweep across continents and there are only a few people involved, but it has taken up as much space in my life during this writing as the larger weave. On that same land where bruja continues to thrust up seedlings in spite of herbicides, machete blades, and uprooting hands, I was ritually abused by a group of mostly

male adults for a period of about six years.* These men had everything in common with their conquistador ancestors, with their
slave-holding ancestors, with men who tortured as both routine
policy and sadistic pleasure.

It was not my original intention to include this second story
here, but throughout the writing of *Remedios* I was simulta-
neously engaged in two tasks: digging up the histories of Puerto
Rican and related women and their responses to the often brutal
conditions of their lives; and recovering the buried memories of
my own experience of, and responses to, brutality. I used my own
history to help me understand the choices of women long dead,
and increasingly the lives of these women from different centuries
and lands gave me insight and strength to face what had happened
to me. In fact, I began therapy and the graduate school program in
which I researched and wrote *Remedios* within two weeks of each
other. I do not think this was accidental. I created for myself the
possibility of healing my own wounds as I explored the collective
wounds of Puerto Rican women's oppression and the medicinal
powers of history. I became my own laboratory.

It is the laboratory of an herbalist. One who gathers what is
growing wild, and with the help of handed-down recipes, a little
fire and water, and a feel for plants, prepares tinctures, concentrating faint traces of aromatic oils, potent resins capable of stopping a
heart or healing it. The history I gathered here is like the medicinal
plants growing in a long-abandoned garden. The herbal is lost,

---

* Ritual abuse involves the sexual, physical, and psychological torture, usually of
children and women, by a group of adults who use some sort of ritual as an explana-
tion and context for what they do. In my case, this was not a Satanic cult, but a group
using an eclectic blend of old European folk ritual with some odds and ends of Caribbean practice thrown in. The people who abused me were not in any way con-
nected to my family.

burnt by inquisitors. The plants that cure scurvy, tone the kidneys, purge parasites are buried in the tangle of weeds whose pollen sweetens the air but which do nothing for human bodies. I must taste the leaves, looking for that trace of bitterness, that special aroma of sweetness. I must let the plant act in my body in order to know what it is.

There are compelling reasons to do this beyond my own need for a tonic, for digestive bitters. Between seven and five hundred years ago, a series of devastating blows fell upon humanity. They were not the first, or even necessarily the worst, such blows to fall in the course of human history. But these are the wounds we have inherited, the foundation of our current world order, the unhealed injuries that fester in contemporary life. During that period, the elites of Europe launched a series of wars upon their own people. The peasants were driven off common lands and into wage labor. At least hundreds of thousands and possibly millions of European women were attacked, tortured, and killed as suspected witches. Throughout Europe we saw the rise of new ideologies that severed peoples' ties to the land and to their own bodies, that burned women at the stake for knowing plants, feeling kinship with animals, and knowing how to heal each other and birth babies without having to look up procedures in books.

The Crusades and long-standing economic competition with the Islamic world had set up a racist frame of reference for conquest. In Spain, the Christian re-conquest of the peninsula from Islamic rule gave rise to the extreme nationalism of a newly assembled country, with all of its accompanying bigotry and religious intolerance. Jews and Muslims were expelled, forced to convert or die, barred from practicing their crafts and trades, and had their belongings confiscated.

Out of this world of famines, epidemics, evictions, and multiplying numbers of landless beggars, a tidal wave of pillage swept out over the planet. The rise of European merchants, companies,

and transnational corporations into dominance has been disas-
trous for all the world's people. Africa was and continues to be devastated by three centuries of mass enslavement and even longer colonial occupation. The Americas and the Pacific Islands were
invaded, their lands and resources stolen, and their peoples destroyed or reduced to exile and poverty in their own countries.
Great portions of Asia were also invaded, captured, and occupied
for European markets. And people were not the only sufferers.
Great forests, herds, flocks, and schools of creatures abundant beyond belief are gone, devoured by a frenzy of greed that killed five
million pigeons, all but exterminated many kinds of seals, whales,
and beavers, and clear-cut forests once many days journey across,
leaving barren, eroded lands. All these events have had immense
consequences for our capacity to live with the earth and each
other.

The stories of women's lives that I have gathered here range
over much of the time and geography of these events. In finding
and distilling them, I am moved by an urgent sense that in order
to invent new strategies and ways of living together, in order to
find those paths that lead to the continuation of life on earth, we
must come to understand the nature of these blows: how and why
they fell, what was lost, what was hidden away and saved, and,
most of all, what we, the majority of humans, have learned from
the long process of resisting, surrendering, accommodating, and
transforming ourselves so that we could live. In these stories, I am
seeking information on how to tip the balance toward survival for
all of us.

Or, to return to the herbal metaphor, the medicines I seek as I
wander in these long-abandoned gardens (I found most of these
women in footnotes and appendices, in single lines buried in
books about men) are not only the home remedies and daily comforts that heal scratches, stomach aches, and runny noses. I am
particularly looking for that special class of plants called adapto-

gens, plants that contain substances capable of altering our bodies' ability to resist attack, to withstand stress, to defeat toxins and
tumors, substances that can enter into the core of nearly over-
whelmed immune systems and bring energy and hope.

One of the ironies of my own history of abuse is that it took
place in Indiera, a place of refuge for indigenous and African
people escaping from enslavement and control in the fertile
coastal zone of Puerto Rico. As a child, I once found shards of Arawak pottery buried in the clay and, another time, carved and
painted images on a rock. Indiera was the site of a settlement of indigenous people, both those from the island and those brought by
force from Tierra Firme who, according to the chronicles, re-
treated farther and farther from the Spanish until they reached the
crest of the cordillera and made a community with their mixed-
blood kin.

The people who abused me were not necessarily from Indiera.
One was a elementary school teacher whose family lived in a
coastal town and was probably descended from some of the Spanish conquerors of the Canary Islands. Another was a doctor from
the United States. Most of them were not known to me outside of
the context of the abuse, where they often wore masks. They were
invaders, anonymous in their power.

In writing about what happened to me, I have found myself
identifying with the original inhabitants of the land on which I
was born and raised, and with all the runaways and rebels that
found their way there over the centuries. As a child, I was proud of
the heritage of resistance that seemed to linger. I could imagine
them in the deep, wild valley to the north of our house, still living
off wild guavas, green bananas, and stolen chickens. My parents,
communists who were frequently under surveillance and harassment from the authorities, were obvious inheritors of this tradition; it was fitting that we lived within a mile of where Matias
Brugman, a leader of the uprising against Spain in 1868 and a

probable descendant of Jews, was killed by Spanish soldiers. These heroic ghosts stood near me at the worst moments of abuse, and I could imagine that the red clay recognized me as one of them. It gave me courage, not to feel quite so alone.

It was also the land itself, its burgeoning life, its sweeping views of distant sea, often shrouded and half-hidden by cloud, its abundant sweetness, its thick, viscous mud, the cleansing rains, the smell of water and greenness, chattering birds, hot yellow sun in tropical blue sky—all of these things provided me comfort and consolation, mute friendship, when I could not tell anyone what was being done to me. In its complexity, its contradictory strands, in its beauty and hardship this book springs very much from the rain-drenched red earth of Indiera.

❦ INTRODUCTION: REVISION

Let's get one thing straight. Puerto Rico was a women's country. We outnumbered men again and again.* Female head of household is not a new thing with us. The men left for Mexico and Venezuela and Peru. They left every which way they could, and they left us behind. We got our own rice and beans. Our own guineo verde and cornmeal. Whatever there was to be cooked, we cooked it. Whoever was born, we birthed and raised them. Whatever was to be washed, we washed it. We washed the ore the men dug from the mountains, rinsed a thousand baskets of crushed rock. We stood knee deep in the rivers, separating gold from sand, and still cooked supper. We washed cotton shirts and silk capes, diapers and menstrual cloths, dress shirts and cleaning rags. We squatted by the river and pounded clothing on rocks. Whatever was grown, we grew it. We planted the food and harvested it. We pushed the cane into the teeth of the trapiche and stripped the tobacco leaf from the stem. We coaxed the berries from the coffee branch and sorted them, washed them, dried them, shelled them, roasted them, ground them, made the coffee and served it. We were never still, our hands were always busy. Making soap. Making candles. Hold-

---

* This was not true in many times and places. Overall, there were more male than female slaves, for example. But in San Juan, women often outnumbered men by this much, notably in the 1600s and in the slave population just before emancipation. Also possibly among rural subsistence farmers in the mountain regions.

ing children. Making bedding. Sewing clothing. Our stitches held sleeve to dress and soul to body. We stitched our families through the dead season of the cane, stitched them through lean times of bread and coffee. The seams we made kept us from freezing in the winters of New York and put beans on the table in the years of soup kitchens. Puerto Rican women have always held up four-fifths of the sky. Ours is the work they decided to call unwork. The tasks as necessary as air. Not a single thing they did could have been done without us. Not a treasure taken. Not a crop brought in. Not a town built up around its plaza, not a fortress manned without our cooking, cleaning, sewing, laundering, childbearing. We have always been here, doing what had to be done. As reliable as furniture, as supportive as their favorite sillón. Who thanks his bed? But we are not furniture. We are full of fire, dreams, pain, subversive laughter. How could they not honor us? We were always here, working, eating, sleeping, singing, suffering, giving birth, dying. We were out of their sight, cutting wood, making fire, soaking beans, nursing babies. We were right there beside them digging, hoeing, weeding, picking, cutting, stacking. Twisting wires, packing piña, shaping pills, filling thermometers with poisonous metal, typing memo after memo. Not one meal was ever eaten without our hand on the pot. Not one office ran for an hour without our ear to the phone, our finger to the keyboard. Not one of those books that ignore us could have been written without our shopping, baking, mending, ironing, typing, making coffee, comforting. Without our caring for the children, minding the store, getting in the crop, making their businesses pay. This is *our* story, and the truth of our lives will overthrow them.

Let's get one thing straight. Puerto Rico was parda, negra, mulata, mestiza. Not a country of Spaniards at all. We outnumbered them, year after year. All of us who are written down: not white. We were everywhere. Not just a few docile servants and the guava-eating ghosts of the dead. The Spanish men left babies right and left. When most of the indias had given birth to mixed-blood children, when all the lands had been divided, our labor shared out in encomienda, and no more caciques went out to battle them, they said the people were gone. How could we be gone? We were the brown and olive and cream-colored children of our mothers: Arawak, Maya, Lucaya, stolen women from all the shores of the sea. When we cooked, it was the food our mothers had always given us. We still pounded yuca and caught crabs. We still seasoned our stews with ají and wore cotton skirts. When we burned their fields, stole their cattle, set fire to their boats, they said we were someone else. What was wrong with their eyes? We mixed our blood together like sancocho, calalú. But the mother things stayed with us. Two hundred and fifty years after they said, "Ya no hay indios," we had a town of two thousand who still remembered our names, and even our neighbors called the place Indiera. When they wanted more slaves from Africa, they complained that we had all died on them. They called us pardas libres and stopped counting us. Invisibility is not a new thing with us. But we have always been here, working, eating, sleeping, singing, suffering, giving birth, dying. We are not a metaphor. We are not ghosts. We are still here.

Let's get one thing straight. We were everywhere. The Spanish, Dutch, English, French, Genoese, Portuguese took captives up and down our coasts, inland by river, overland on foot. They brought us here through every bay deep enough to hold a slave ship. Legally, through the port of San Juan, all registered in the royal books. And dozens more, unloaded at night, right there in the harbor, sold but not written down. But that was the least of it. We came through Añasco, Guánica, Arecibo, Salinas, San Germán. In sloops from Jamaica, St. Christopher, Curaçao. We came by the thousands, bound hand and foot, uncounted, unaccounted for, while official eyes looked the other way. And we came as fugitives from the other islands, because the Spanish let the slaves of their rivals live here free. From Saint Croix and Tortola, from Jamaica and the Virgins. There were many more of us than were written in their registers. Untaxed, unbaptised, hidden in the folds of the mountains, in the untilled lands. There were many more of us than the sugar planters knew or would say, always sobbing to the king about no one to do the work. We were here from the start, and we were here more often. They were always running away to seek better fortunes. We ran away, too. We ran to the swamps and we ran to the cordillera. We ate their cattle and set fire to their cane fields. If they caught us, the judges were instructed to cut off our ears. (Police brutality is not a new thing with us.) Spanish men left babies right and left, café con leche children. But in their imaginations, they were all alone in their big white houses, dreaming of Peru or the voyage back to Spain, while on their threshold a new people was forming. How could they not see us, nursing their babies, cooking ñame, frying balls of cornmeal, banana, yuca; stewing up crabs and pork and guingambó. Wrapping cotton rags around our heads. Throwing white flowers into the sea. How could they not hear us, telling each other our stories with the soles of our feet on the clay, with the palms of our hands on tree trunks, on goat-hides. Carrying their loads, laundering for strangers to earn them cash. We have always been here, longer and steadier, working, eating, sleeping, singing, suffering, giving birth, dying. We were not contented. We were not simple souls ready to dance and sing all day with innocent hearts. We were not lazy animals, too dull-witted to understand orders. We were not hot-blooded savages, eager to be raped. We were not impervious to pain. We felt every blow they struck at our hearts. We were not happy to serve. We didn't love our masters. We were slaves. We were libertas. We were free mulatas. We were poor and hungry and alive. When they needed hands, they brought us. When they needed jobs, they threw us on boats to New York and Hawaii, threw us on food stamps, threw us drugs. But Puerto Rico is African. We made it from our own flesh.

Let's get one thing straight. Puerto Rico was a poor folks' country. There were many more poor than rich throughout its history. More naborías than caciques. More foot soldiers than aristocratic conquistadores. More servants than mistresses. More people wearing cotton and leather than people wearing silk and damask, velvet and cloth of gold. They did wear those things, and they ate off silver plates. But most of us ate off higüeras, or wooden trenchers, or common clay. There were more people who ate plátano and cornmeal and casabe every day of the week, with a little salt fish or pork now and then, than those who had beef and turtle and chicken and fresh eggs and milk, with Canarias wine and Andalucían olive oil. Most of us had no money. Many of us were never paid for working. Those of us who owned the fruits of our labor traded it to the merchants for far less than it was worth, and bought on credit, and ended up in debt. We were the ones who cleared the land so it could be planted with sugarcanes from India, and coffee bushes from Ethiopia, and bananas and plantains from Malaysia. We were the ones who grew food. We were the ones who were glad when a store came to the mountains, and then watched our future harvests promised for the sack of beans, the new blade, the bag of rice or corn meal. We were the hands of Pietri and Castañer. We were the hands of Ferré and Muñoz. We washed and ironed the shirts of the politicians. We scrubbed the pots of the governors and their wives. We sewed those fine christening gowns for their babies and fetched the water for their baths. They said, This governor built a wall, and that one made a road. They said so and so founded a town, and this other one produced a newspaper. But the governor did not lift blocks of stone or dig through the thick clay. The capitanes pobladores didn't labor in childbed to populate their villas, or empty the chamber pots. The great men of letters didn't carry the bales of paper or scrub ink from piles of shirts and trousers. We have always been here. How could they not see us? We filled their plates and made their beds, washed their clothing and made them rich. We were not mindless, stupid, created for the tasks we were given. We were tired and angry and alive. How could they miss us? We were the horses they rode, we were the wheels of their family pride. We were the springs where they drank, and our lives went down their throats. Our touch was on every single thing they saw. Our voices were around them humming, whispering, singing, telling riddles, making life in the dust and mud. We have always been here, doing what had to be done, working, eating, sleeping, singing, suffering, giving birth, dying. Dying of hunger and parasites, of cholera and tuberculosis. Dying of typhus and anemia and cirrhosis of the liver. Dying of heroin and crack and botched abortions, in childbirth and industrial accidents, and from not enough days off. This is our history. We met necessity every single day of our lives. Look wherever you like, it's our work you see.

❧ BISABUELAS

❧ Gingko

We have need for memory. For something that can reach back
before the first symbols were scratched into tablets of clay, more
pliable and enduring than paper. Something with the power of
a dream or a smell that can bring back, from the tiniest traces,
whole submerged lives. The living fossil. The ancient garden.
The gingko tree.

Flat, broad leaves like open palms, like hands offering
something up. Like fans, stirring the ancient air, wafting just
the hint of a fragrance, Paleolithic pollens from long fossilized
flowers encased perhaps in amber. Gingko remembers. Gingko
restores. Gingko for stroke, for loss of memory, for bringing back
that which is too old, too far gone, too deep in the past to find
any other way.

Gingko waved leathery hands at the dinosaurs, long
before grass. Gingko lifted branches to the horny feet of the
pterodactyl. Gingko offered shade to the first skittering
mammals. Gingko remembers our mother.

First Mother—
Sub-Saharan Africa: −200,000

We began in her shade, running at her callused heel, strapped to
her strong back, the first mother, the one woman we all hold in

common out of that band of a thousand ancestors from whom humanity came, rising like a dust storm out of the heart of Africa.

First Mother was never the golden-haired Eve in Renaissance paintings whose flowing locks fall across perky breasts, munching apples with the snake. She was walnut-skinned with hair like a thundercloud, and her breasts hung long and slack and leathery from nursing many babies. She lived at the rim of the wide and green Sahara, a land of many rivers and flowering meadows, and she did not eat apples. She ate dates from the palms and sweet berries from shrubs. She ate nuts and seeds, wild grubs and honey. She had antelope when she could get it. Fish when she could catch it. She did not live in a garden, alone with a man. She lived with a band of kin, and they walked wherever they pleased, on the green and yellow and brown earth, gathering, and dropping seeds, hunting, and scattering bones, drinking, and going dry, growing older and bearing young.

Her children spread outward like a fan of fingers, filling up continents. Some lived at the edge of the sky, in high cloudy valleys among snowy peaks, and their chests grew broader and deeper in the thin air, their blood richer. Some lived in the dense dimly lit forests, where warm rain dripped from a canopy full of the swinging shadows of monkeys, and these became quick and light on their feet, small and compact, with smooth and hairless skin, the better to stay cool. Some lived in places of long winter and few plants, of mammoth Arctic nights and blazing days, and they padded themselves with fat against the bone-cracking cold and learned to eat the oily flesh of whales. Some lived inland, houses pitched against the winds of winter sweeping the plains and steppes for endless months of darkness, far from the fish oils that could strengthen their bones, and these grew pale, translucent skin, made to suck up the meager daylight. Some stayed in the latitudes of the sun and gathered up even more of the darkness of earth to keep themselves from burning. They were tall and thin, arms long enough to pick fruit of savanna trees, legs swift enough to follow the distant herds, with a blue-black sheen that gave their bodies shade.

But everyone in the menagerie came from the same litter, suckled at the same brown breast; and in every one of her daughters, unchanged through the generations, a tiny fragment of her flesh persists, a grain of earth she gave us,* with our humanness, in the wide Saharan garden, at the beginning of human time.

WOMEN OF YAMS— WEST AFRICA: −50,000 TO 200

−50,000: Kindling—African Continent

In the long, long ago of the great-grandmothers fire came among the people. The people had gone far from the place of the first mother and had already begun to be different from one another, when fire came. We had learned to carry things with us. Bundles. Baggage. Choppers and scrapers and animal skins. We took shelter among tumbled rocks and hollows. We moved into caves made by long dried rivers that once ran underground. The rivers vanished, eaten up by drought, or took shortcuts and ran elsewhere. The empty beds they left behind were clean and dry and out of the wind, and we slept there. Then, sitting at the mouth of such a cave, watching the play of lightning in the sky, one night fire came to us.

---

* Examining samples of mitochondrial DNA, passed down only from mother to daughters, allowed researchers to come up with the "Eve theory," that although we also have many other ancestors, all human beings have at least one common female ancestor, part of a small band of several thousand humans from whom we evolved, living in sub-Saharan Africa, about 200,000 years ago. The Sahara has at various times been a place of green pastures and rivers. I have taken the poetic liberty of placing our mother in one of those times.

Not the spark that falls from the sky and sets the dead log ablaze. The spark we summoned ourselves, from flint striking flint, from a point of dry stick whirling in the socket of parched wood. We learned to tickle the spark into a little heap of yellow grass, curled threads of bark, brown moss. We learned to kindle.

With fire, we could make our camps in more places. We could hang meat in the smoke to dry, or roast it just above the flames. We could grind seeds, mix the meal with water, spread it on a flat stone set in the coals, and bake bread. We could roast roots among the embers.

Fire was a tool like no other. But even more, fire was a place. At the edge of fire we gathered, with shadows and light dancing across our faces. With fire came story. With fire came song. Like sparks, people's thoughts and dreams flew from behind their black eyes and blew across the flame-lit circle. Our hungry hearts, our waiting faces were like soft shredded bark, like dry grass. We learned to summon the spark, and we ourselves became kindling.

— 8,000: Forests—Nigeria

What use is it to know the life lived ten thousand years ago at the edges of the rainforests of West Africa? How can simple truths make a dent in lies that are centuries thick? That the people of the Niger and the Kongo forest were not very different from the people of the Rhine or the Thames, the Euphrates or the Yangtze. They spoke different languages, hunted and gathered in the forests, began farming as people all over the hemisphere began farming: yams, Mandinka rice, malagueta pepper, melon, coco-yams, palm oil. That like people everywhere they invented the tools they needed: axes, sickles, picks, and hoes. That like people everywhere, they adapted to what was there, and so their blood cells curved into the shape of sickles to fight malaria.

What is there to say of the people at the forest rim three thousand years ago? Like people everywhere, they tamed animals and plants and kept on inventing. Dwarf cattle and goats that resist the sickness carried by the tsetse fly. Cowpeas and kola nuts, coffee and okra, akee and gourds. Slash and burn farmers, making a clearing and then giving it back. That they made soap and charcoal, pottery and rope. That they took supplies from the forest. Beeswax and tree gums, bark and vines. That they dug from the ground. Clay and building earth and grindstones. That they got sick like people anywhere else: malaria, yellow fever, dengue, yaws, parasites. And like intelligent people everywhere, found medicines in the trees and herbs.

That they became travelers along the rivers and nets of footpaths, and let green walls of forest enclose their villages and keep them safe. That they began to trade. That they hunted and trapped: elephant, baboon, monkey, bat, giant snails. That the rivers, lagoons, and coastal waters were full of fish, and so naturally they netted and speared them. That because they were people, they made art. Sculptures of clay famous for their beauty. Iron tools, simple and elegant.

That what happens, happened. Families became tribes, tribes began inching their way toward nationhood. It was no different here than anywhere. Nations always rest on the hearts of the mothers. Nations eat the lives of women and girls. Out of the long history of the forest-edge peoples, someday great cities will rise, where the bodies of dozens of girls, all killed in a single day, will be built into the foundations of Ife. Like cities, like civilizations everywhere, life will rise on pillars of women's bones, rest its splendor and dignity on the dark stains of women's blood.

⚘WILD YAM

Wild yam makes what the body makes. Something golden and potent slipping into the bloodstream to ripen the eggs, preserve the skin, grow babies, erase pain, make all things work right.
Wild yam pounded into paste, delicious with seasoned palm oil,

brings an abundance of twins, good digestion, energy, and calm. What does it take to believe in the plentifulness of life, in such generosity, in daily pleasures sustained throughout generations? Here, taste the starchy root dried to chalky slices, the medicine of trust.

— 4,000: Colors—West Africa

Indigo. Ochre. Red clay and yellow clay. Mineral earth and mussel shells. The leaf that stains cotton into pale green, the fruit that is like violet ink, the root bark that turns orange and the vine that makes brown. In West African villages women steal the rainbow from the backs of parrots and dye fibers into blazing colors. With carved wood and lengths of vine they stamp and tie and twist the cloth of life and give it back iridescent and dancing with stories. Birds and fish, diamonds and spirals, patterns like the rows of planted millet or the braids on a sister's head. Scallops like waves on western beaches, undulating lines like sand dunes, zig-zags jagged as lightning under heavy clouds or the spikes on a crocodile's back. Triangles set in intricate patterns to evoke the scales of river fish and circles scattered inside larger circles like huts in a village, like rain on water. The women rinse the cloth and dry it in the sun, tie it around their waists, their buttocks, around their shoulders as slings for firewood and babies, wrap their heads with it to catch the sweat of the day. Color settles down like a huge extravagant bird in the midst of the cooking fires and sets the people of the villages smiling and giggling and humming as they work.

— 2,000 to 0: Bantu Women Cut Bananas—Africa

Imagine a two-thousand-year walk from the Cameroon of northern West Africa, east across the belly of a continent, first grasslands, then forest, then thicker forests still. The Bantu-speaking peoples fill up the available space, pushing and shoving and elbowing aside, settling along the way. They dig and smelt the red-

dish ores and forge iron blades with which to cut a path. Sliding down the eastern flank of Africa, they find new fruit of unsur-
passed sweetness hanging in yellow bunches like a multitude of
hands reaching out from the thick green stem. With the knives
they carry at their hips, Bantu women slice bananas from the
heavily laden plants, eating as they walk south to Zimbabwe and
curve west toward a memory of the Atlantic. Around the same
time that a Jewish prophet declares himself a fisher of men at the
point where Africa curves into Asia, the women of the walking
people arrive at the place that will someday be Angola and dip
their weighted nets into the waves. Their daughters will plant their
feet over all this land and half the world, carrying the knowledge
of sweetness in one hand and the taste of iron under their tongues.

✺Banana Peel

Below the thick yellow jacket that covers melting sweetness,
inside the lining, is a layer, pale brown and potent, that can
carry your burdens, take up your scars. It will devour warts
and blisters, suck them into itself, leave only dry scraps that fall
away. Banana Peel is the scavenger that cleans up the damage,
that scours the residue, that chews up the no longer needed.
Banana says leave it behind, cast it off, time to move on. Slip
Banana Peel into your shoes and leave the past behind. Wrap it
around your finger and watch the open cut shrink to puckered
skin, the scab disintegrate. Go ahead, says Banana Peel, don't
wait to be ready, don't wait to pack. You don't need these old
clothes. Go naked on your journey, like the tender banana, sweet
and available to life.

200: Salt—Northwest Africa

Here is the crystalline sweat of the earth, gathered up from the
dried salt beds of her armpits, the pooling places of her navel, the
creases between belly and thigh, here is a remembrance of the

oceans we crept from beyond all memory of memory. Here is a necessity of life. We scrape it from the coastal rocks, from the desert deposits, and fill cotton bags and leather pouches. We load it in sacks onto the backs of camels and carry the precious burden across places where water evaporates in a soft hiss from our skins and even our imaginations.

When the salt harvest arrives in the villages of the Berber peoples, the women celebrate in a great mock battle, whacking with clubs and hurling stones against their adversaries, letting out cries as fierce and biting as the salt itself. This is their ferocious answer to the gift of salt, potent enough to seal a binding promise, to drive away ill luck, to enforce hospitality among rivals, older than us by far. The sound of their exultation carries miles in the dry air, out into the stillness of the Sahara, where it is eaten by wind and dust, and out over the blue sea, where it is echoed in the harsh cries of gulls.

WOMEN OF BREAD—
THE MEDITERRANEAN: −12,000 TO −1,500

THE DEER MOTHER

−12,000: El Juyo, Spain

> *Throughout ancient Europe, people showed reverence for the cycles and abundance of life by worshiping the Goddess, often in the form of an animal. They made paintings and sculptures depicting her and offerings of various kinds, including the bones, feathers, fur, antlers, or whole bodies of her sacred beasts. In northern Spain, archaeologists found the body of a deer buried in a ritual manner, probably as such an offering.*

She is the mother of all life, and
she runs through the forests as a deer
her belly swollen with young.

We call her to us with the bones of deer.
We call her to us with antlers.
We ask her for the berries to be plentiful
and that the babies live through the winter.
We ask for the birds to lay many eggs.
We ask for the fish to come into our nets.
We ask for the deer to fall to our spears.

We call her to us with gifts.
First, we shape a hole in the earth,
round and long like an egg
or the womb of a mother.
We call her.
In the womb of the earth we lay the body of a deer
so she will come.
We call her with gifts.

We paint the deer with red ochre,
the color of fire where we gather.
We cover the deer with precious
mineral flakes of purple, orange, red.

We call her to us with her own body.
We call her with bones.
We decorate her body with borrowed antlers.
We seal her into the womb of the earth.
So she will give birth to herself.
So she will give birth to the fish.

So she will give birth to the berries.
So she will give birth to many eggs.
So she will give birth to the swift deer.
So she will give birth to us.

— 6,500: The Peaceful Land—Southeastern Europe

For how many centuries have they told us that only Europe the conqueror, Europe the invader, Europe the accumulator of other people's wealth was worth celebrating. We who have rejected again and again the insidious voice of the conquistador and searched for our dark abuelas in the mirror, we who have managed to embrace our mestizaje, proclaimed our despised ancestry among the conquered and enslaved, how do we love what is pale-skinned in us? Listen, daughters of Spain, inheritors of ancient Europe: once there was a time before war. Once upon a time, it was Europe that was free and flowering, Europe that was indigenous, Europe where women were honored, nature respected, the hoop unbroken.

Imagine this. From where the Dneiper runs south through the grasslands of the Ukraine to the Atlantic waves breaking on the shores of Brittany, and north to the cold rim of the Baltic, Europe stretches, fertile and green, and undisturbed by war. The people leave behind no ruined fortresses, no walled towns on the crowns of hills, no tombs of warriors filled with weaponry. There are no forts, for there is nothing to fortify against. Towns are built among the fields, near the rivers, for use and for beauty, not defense. There are weavers and hunters, farmers and potters, and they leave behind only the tools of fishing and tilling, baskets and spindles and hoes.

The names are lost deep in time. We call the tribes for the modern towns where they have left behind bowls painted in intricate, beautiful patterns of spirals and lines, vases shaped like birds or deer, red jars decorated with the eyes of the goddess. We could wander for millennia in that ancient peaceful world, searching for familiar faces, gestures we recognize, the whole from which the splinters of our inheritance came.

While famed Jericho has at most nine hundred people, the Turkish city of Catal Huyuk teems with seven thousand. From the rich plains, women fill their baskets with three kinds of wheat and also barley, greens, root vegetables, and fruit. There are herds of cattle and goats, and the women make yogurt and cheese while the men hunt wild pigs and deer. Travelers are always coming and going, trading for obsidian to make knives and mirrors, marble for jewelry and figurines, iron oxide paints, crystals, shells, and semi-precious stones. A market town, a peaceful town, a place full of skilled craftswomen and well-fed children. A town repeated across river and field, mountain valley and lakeside meadow for a thousand miles.

Someday soon the sound of hooves will echo here and everywhere across this wide flowering land. The graceful pottery will lie shattered, the fields trampled, and the great hoop of life will be twisted into the shape of a battle shield. Sky gods will walk across the belly of the earth mother and the conquistadores will begin to be born between the broken stalks of barley. Death will no longer be a dark and merciful mother.

But in these peaceful days, the people of Old Europe keep the great circle from birth to rebirth. In Catal Huyuk the dead are given to the birds who eat what is useful and leave only clean white bones that are buried under the floors to keep the beloved close. The red pottery and owl eyes of the bird goddess keep watch over the dead of ancient Spain, laid in round chambers at the ends of tunnels, under little hills of earth.

In what chamber of our Spanish hearts do her wings still flutter? Underneath the floor of which room in the ancestral house does she live, the ancient European grandmother who was neither ruled nor ruler? What birds have eaten the old world and nour-

ished with their droppings the roots of our American tree? In what
tropical fruit, behind the black eyes of what mestiza face does that
abuela, white as a sickle moon, still curve up singing toward the
sky?

PIG MOTHER

—6,000: Europe

> *The Mother Goddess of ancient Europe was worshiped in
> many forms and her presence has persisted through many
> invasions and transformations. As Christianity came to
> dominate the region, Christian rituals and sacred places
> often settled on the old foundations: pagan rites that
> marked with fire, water, greenery, eggs, and grain the cycles
> of the natural world merged with Christian birth, death,
> and resurrection stories, and churches were built over the
> holy wells and groves of the Goddess. In Christmas trees,
> Easter eggs, and the attributes of the Virgin and the saints,
> her worship persists.*

Mother of the planted fields,
mystery of the grain that rises
and falls and rises again,
mother of the changing and unchanging
ancient and deep.

By all that is fat and fruitful,
by all that grows quickly and ripens,
by all that has abundant squirming litters
suckling at a dozen teats
we call the earth to feed us.

We are wearing masks
with the fat cheeks of pigs.

We are carrying pots
with the fat bellies of pigs.
We shape mud into fat earthy pigs
and decorate them with swollen grain.

You will not disappear.
You will remain in the ground.
After the horse men come with their sun gods,
after the armies come trampling fields
and dragging their soldier
gods behind them,
after they raise your fragile son, the grain king,
raise him and eat him and set him above you to rule us,
you will remain.

You will be Demeter and Zemyna and Mother Moist Earth.
We will call you Radegund and Milpurga and Marija, Mother of God.
You will be the Black Madonna, the color of river mud,
and we will not forget you.
Even in the grey cathedrals erected over your sacred springs,
your worship will remain, flickering in the light of many candles,
where the women leave you wreaths.
The earth will still sprout green after rain,
and you will still suckle your grunting young
and we will make our offerings to you forever.
Your mysteries will not end.

— 3,500: Mare's Milk—Ukraine

In the grasslands of the Ukraine, in the very places where my Jewish ancestors came thousands of years later and died, some of
them, massacred by Nazis, is an ancient burial site where the bones
of horses sacrificed to warrior gods lie where they fell. This is the
place where the bit was forced between the mare's teeth and the

stallion was bridled, where the wild beauty of the herd was transformed with leather and iron into the wealth of chieftains.

In the town of Kremenchug, thousands of years before the day
my great-grandmother's grandmother defied the rabbis and stood
up in temple to proclaim, "Your God is a man!" other men of the
steppes, straddling the backs of horses, tore the sacred from the
earth and made it a knife blade slashing across heaven. In this
place, where our relatives the horses were butchered to uphold the
rule of the violent, the old women who had born them were
stripped of honor and authority, diminished into widows, and
thrown, throats cut, into the graves of their mates who were no
longer their lovers but their lords.

The men of the wide grasslands sat aloft on the backs of their
kin and raided each other for more horses, for cattle, for goods, began stealing women from each other like so many head of live-
stock. The people of the herds drank fermented mare's milk and
worshiped what they wished to control: the wild power of horses,
the flight of the sun. Their heels digging into the flanks of their
steeds, they followed the sun west into the settled lands, the green
fields of the villagers, and tasted the rich fruits of the farmlands.

It was from this place, more than six thousand years before
leather-booted men set fire to the shtetls of my people, that the
world was turned upside down. The black breast of the Mother,
her dark earthen womb, became the abode of death, the under-
world, lifeless home of a harsh god. The snake who sheds her skin
and reminds us that life is ever renewed, the little serpent and
friendly guardian of children and flocks suddenly became an evil
lurking in whirlwinds, sign of everything untrusted, image of betrayal. Ivory and gold, those old bone colors of death, became the
banner of the God of the Shining Sky. Here where in 1941, thousands dug their graves and were shot into them, the sacred female
became the sacred male, and the idea of war sprang half-grown
into the saddle and galloped west.

− 2,700 to − 2,000: Deserts—North Africa

Like shells washed up from unimaginable depths to lie, bone-dry
and bleached on the shore, memories of a lush, green land are scattered on the walls of desert caves. Once there were rivers full of
fish; dense grasslands from which huge flocks rose, wings clapping
like thunder; herds of wild cattle with curved horns and swift
antelope. On the walls of caverns that now lie many days into the
deep Sahara, galleries of images still fly across the rock, the bright
paint barely faded in the nearly moistureless air. A forested land
of cypress and oak, fertile meadows full of grain and orchards of
fruit—a land of figs and honey.

But the rains ceased to fall on this garden and the world
changed. Perhaps the birds left first, migrating to wetter places.
Then the antelope. The rivers fell back into their beds, leaving the
bones of fish to crumble into the diminished soil. Grain burned in
the sheaf, the fruit shriveled on the branch, the trees withered and
died, and the people scattered.

Out of the dried lands they whirled like dust, west into the high
Atlas, north along the coast of the blue sea, learning to live under
a blaze of fire in the newly born deserts. Swathed in cloth that kept
away sand and flies, the people crossed the Sahara carrying ivory
and gold from the south, copper and tin from the north. The ancient flowering meadowlands had gone to bone-pale rock and
sand and its people filled the marketplaces of the Phoenicians,
sailed upon the backs of camels, learned to ride the wind on Bar-
bary horses, the swiftest and most beautiful.

The Berber peoples became both settled and wandering, a mo-
saic of separate tribes, each with its own tongue. In the villages
they grew garbanzos and wheat. In the desert they pitched their
tents over the fossils of parched rivers and gathered dates at the
infrequent springs. The women wore bracelets of bronze and
tiny bells that tinkled like the ghosts of falling water when they
walked.

Others moved south, all the way to edges of the great, dense rainforest, to the still moist plots of rice and melon and yam. They joined the villages of the Sudanese grasslands and together built trade cities stacked with salt and leopard skins and West African gold.

And some pushed east into the rising sun of Egypt, to the still glistening lands barely emerged from the mud, and elbowed their way in at the crowded edges of the Nile. There the people of the vanished gardens became farmers of the silted lands, watched the temples and palaces rise and helped to raise them, joined in rebellion when rebellion came, and endured the dynasties of the Pharaohs as best they could.

— 1,500: Cutting—Northeast Africa

No one knows exactly where or when it began. But sometime before the Pharaohs built the last of their pyramids, and somewhere between the Red Sea and the Sahara, men began to insist that women be cut in the tenderest places.

The procedure is described in the oldest scrolls, on pieces of papyrus, in the commentaries of visiting Greek scholars, in account books that record the payments to practitioners. It is described by European priests and anthropologists. It is reported in the medical records of a dozen African nations. It is happening to little girls as you read these words.

The one who cuts wears many faces. An Egyptian surgeon, a doctor in Dakar, a team of male nurses in Mogadishu, the grandmother, the aunt, the old and honored village woman. The girl (it is usually a girl, but sometimes it's a newborn infant, sometimes it's a young woman awaiting marriage) is held down on a stool with her legs pinned apart, open, vulnerable. The cutter reaches between the moist folds of pinkness and grabs the sweet clitoris, maybe with tongs or with sticks or with fingers. There is nothing given to deaden the pain. With scalpel, or sharp stick, or kitchen knife, or razor blade, the most sensitive, nerve-rich part of the human body is sliced off, rooted out, torn away. The cutter digs with her fingernail to make sure nothing, nothing at all, is left. The other women also poke their fingers into the bloody hole to check. The women chant or sing or bang on drums to drown out the screams of the victim. No one comforts her.

The cutter continues, carving off the delicate inner folds. The child must be held down by many arms, as she is often in convulsions from the pain and fear. Now the cutter scrapes away the outer lips, the thick folds of tender flesh around the mouth of the vulva. They must be raw, open wounds. The bleeding places are clamped together with thorns or pins. Only the smallest hole, no bigger than a kernel of corn, is left open, for the seeping out of menstrual blood and urine. The cutter introduces a splinter, or a small stick of bamboo into the wound, so it will scar around the wood. Then her legs are crossed and tied in place. Sometimes she is bound from knees to waist in goat hide or bandages. She must stay still for several weeks, tied in her rags, lying rigid with shock in the stench of spoiling blood and her own wastes.

Now she is suitable for marriage. Now that her own desires have been tortured to death, she is desirable. She will not have sexual feelings for the wrong people. She will not bear the wrong children. The men who say this is good, congratulate themselves. They say it will be a relief to her. That she must have been tormented by all that excess sexuality, that unnecessary aliveness, that her clitoris was dangerously overgrown and would have led her to behave like a man, even, perhaps, made her wish to make love to women. Now, they say, she is decent. When the time comes to marry her, her husband will use a knife, or his own muscle power, to break and enter. When she is made pregnant, she will be stitched up again. When she gives birth, the midwife will rip and cut her open again. By the time they are finished with her body, she will be a mass of scars. She will not remember that anything but the most horrific pain ever lived between her thighs.

Great civilization of Egypt, light of the ancient world, center of learning and science, pride of the Mediterranean, what have you done with the joy of women? Where among your tombs and monuments have you buried it? In what deep chamber do the dried genitals of mummified princesses lie like rose petals, turning to dust? Did you throw the severed tidbits of common girls into the Nile to fertilize next year's crops, to feed the fish and make them plump and sweet?

Across the millennia we call you now to account for this legacy of torture you have left to us, the millions of African women, the centuries of pain, the complacency of kinsmen, the complicity of mothers, the nightmares of children echoing throughout the generations. We tell you that you have blunted the power of a continent, whose women have even so been its strength. We stand before your oversized statues, your slave-built palaces, the enormity of the crime, and promise to be implacable against you. We say it will end. We touch our own electric, living, flowering flesh and make the rain come down on the parched lands.

✿Morivíví (The Sensitive Plant)

What do you do for a wound as deep as the roots of being? How do you bring back sensation to flesh whose last memory was of agony? To a body blunted by pain? Would morivíví do it? Would the essence of the sensitive plant be a cure? The small plant with feathery leaves that fold together at the lightest touch, whose stems curl protectively in upon themselves. Morivíví means "I died—I lived." Surely morivíví, the one that unfolds in still, warm air, opening and reaching for the sun, surely a tincture of the clinging roots of morivíví can bring back, if not the torn and cut away body, at least the shadow of a sensation, a shiver of the lost pleasures, the feeling, the feeling.

Scars

I will not tell you what was done to me. Only that the men who used my body also wanted me to feel fear and pain and pleasure at their command. That in order to complete their control they deliberately crossed the signals, confusing one with another. That it took decades to understand that what I thought was desire was sometimes panic. That what I took to be anxiety might be excitement. That there could be pleasure without the razor edge. I have had to walk back, inch by painful inch, to the place of joyful release.

In my struggle I hear the voices of my grandmothers, chorus upon chorus in a hundred tongues. *For how many thousands of years have they feared this in us—the masters, the war chiefs, the fathers of clans? That we can ripple with pleasure again and again; that we can grow children in our bellies and fill our breasts with milk to feed them? For how many lifetimes now have they sought, more hungrily than any trade route or lost treasure city, some foolproof way of owning this power of our bodies?*

This is the birthplace of war and of sacrifice, of bloodletting and corruption. I hear generations of women cry out. The jealous sons have slaughtered their abuelas, lost track of their kinship, violated the sacred in search of a power that cannot be seized. They are deluded. They imagine that because they can destroy life, they control it. That the rituals of harvest are sacred, not to the deep renewing mysteries of earth and seeds, but to the sharpness of the sickle.

They wield sharp blades against all the abundant places of life, not seeing how it slips between their fingers again and again, the living pulse becoming shed blood, empty of what they try in vain to grasp. They are wracked with the hunger to return, to reenter the holy web. In their delirium they transform their longing into rape: hurling themselves upon us they dream they have entered the temple, but the doors are barred against them. Enraged, they commit horrors on our flesh, but the thing they seek eludes them.

They did not cut away portions of my body. They were content to corrupt the sure, sweet knowledge of how pleasure builds to pleasure, to clip its wings so it fell back wounded to earth, to claim that my every response belonged to them. Feather by feather I repair the wings of this quivering injured bird, and learn, perhaps more deeply than those never captive, the delicate tensions between freedom and surrender, soul and sex.

But there are women whose bodies will never wake to flight again, whose capacity to take pleasure was pulled up by the roots, who were left with nothing but dead skin. They can no longer feel the intimate center of touch, delicious wet sliding, the tingling, breathless edge. Those nerves are dead. Rape has been carved into their innermost muscles. Their scars are the signatures on a contract of control. I am abashed before them. What do I know about such irreversible harm? I do not presume to represent them. But I know in every wound of my own more subtle tortures, and in the glazed eyes of those who cannot bear to know, how they represent me.

WOMEN OF YUCA—AMERICA: —15,000 TO 500

—15,000: Pikimachay—The Andes

We live where sky and water are born, between snowy peaks where the vicuña runs in a cloud of golden fleece and the wild hare of the rocks leaps in the sun. Our thoughts are full of wind. We make flutes out of the bones of swift guanacos to play the songs we hear among the stones. We walk among clouds, snaring birds, digging up wild potatoes, shaking the thick heads of quinoa for their nourishing seeds.

In spring, water gushes from the edges of the snow fields and fills the meadows. It spills over the edges of the high land and tumbles down the morning face of the world, into the emerald forests far below. The sound of trickling and rushing surrounds us. Water falls off cliffs in green and white ropes, rumbles through canyons full of stones, pulls soil from the roots of trees, and plunges down impossible precipices. We follow the melting snows through narrow little valleys. There are brightly colored ducks that dip and dive in the pools and clouds of small fish that dart away from them. Some days we go no farther. Some days we do.

From halfway down we can hear cries of monkeys, screaming of parrots. We tell each other stories about the green world, about hunting giant guinea pigs, about pulling sweet and succulent fruits from tree and vine, about the nourishing roots and strong medicines to be found, about wood. We tell about Condor and Anaconda and Jaguar and the beginning of the sun. But we rarely descend.

At night in our caves, fire bright between us, we wrap ourselves in soft skins and dream. The eyes of Jaguar burn like fiery stars among the black branches, warm rain falls, and slower, deeper rivers cradle mysteries and dangers in their brown embrace. Some nights we want nothing more than to follow them and wander in green twilight. But in the morning we change our minds. How could we ever leave the bright thin air, the slopes all white and gold and blue, or the voices of our mothers in the wind?

৯৯POTATOES

Small, round teachers of possibility, how you shine in all your
endless variety in the cold highlands where you first came into
our lives. In each small plot of Andean soil, the ancestors bring
forth from your infinite adaptability new varieties perfected for
just that combination of sun and soil and water. You come in
white and yellow, purple and red, orange and brown. You can be

sweet or earthy, floury or slick, delicate and fragrant or too bitter for anyone but the llamas. You ripen fast or slow, moist or dry, for quick consumption or long storage. Tuber of the three thousand forms, you remind us that there are always more choices, more unexplored paths, is always more potential than we can imagine from the present moment. Papita de los Andes, you roll into our hands shouting, "Diversify! Be colorful! Have fun!" You offer us the unknown, the multiple pathways, the different seasoning, the doorway to discovery, the unexpected bonus, the unqualified disaster, the privilege of making many fruitful mistakes.

Only when this lesson is refused, when those who cultivate you reject the rainbow and repeat themselves endlessly, planting the same seed in the same ground, acre upon acre, season after season, does famine follow on your heels. Choosing safety, you say with a wink, is not always safe.

— 4,000: Rainforests—
Upper Amazon and Orinoco Basins

This is the fruitful belly of the world and everything we need is here. Every day the sky spills and the rivers swell, full of fish and turtles and manatees, big enough to feed a village. The forest has every kind of fruit, sweet and sour and juicy. They hang from branches, jut from trunks, dangle from vines, even spring from the heart of a thorny nest on the ground. There are spicy peppers and speckled beans, wrinkled brown nuts in hard shells, and honeycomb in the trunks of rotten trees. With a good stick you can loosen the earth and pull up manioc, batata, jícama, peanut, ararú.

Tobacco smoke and the pungent steam of a thousand medicines rise from our fires. Tangles of white cotton to pull from the pod and twist into thread, wood for our looms, dyes for the cloth we weave. Hundreds of fibers to make into rope, bags, nets, baskets decorated with feathers. There are gourds to keep things in, or pots of river clay. We sleep suspended from the trees, in hammocks hung beneath roofs of palm leaf so the rain makes curtains around us in the dark. And we burn away the hearts of tree trunks to make boats, and float like seedpods on the endless rivers, fishing, trading, visiting.

The forest is nearly forever. A woman could walk for years, cross many rivers and streams that flow toward morning, and not find the end. But there is an end. A place where all the rain in the world, all the clouds, all the rivers and pools and lakes run together and there is nothing but water and a few green specks of land. Our relatives who live there speak strangely, differently. They go out in their log boats on that immense, heaving water whose current runs sometimes in and sometimes out. They go so far they look like twigs tossed on the ripples of a pond. They go to the big islands near shore, but they say they can see other ones, right at the edge of the sky. They say there are more islands, with good fishing and sweet forests. They say the islands keep calling them from just out of sight. They say someday they will go.

— 4,000: Corn—MesoAmerica

This is the world. Green valleys fed with ashes from the fiery heart of the earth. Blazing sun. Black beans, brown beans, red beans, white beans, beans mottled in shades of red and white and brown, stored in clay jars. Pumpkins and squashes and peppers, red ones, green ones, yellow ones, some sweet as rain, some hotter than lava. But especially, there is maize, the green grandmother with the golden heart and the silken hair who feeds the people. Yellow corn, red corn, blue corn, white corn. Corn for eating green in soup. Corn held over the fire to puff into little white flowers of goodness. Corn dried and ground and cooked as gruel, flavored and steamed in the husk, flattened into bread and baked on hot stones. Long before the temples and the cities, the slaves and the tortured captives, the carved jade and the crafted silver, the bloodletting and the sacrifice, comes the simple goodness of the corn, sweet and nutty and nourishing as the sun in the morning.

— 1,000 to 500: Temples—Central and North America

Ah, but now it is time. From the silt-rich flood plain of the Coatzacoalcos River where the Olmecs carve their massive heads of stone, to the Ohio River Valley where the Adena lift mounds of earth in the shapes of animals, people begin to build temples. In Tabasco the Olmecs carve Jaguar and Harpy Eagle, Serpent and Shark into the flanks of buildings. In the forests of the Yucatán and the Petén, the rain god Chac looks outward from the sacred steps of pyramids. In the great metropolis of Teotihuacan, on the hill of the Toltecs at Tula, on the raised earth of Etowah in Georgia, across America the temples rise, lifted by many hands. Goddesses and gods of rain and night, dawn and moon, feathered serpent and grinning monkey, raven and fish, corn and yuca, earth and sky, green growing things and bone-white death are carved in stone and shell, hammered in gold, shaped in clay. And with these deities and observances, altars and holy places, come priests and lords, nobles and slaves, conquest and tribute, warriors to be honored and prisoners to be sacrificed. Only in the small, the wild, the intimate magic of tribal people does the memory of our kinship and equality still linger, far away from where stone rises upon ornate and bloody stone.

৬৯ TOBACCO

Fragrant nicotiana is an elder who offers us a test. In one hand she holds reverence; in the other, addiction. Tobacco is the herb of balance, of restraint, of reciprocity. Tobacco teaches sustainable use.

When you offer tobacco with prayer, with gratitude, with respect, you are spared. Tobacco honors the giver and the receiver. But if you try to stash away honor, crave unearned respect, turn tobacco into a smoky facade of sophistication or cool to dazzle others and fool yourself, watch out! Tobacco will eat into your lungs, set wild fires raging in your throat, choke your heart with mud slides, release packs of wild cells that will multiply out of control, invading and devouring your flesh.

Tobacco holds the scales and puts you in charge of the consequences. Honor others. Honor yourself. Take what you need. Take only what you need. Count your blessings, name your friends, offer your integrity freely to the world. Tobacco says for the life you receive, give life. Tobacco says gluttony and greed and ingratitude will tip the scales toward misery. Like the great cities of the ancient worlds you will learn that hunger comes from starving the fields, fiery destruction from enslaving the people, and disrespect can lead to death.

0: City Girls—Teotihuacan, Mexico

All you big city girls with hearts that sing to the bustle of crowds, let me tell you, it didn't begin in Manhattan, didn't start in L.A. Teotihuacan may not have had subways or Central Park, but you could walk for hours round the rim of that lake, watching farmers raking lake weed onto the raised beds to feed crops for market. There were no department stores, but who needed them with all the craftspeople's quarters where you could shop for obsidian mirrors, jade jewelry, feather garments, and polished beads? The tools they made in the volcanic glass workshops went out across the continent and Teotihuacan had as many foreigners, as many languages and ethnic foods as New York any day. Just like New York, Teotihuacan had neighborhoods. The Avenue of the Dead was like Park Avenue, full of ritzy penthouses and courtyards open to the sky. There were whole sections of town with nothing but apartment buildings, pretty nice if not too fancy. And, of course, the barrios full of tenements, dark, smelly, overcrowded rabbit warrens packed to the brim with poor folks struggling to make a living. Granted, New York is a lot bigger and has better dance clubs; still, two hundred thousand people was nothing to sneer at back then. You could definitely get lost in a crowd, make sure your business stayed your own, get out and meet people your family didn't approve of, and still come home to a street where everybody knew your name.

0 to 500: Turtle Women, Women of Trees—
The Caribbean

This is what we are left with: fragments of shell, splinters of wood, shreds of bark, stories changed almost beyond recognition after passing through so many other mouths: the men, the warriors, the priests. It is all we are left with to tell us how the women of Boriken began.

This is what we have. In the beginning, our mother was a turtle, and we all came from her back. Not the tiny painted turtles you can get at pet stores, but the great green sea turtle, the hawksbill, the carey. The one they hunt for turtle soup, for the virility they seek in her eggs, the one whose shell is covered with whorls that map the universe, that they use to frame their eyeglasses, hoping to see.

This is what we have. That somehow the men, traveling up the chain of islands from the great continent to Boriken, were left without women and found us, shining among the trees, creatures supple as saplings, glowing red-brown under our bark, but without sex. That it was the carpintero, the woodpecker, who came and opened us, and in a flurry of red and black and white feathers, beating wings and yellow-rimmed eyes, the birds made new places, tender and pink, for our touch. That they made us flower, wider and wider, until from the sap-filled crevices of our bodies, from the sticky pleasures we took together, a people was born, made of sea water and earth, feather and shell and trees.

✋ ABUELAS

West African Women

600 to 1400: Market Women—West Africa

In the marketplaces of West Africa, it is women who spread their wares on colored cloth, pile surplus grain and fruits and fabric in painted baskets, and barter and haggle, laughing and argumentative. Men may travel the long trails across the deserts, go to the ends of the known earth for exotic copper, forged iron, painted clay. But the trade of the town square belongs to women.

Even after centuries of invasion, after the bloody uprooting of villages into the holds of slave ships, after generation upon generation of captivity, rape, torture, and endless labor in the sugar fields, kitchens, and laundry rooms; even after the tight web of kinship is stretched and torn in the slave markets of a hundred towns and cities, West African women freed from shackles into poverty will still be traders. From scraps and ingenuity they will find something to craft, cultivate, cook, spread out on the ground before the eyes of strangers. Baskets and embroidered blouses, coconut candy and palm leaf hats, sweet peppers and fermented maví—African women will fill the plazas of Puerto Rican towns with their voices, bartering and haggling for their livelihoods. For a couple of coins, the price of a chicken, a pound of beans, a length of cotton, they will flatter and harass and persuade, sell whatever there is to be sold, and fill bellies one miraculous day at a time.

700: Not All Tribes Build Upward
Toward the Sky—Nigeria

Those who have lived too long in the shadows of empire look only for kings and monuments and pass the villages by. They run after glittering stories of Greater Ghana, Mali, and Songhay, of mani-kongos and sunnis, of Mansa Musa and Sundiata and the lords of Benin. There they will find the familiar power struggles of dynasties and war parties, conquests and looting. But we will step off that path and take a walk among the small societies, where Africa is born again each season and balance is found again and again.

Kingship is a blunt and clumsy tool compared to the intricate and flexible life of the villages. Power does not pile up at the top where it can topple and fall in ruins. Power falls like seed planted in a field. Each head of a family, each leader of a clan has no more than can be held in two hands and scatters it no farther than it can be thrown in a single gesture. Each village runs its own affairs, but no neighboring village stands alone. The people of the small societies make patterns of loyalty and mutual obligation, as elaborate and elegant as the regalia of royalty and of far more practical use.

Among the Igbo, the Tiv, the Tallensi, respect is not servility and birth does not confer advantages of class or rank. In the fertile lands of the Igbo, people grow faster than yams, and everything must stretch easily. Families break away to plant new villages. Villages join together and combine into one. The rule of men over women is not as hard and fast as in the places where great profit is to be had. The ancestors mediate disputes and speak with the gods on their children's behalf. Within the net of responsibility, there is room to move around, many ways to find prestige, many paths of service to the clan. Here in the villages, African democracy is being woven with local ingredients: a weft of self-confidence and kinship, a warp of many places to enter and many ways to leave.

While the heads of merchant city-states reach for the sky, building higher and higher walls, the people of the villages make widening circles with their arms and notice who stands on either side.

600 to 1400: Slave Road—Africa

It's an old and bitter road, the slave road out of Africa. Thousands of bare feet carrying heavy hearts, the numb eyes of women, the frightened faces of children, these more than any walk there. In the first years of the T'ang dynasty, before the Hijira of Mohammed, before Teotihuacan went up in flames, before Spain became Arab, before Islam became empire, there were Black African slaves in China. Eight hundred years before Portuguese ships began devouring the coastal villages of the Guinea Coast, West African women were dragged across the Sahara and sold in Persia. Five hundred years before the Spanish began raiding the Berbers to work sugar plantations in Canarias, most of the wealthy families of Canton had Black slaves.

And where Islam entered, the road grew wider, the traffic heavier. Bantu-speaking traders sent slaves to Red Sea Arab ports, and with ivory and iron, amber and leopard skins, rhinoceros horn and tortoise shell they made their way to India, to China, to Italy and Spain, to the homes and businesses of wealthy men throughout the Muslim world. Oh, it was far from the six-lane highway it would become when Europe tore open every dip in the coastline where a slave ship could anchor, but it was no longer a footpath of misery. The defenders of the faith made a road trampled hard and bare and wide enough for ten thousand to walk away in chains.

They are still walking. Even after the Atlantic abduction of nations left ruins beyond repair, after the bloody trade was ended, after abolition, after independence, the beast is still not dead. From the Red Sea, descendants of Arab traders still raid south from Khartoum deep into the Sudan to the marshes of the White Nile, stealing dark women and children, keeping them as slave labor, beaten, starved, forced to work; and whoever writes their stories, protests their bondage goes into exile or into jail.

And what of those who live far away from such extreme penalties? Who is willing to tell this shameful truth? Who will take the human rights report to the street corner and raise hell?

Silence and oil and the power-brokering of guns and trade and religious alliances. Silence and the shame of the oppressed to tell the world that the slaver's taint is also upon us. The cynical readiness of the entitled to blame first and foremost the enslaved, or those who are closest kin to them. And yet, in all truth, it must be said. In the United States, the great-great-grandsons of African slaves, men who have chosen Islam for its dignity and rich heritage, choose not to rock the boat of Muslim donors for these kinswomen's sake. What Minister Farakhan gained from the march of half a million men, he will not risk for the girls and women of the Sudan. One thing weighed against another, money and influence, suffering and grief, conscience makes its peace with slavery once again.

1352: Ibn Batuta Writes Home—Mali

Islam spreads into West Africa in the saddlebags of merchants and is diplomatically adopted by townspeople in all the centers of commerce. Islam makes a net of common customs, blurring the lines of nations, overriding tribal equities with new hierarchies of influence and benefit, empire and trade. But even in the courts of Muslim kings, the old religions persist alongside the new, and the heritage of Mohammed is strangely unfamiliar when dressed in West African garb.

Ibn Batuta travels south along the merchant road from Sijilmasa to the salt-making city of Taghaza, where even the mosques are built of glittering blocks of the crystalline stuff, and on across the true desert for more than a month, until he reaches the oasis of Walata and the settled lands of Mali that lie beyond.

The kingdom of Mali has been Muslim for a hundred years, but Ibn Batuta is shocked to see the casual nakedness of unwed women, the sociable self-confidence and easy discourse of the wives, the tribal sprinkling of dust on the heads of those who prostrate themselves before the rulers. In the Muslim cities of West Africa, women are not secluded, women are not hidden, women who live by the laws first written in far away Medina still walk upon the ancestors' earth, talk to the ancestors' spirits, bare their breasts to the sun.

1440: People, Pepper, Ivory, Gold—West Africa

The wealth of Africa is apparent to the naked eye. In the city of Benin, Portuguese traders may barter for precious pepper to disguise the rotten smell of putrid meat, for gleaming ivory and the currency of half the known world: West African gold. The cities that sit along all the shores of this continent are dazzling to the visitor's eye. Kilwa and Mombasa, Brava and Zeila glitter with the accumulation of centuries of Asian trade, brilliant with silk and gold-embroidered clothing, rich carpets, delicate porcelain, storehouses full of silver and pearls and bolts of fine cloth. Gao and Timbuktu are still centers of learning where one may purchase scrolls and priceless manuscripts from many lands. And everywhere there are people, unaware that their hands and backs, wombs and bellies will represent a greater wealth still, but not for themselves. This vast and prospering continent, whose riches are only just dawning on its neighbors to the north, will not yield easily to invasion. Not until Europe breaks open the nearly bottomless treasuries of America will it suddenly and unexpectedly surge into power enough to crack the bones of Africa and suck the marrow dry.

AMERICAN WOMEN:
700 TO 1400

700: Mayas—MesoAmerica

Others will tell you of the magnificent pyramids, the exquisite carvings, the majestic courtyards now overgrown with vines, or the observatories where they tracked the intricate dancing of the stars and mapped the orbit of Venus. They will call it mysterious that this grand civilization, so strong, so brilliant, so accomplished should have dwindled back into the forest, its cities abandoned to the monkeys. It was no mystery. It was both simple and harsh. They took more from the land than the land could give and gave back less than it needed. Like the salt-encrusted deserts of Sumer, the eroded hills of Greece, the naked, deforested sugar lands of Northeast Brazil, the message of the great Mayan ruins, long since abandoned for tiny holdings in the hills, is both devastating and direct.

You who have built huge avenues and temples of commerce, who use giant lenses and radio signals to study the stars, what we who were your equals in achievement have to teach is neither of architecture nor the sky. Our lesson is of the broken circle of the earth. The aching land we disregarded. How, exhausted by our demands, the land sickened and faltered until, unable to sustain themselves on our grandeur, our cities died.

975: Against the Knife—Mexico

The Chichimecas, the Children of the Dog, who came south out of the dry lands many generations ago into the valley of Mexico, have built the city of Tula on the crown of a hill, and Topiltzin, son of Mixcoatl and a man of peace, rules under the sign of the Serpent. The people have become the Toltecas, an empire spreading over wide lands. Topiltzin encourages architecture, and they become master builders. He encourages farmers to experiment, and they develop improved strains of maize, squash, and cotton. He encourages artists, and the Toltecs craft fine work in silver and gold, invent new forms of pottery, weaving, feather-work, and writing. Topiltzin takes the name Quetzalcoatl, bird-snake.

But now the children of the Feathered Serpent have been swallowed by the children of Tezcatlipoca, ruler of the night. Quetzalcoatl has dared to stand against the knife and oppose human sacrifice. Hidden in the hissing, living skirts of Coatlicue, the Snake Mother, her children must flee south. Behind them the blood continues to spill across the temple stones, until Tula itself falls and other blood-stained cities rise in its place. The people of Quetzalcoatl find a home among the ruins of Maya and there is a new flowering of life in the Yucatan, without sacrificial torments, without still-beating hearts set to char among the flames.

Ancestor of my heart, I have stood beside the place of sacrifice and smelled the burnt offerings, the anguish of the captives. You did not end it. Across MesoAmerica the mothers were dishonored, widows sent to their deaths, and the Aztec heirs to the blood rites proclaimed that the sun was lifted each morning by the spirits of young male warriors tortured to death and dragged down into darkness each night by the souls of women dead in childbirth. But the peace they drove out continued to haunt them. When, five hundred years after your flight, new invaders came, unlike any seen before and destined to be the bloodiest yet, the people whispered your name, murmuring hopefully, "Perhaps he has returned at last, Queztalcoatl, the Feathered Serpent, the one who stood against the knife—the bringer of peace."

1000: Bone and Hair and Shard—North America

How do I sift among the many broken stories for the one that reflects a fragment of your face? Shall I tell you of the Anasazi living in the canyons of the Southwest who vanished in a time of drought? Or what about Cahokia, the largest ancient city north of

Mexico, whose people grew sunflowers in the river bottoms and may have succumbed to tuberculosis? Perhaps you would rather hear tell of the Iroquois, of the longhouses and the clan mothers and the league of nations. Here I sit, a storyteller looking back across places that have been altered beyond recognition, looking for the lives of women in a splinter of bone, a single hair, a shard of pottery. The bone suggests the graceful movements of an arm, the hair the sound of someone breathing in their sleep, the shard the curve of a vanished bowl. But perhaps the arm was clenched in anger, the hair shaved from an enemy's head, the shard from a chamber pot. The messages were all but lost in transit. I cannot find our mothers in the archaeologist's reports. All I can offer you is the soil of North America, planted everywhere with histories that touch our own like fingers in the dark.

1400: Caciques—Boriken

You would think we had always had caciques, but it isn't so. In the long ago of our people, family was family and clans lived side by side without trying to boss each other. It was the same as everywhere, the slow gathering of more than their share, the dream that those with more are more fit to rule. To choose the song we will all dance to. And as in most places, when cacique was invented, warrior and husband were not far behind.

Bad habits tend to start at the top. When caciques began to make rules and inheritances, at first we women had an almost equal share of inequality. Fatherhood was no big deal. The accumulated wealth was passed to sisters' children. But the scales had already begun to tip. The more naborías generated wealth, the more wealth had to be defended. The more wealth had to be defended, the more important warriors became. And long before the white-sailed caravels began circling the islands like hungry sharks, men had begun to wrest the power of lineage from the mothers. Oh, the abuelas still had honor among the people. But

generations before the one that saw invasion, the wives of dead caciques were being sacrificed, sent with their husbands into death,
forced to surrender their authority to their sons, pushed out of
the way of what the lords of the land, as they always do, called
progress.

Mediterranean Women:
600 to 1400

620: Arabian Nights—Arabian Peninsula

We are all storytellers trying to save our lives. Like the captive
bride of the Sultan, lengthening her life one tale at a time, we hold
death entranced by our liveliness. At night the bright stars wheel
overhead, across desert and oasis and sea coast, over tents of rough
cloth and hide, over cities of stone, over open campfires and night
travelers on camel and on foot. The women of the Arabian night
come forward into the firelight, one by one, wearing names both
familiar and strange, Aixa, Yamila, Fatima, Hind, Yasmin. The
rough ceiling gives way to constellations as they speak, and the
dim roar of traffic becomes the wind whispering across dry land.

Jahilia wedding nights, the singing and dancing and feasting.
There are many kinds of marriages made under the moon. Some
women marry one man, some marry many. Such a woman's husbands, wedded to her alone, take turns visiting the marriage bed.
She has many lovers, a full kitchen, a generous home. But soon this
lush oasis of pleasures, this grove of date palms will be cut down,
and only men will have an abundance of lovers.

Here comes a wealthy widow of Mecca, a woman with confidence, running her own business. Her caravans carry goods into
Syria and bring back Syrian merchandise to sell. Khadija is forty
years old when she proposes marriage to her young overseer, a man

of twenty-five. Freed by her wealth from any need to work, Mohammed enters a life of contemplation. Fifteen years later, in a cave near Mecca, Mohammed wakes shivering from a vision of the angel Gabriel, and it is Khadija who wraps him in blankets and assures him that he is sane, Khadija who takes him to her scholarly cousin for help in understanding what has happened. She is the first Muslim woman, his first convert, but her marriage is not Islamic. No male guardian arranges the wedding. She is neither veiled nor secluded. Her independence is unchallenged, her husband young and, as long as she lives, without other wives. But she passes into her tomb in the hill called Hujun.

Now a little girl comes skipping through the night. She stops and looks over her shoulder. She turns serious dark eyes toward our firelit faces. I was six years old, she tells us, when my mother called me in from my games with my friends and told me I must go inside the house, and so it fell into my heart, she says, that I was married. 'Aisha is the third and most beloved wife of the Prophet. She is nine years old when her mother takes her down from her swing, washes her face, takes her in, and sets her on the Prophet's lap so that their marriage may be consummated. Now, looking at us from the shadows, she is a grown woman, her eyes challenging us to understand her story. That she had his respect and trust, that he depended on her and she on him, that she was no cowering, passive wife. That she had much more to say, and said it, than the chroniclers ever reported. That she did not go willingly into seclusion but, like all the wives, protested to the verge of divorced en mass. That when Mohammad lay buried beneath the floor of her bedroom, it was she who was consulted and gave decisions on matters of sacred law and custom. That her life, like ours, was woven of constraints and freedoms.

Into the warmth of the crackling blaze step the wounded priestesses of Kindah and Hadramaut. The dancing flames seem to restore flickering red hands to their severed wrists. When the news came of the Prophet's death, six women of power dyed their hands red with henna and began playing on drums and tambourines. Twenty more, whom the chroniclers call harlots, joined them, dancing and chanting and calling the people to rise up and throw off the rule of Islam. Although the men of Kindah and Hadramaut fought to defend them, the soldiers of Abu Bakr came thundering through on horseback and cut off the hands that drummed and curved in the air. But in this circle where all the stories are told, fingers of fire pluck the wind and tap on invisible tambourines once more, a glimpse of rich worlds gone up in flames.

The priestesses blow away in the wind and here comes Salma bint Malik, riding like fury on her mother's camel, leading her soldiers into battle against the heirs of Mohammed. Her mother, too, led warriors against Islam and, captured, was tied to two wild beasts and torn in half. Salma was given to 'Aisha and served her, even marrying a relative of the Prophet's, but when he died, she returned to her own people, now in rebellion, returned to lead them and to avenge her mother's cruel death.

Here are women, one after another, stepping in and out of the light in turn. Those who wrote stiff contracts before their weddings and protected their rights by wielding the law. Those who were put to death for taking lovers and those who were widowed and ran the store. Those who resisted the push of Islam, who forced the Prophet to authorize the worship of the goddess Allat. Women who whispered sedition from behind their veils, and those who lay in each other's arms in the women's quarters. Women who made bright gardens in small walled spaces, and women who lost the ability to speak because no one listened. The embers die down to dim coals, and like Sheherezade, the vizier's daughter, we are still singing in the dark, while the voices of long-dead women fall round us like showers of shooting stars.

900 to 1400: Bread, Oil, Wine—Christian Spain

The cycles of the year weave through each other. The cycles of the earth, of planting, flowering, harvest, and seed, the rhythms of work, are marked by Saint's days and Catholic feasts, by the lunar patterns of candles, wine, and ancient prayers of Jews, by the muzzein's call, the cleansings and fast days of Muslims and the frowned-upon worship of the hidden goddesses and gods of the land. But here in the North, the Church is ascendant, the reconquest of Iberia underway. The peasant women of Spain move through the dance of the year to many melodies, but more and more to a Christian beat.

The first feast after Christmas is Candlemas. The ancient festival of fire has become the Purification of Mary. The church is filled with candles, the hills sparkling with bonfires. The men go away in early spring to work in the olive groves and wheat fields of the landlords, to dig and plow and tend the trees. At home on small plots, women weed their vineyards, do the second working of the soil after last year's harvest, see to the vines.

Ash Wednesday, and then it is Lent—the sober tightening of belts as the last of the old year's food is used. The time of repentance and abstention. If the season is hard and the priests vehement, as the time of the Crucifixion draws near there will be attacks on Jews. But the time of fertility and rebirth is coming. Days after the equinox is the Feast of the Annunciation, the miracle of divine pregnancy as buds begin to swell. Jews celebrate deliverance and pray for it over *pesach* wine. On the first Sunday after the first full moon of spring, the Christian world throws off its sorrow and is reborn.

In April and May there is weeding to be done and the fallow fields get their first plowing. Flowers bloom, lambs appear, and the cherries, both sweet and sour, are in season. May Day, the old holy day of the flowering earth, festival of fertility and love, peeks out from under the blue cloak of Our Lady and the Feast of the Ascension. Midsummer night is a pagan feast, but three days later is the Day of San Juan. As fruit begins to form on the bough, people flock to the markets and plazas to sing and dance.

In July they have the days of Maria Magdalena, the sinner who broke all the rules and was saved, and Santa Ana, patroness of housewives and women in labor. They matter more to ordinary women than Santiago, fierce patron of Spain and its conquests, whose image is carried through the streets at the end of the month. Magdalena is especially dear to them, her popularity growing as those troubled by their imperfections seek solace in plays and songs about her repentance and redemption.

In summer, in the hottest weather, the wheat is reaped and winnowed. The sheaves are bound and stacked, grain separated, sacks filled to bursting point. Everyone gathers in mid-August for the Feast of Mary's Assumption. Under hot blue skies the faithful contemplate her bodily ascent into heaven, there to be Queen. Late summer, grapes are cut from the vine, the first pressing is done, and the barrels are filled. Now there is plenty of everything: figs and apples, pears and prunes, bread and milk and honey.

Michaelmas, feast of the Archangel, is the harvest festival, one of the great markers of the turning year. There are prayers of thanksgiving and blessings of the gathered crops. Jews eat fruit and honey, invoking sweetness for the New Year, and begin the purification of the High Holy Days. In this time of abundance men return from far-off fields to their lovers' beds again. Women sell their wine and the fruits of their small orchards to pay off debts and buy what is needed before winter: a new ax blade, needles, wheat, and last year's oil from the patrones.

The year turns from golden to brown. In October the wheat fields are plowed under and planted again. There are still figs and grapes and the autumn crop of nuts is ripe. There is firewood stacked in the shed, apples and dried fruit, cheese and sausages, crusty bread, oil and onions and red wine. Now the men stay at home, turning the soil in the vineyards once again and pruning back the vines for winter. Time to remember the dead, as death hovers over the chilling land. It is Yom Kippur, Day of Atonement for the Jews. It is All Hallow's Eve and the days of All Saints and All Souls. It is the turning place, when spirits of those who have left us approach the living once more and are fed.

November and December the olives are ripe, and women go off to pick them, filling heavy baskets and loading wagons that will carry the fruit to the press. Some women discover they are pregnant after the harvest-time reunions and say a special prayer at the Feast of the Immaculate Conception. Soon it will be Christmas, with the promise of light in midwinter darkness, the joyous rebirth of the sun, the miraculous infant born in poverty and kneeled to by kings. From the dark wooden presses, this year's supply of aromatic green oil drips into the waiting tubs to fill the lamps, flavor all food, ease childbirth, and lubricate the ever-turning wheel of the year.

⁊ OLIVE OIL

Olive oil is like that certain neighbor, that particular relative, la entremetida, always poking into everything, chattering, lubricating the life she touches with that pervasive scent of hard-pressed experience, the eyes that know, the camaraderie of being alive. Olive oil brings you the newspaper column that mentions five solutions for the problem she thinks you have and a little something she cooked up because nobody should be so skinny as your third child, bless him. Olive oil is impossible to close your door on, impossible to reject, sneaks what is good for you into your house, slips medicines under your tongue, eases the baby's head through the tight spaces of your pelvis so that nothing tender gets torn. Sometimes the smell is so rich, so unsnubbable, that you crave a cool and scentless safflower, a moment of privacy, a rest from her pushy love. But when she takes off for a

visit to her niece and is gone for a week, you can't wait for her
golden green oily touch to fill your nostrils, your cooking pots,
your family life, all the dry crevices of your longing.

900 to 1200: Poets of al-Andalus—Muslim Spain

'A'isa Bint Amhad B. Muhammad B Qadim of Cordoba is the
daughter of a wealthy family. It is said that in all of al-Andalus she
has no equal in intelligence, in knowledge both sacred and profane, in poetry and rhetoric, and in virtue, eloquence, and good
judgment. She composes praise poems to kings, and her fluency
opens a way for her where few have gone. None refuse her media-
tion. She has beautiful handwriting and has copied Korans and
other texts. She collects books and has an abundant library. In the
Euro-Christian year 1009 E.C.C., which is the year 400 of Islam,
she dies without ever having married.

   To a poet who had asked her to wed him, she replied:

I am a lioness
and have never been pleased with the lairs of others—
and if I had to choose someone
I would never answer the barking of a dog, I
who have so often closed my ears to lions.

A hundred years earlier the slave woman Qamar, a native of Baghdad, is a singer at the court of Ibrahim b. Hayyay, lord of Seville.
A skilled musician, knowing many verses by heart and with a
voice of great purity, Qamar leaves behind only two fragments of
poetry. One, cold and formal, praises her master. In the other she
writes:

Ay! I weep for Baghdad and for Iraq,
for women like gazelles,
and for the enchantment of their eyes,

for their long walks along the Euphrates
faces rising like moons above their necklaces,
beautiful women who saunter
languidly, through a life of delights,
just as if they felt a hopeless passion.
Oh, I would give my soul for my own land!
Everything bright comes from its splendor.

Butayna Bint Al-Mu'tamid is the daughter of the king of Sevilla. In the endless wars between factions, the Almoravids besiege the city, sack the castle, and Butayna has disappeared among the many captives sold into slavery. Her grieving parents know nothing of her until they receive some verses, which will later become famous throughout the Muslim West. In them, she tells how she has been bought as a concubine by a merchant who has given her to his son. She writes how she was prepared for him, but when he came to her bed she refused him. In her verses she describes how she spoke to him of her lineage and swore she would not allow him to touch her unless they were wed with her father's consent. How she insisted that the merchant send her words to her father and writes that she now awaits his response. The verses reach her father in exile and her parents rejoice to learn that their daughter is alive. Unable to rescue her, her father gives his consent to the marriage and writes, "Be affectionate with him—the times decree that you accept him." Wielding poetry in self-defense, Butayna has won some dignity in her captivity.

Cordoba is a city in turmoil, in these years between 1009 and 1031. Life is uncertain, and for Wallada, daughter of the murdered minister al-Mushafi, this leads to unusual freedom. She is an acclaimed poet, the center of an admiring circle, a well-known cultural figure in the tumultuous town. But some attack and criticize her disregard for convention and decorum.

The great poet Ibn Zaydun is her lover, his poems to her among the best-known in all of Spanish-Arabic literature. When he falls in love with her slave, she attacks him bitterly. Her next lover is the vizier Abu Amir Ibn Abdus. Although she never marries, they remain close until their deaths. In her last years she is poor but never humbled. On her right sleeve she has embroidered the verse "I am made, by God, for glory, and I walk proudly on my own road."

1097: Fire at the Gates—Syria

In the cities of Syria, women and men, Muslim and Byzantine, await the coming of the Franj, the Christian invaders from north and west. The Muslim commanders of the faithful know about conquering those of other religions. They are tolerant of outside observances, and both Christian and Jew are generally safe beneath their rule. But the crusaders who come ravening out of Europe are worse then starving beasts. Wherever they enter, they kill and enslave.

The ruler of one city courteously requests that the Byzantine Christian men who may be expected to sympathize with the Franj leave the city for the duration of the siege, and personally guarantees the safety of their families. And when, in years to come, Saladin retakes Jerusalem, he will keep the synagogues and churches open, will compensate Jews and Christians for any losses they have suffered, and, if they wish to leave, will give them money to help them start new lives.

But the civilized Christian knights, the lion-hearted crusaders of romantic tales, begin their holy task of liberation by slaughtering the Jews of Rouen in France and continue as they have begun. When they enter the city of Ma'arra, they butcher every human being they can find, drag their bodies into the fields, boil and roast the people they have killed, and hold a great feast to celebrate the arrival of true religion in the dens of the infidel.

900 to 1400: Juderías—Iberian Peninsula

The Jewish girls of Spain work in their mothers' vineyards, help to cultivate their mothers' plots of land. Like Reguo Benaviste, in 1389, many go into the homes of other Jews, or their converso relations, to work as servants in exchange for food and beds and clothing. Reguo enters the service of Samuel Benaviste at the age of six, for a term of ten years. Samuel promises to care for her in sickness or health.

1182: The blood libel, the myth that Jews perform rituals with the blood of Christian babies, appears at Saragossa and some people are eager and willing to believe. 1215: Jews and Muslims must wear special badges and clothing. 1243: Wagonloads of Jewish books are burned in Paris, while, accused of desecrating the host, the Jews themselves are burned in Berlin. 1264: Jews are invited into Poland to lend the nobles money, to bring their skills in commerce and their Mediterranean contacts. 1268: Jews are attacked by mobs in London and other English cities.

Jewish girls from well-off families are apprenticed to sew and embroider at the age of ten. Bellaire, daughter of Issachus Saragoça, is contracted to Mosé Salamon of Barcelona for the years from 1387 to 1389. She is to learn button-making. Jewish girls cannot expect to work as silk weavers, as silversmiths, or in the making of books. But they can weave ordinary cloth, sew and embroider, keep spice shops, and sell fish and medicine, rags and linens, books and manuscripts. In 1355 Oroceti, wife of Josef ben Shaprut, and Oroshoel, wife of Salomon Aljamin, are well-known throughout Navarre for the quality of their silk and wine and shoes.

1290: The Jews of England are expelled. 1291: They may not settle in France. 1306: The Jews of France are imprisoned, their property seized, and one hundred thousand are expelled.

If she is fertile and willing, and her husband promises not to lie with her for the term of her contract, a Jewish girl may be a wet nurse, breastfeeding the children of wealthy families for a monthly fee. Or, if she is hungry enough, she can find ample employment as a prostitute. Jewish and Muslim men are proscribed by law from having sex with Christian women, but Christians, Muslims, and Jews may all be clients of a working Jewess.

1348: As elsewhere, with the coming of the plague, Jews are blamed for poisoning the wells, angering God, and bringing down this suffering. The desperate populace massacres the Jews of Spain. 1391: Pogroms again, in the wool-trading centers, in the port cities, in the cathedral towns of Spain; Jewish homes and synagogues are burned and Jews dragged into the streets by their neighbors and killed.

If she is fortunate, she may be one of many women doctors, especially if she lives in the kingdom of Aragon. Floreta, widow of Jucef ça Noga and licensed to practice medicine, attends Queen Sibila of Fortía. Bellaire, Pla, and Dolcich, all married to men of the Gallipapa family of Lérida, are licensed to practice anywhere in Aragon. Ceti of Valencia practices at the court of Pedro el Ceremonioso in Navarre. But Jamila of Calatayud, a Muslim woman, is fined for practicing without a license. The course of study is three years and then an examination by a physician of one's own religion. A Jewish woman may also be a midwife. Many are, especially since a Jewish gynecology text was translated from Arabic to Hebrew and has been circulating throughout the learned homes and academies of Iberia.

If she is fortunate, she will not be in the streets when the pogrom comes, will not live in the quarter that is burned, will not be coming out of the synagogue on the day the dam of frustration breaks and her neighbors vent their rage at high prices and unjust landlords on the Jews. If she is fortunate in every way, her grand-

children's grandchildren will survive, to kiss the ground in passion
and grief, when the Jews of Sepharad are cast out and exiled from
this beloved land.

❦Pomegranates

Fruit of a million seeds, jeweled globe of garnets, breast and
thighs of the goddess, garden of delights, symbol of the fruitful
earth. *Rimmon*, Pomegranate, Granada, Grenadine. Each small
grain swells with ruby juices in its own tight place, alone and
nested among a thousand others within the leathery skin, made
to withstand the desert sun. So in the Jewish quarter, each home
with its own Sabbath light, all leaning upon each other, and the
walls and laws around. Pomegranate teaches community,
teaches the delights of love, teaches us to nest in each other's
hearts, to cup the juice of life in our joined hands, union,
communion, community of souls, the true and most ancient
holy of holies where we find each other naked, place of ecstacy
remembered in each cup of wine we bless. When the blow falls
and the fruit shatters, let her seeds scatter far and wide on this
earth and spring up everywhere, a million orchards of joy.

1350: Working Santiago de Compostela—Galicia, Spain

Ay, mija, you'll be so glad you came to Santiago. You'll make out
like a bandit in this town. Ever since St. James first appeared here,
it's been the biggest pilgrimage site, the greatest tourist trap north
of Rome. What would you like to do? Sell ribbons and finery to
the upscale visitors? They also like their medallions made of silver.
You can be a very successful baker, sell at airport prices, even
stretch the flour with a bit of sawdust, and although sometimes
you get caught and fined, the pilgrims mostly pay. You can peddle
chestnuts and fresh anchovies, but we've been warned off from
selling them during Mass. Of course, with so many people in
town you can always sell spice or candles.

We don't have cruise ships, or that Tuesday and Thursday lunchtime stampede for sandwiches and cocktails that you get in Old San Juan. But whenever they pull into town, on foot or horseback or wagon, pilgrims always arrive hungry and ready to pay ridiculous amounts for bread and sausages, oatmeal, wine, and cheese. You know how people spend when they're on vacation! It's no different here, and there's plenty of opportunity to sell expensive snacks.

But my personal favorite is making medals of Santiago, holy souvenirs that sell like hotcakes. Since we're still hundreds of years away from having t-shirts silk-screened with his image or matching salt and pepper shakers, medals are really the most popular purchase in the trade. Every day when I sit in my shop, stamping his image into little circles of lead and tin, scratching it into carved pieces of shell, or working it into more costly items in copper or silver for the ladies and the gentlemen, I never forget to send up a prayer of thanks to Santiago, patron saint of my very own Reconquista. Because while the caballeros are off fighting the Moors, Christendom just keeps getting bigger, more pilgrims come here every day looking for miracles, and the good saint keeps them foolish and openhanded, so they spend and spend and spend.

Premonitions

1478: Unfortunate Isles—Canary Islands

In the legends of the Mediterranean, these are the islands on which good luck always smiles, the blessed and magical archipelago, the fortunate isles. But now their fortune has run out. Fresh from the battles of the Reconquista, the new lords of Andalusía land on the beaches of Canarias, so named by the ancients for their free-roaming packs of wild dogs.

The Guanches are kin to the old Saharans. They have prospered here in the heat and light, surrounded by the sea. But Canarias is about to become a laboratory for empire and their time in the sun is over.

Drunk with exhilaration from victory after victory in the south of Iberia, elated at the fall of the Muslim kings of al-Andalus, the men of resurgent Spain fall upon the Guanches in a frenzy of greed. Everything that will be done to America, they do here first. They capture caciques, marry cacicas, demand tribute, bring African slaves from the nearby coast, and force them to grow sugar.

Don Peraza, conqueror of one island, captures and rapes a Guanche woman, a cacica in her own right. Conquest has not yet made the Guanches numb to such violation. Peraza is dragged from his home and killed. His widow demands justice, thinking justice is the punishment of those who resist. But the royal crown of Castilla y Aragon decrees that the Guanches need the illusion of sovereignty to be good subjects. That in the long run, moderation will save them work.

La Guanche is the elder sister of our mothers. Of Malinche and Guanina, Anacaona and María Caguax, of millions of women across the ocean who do not yet dream of her, busy about their lives in the worlds they know. But she dreams of them. She dreams it again and again, the persistent nightmare, the nightly horror. She sees the wild dog Peraza with his sharp fangs bared, snarling and ravening across the world, leaping from island to island, from shore to shore, a naked woman dangling from his teeth.

1482: Elmina Castle—Ghana

It is a place along the shore where ships can shelter. It is the mouth of a river. A place of small trade. It does not yet stink of burning flesh. It does not yet reek of bowels uncontrolled from terror. It is a small place. It is the tiny cut through which a continent will begin bleeding nearly to death. It is a pinhole, but infection will enter and go festering through the body, poisoning the blood. The veins are there, the well-traveled roads, the smooth Muslim middlemen, the modest trickle of the enslaved moving slowly out from the edges of the forest, north across the deserts. But very soon the forest paths and coastal ways will be choked with crowds of people weeping or stony-eyed from shock, and this small place, like a hundred others, will become a fountain of tainted riches, a gaping three-century wound, a site of unbearable loss, the place of amputation, the mouth of hemorrhage, the scene of the crime. As this river of pain and of human spirit flows out from the shore, Yemaya of the River Niger will grow as wide as all the waters, become mother of all those dragged across the hell of the middle passage.

One out of three will die, become white bones rolling on the ocean floor, spirits trailing after the stinking ships, a track of blood drawn across the waves. Those who survive the crossing transform each place they touch, in blood and suffering, in naked courage and stubborn endurance. The enormity of this atrocity, the lamenting cries of the captives, the angry shouts and cold silences of the captors, the legacy of rage and grief and shame will echo and echo down the centuries, and its voice will not be still.

1487: Maleus Malificarum—Germany

It has been happening for a few hundred years, happening here and there. There have been cases. But for the authors of the new treatise, it has not happened anywhere near enough. Women are the Devil's tool, and, according to them, he has been busy. Hatred of the wombs that bore them rises like a thick steam from the page. You will search her body, they say, for Devil's marks. Search with metal claws, with hot iron, with instruments of pain. You will crack her bones, tear her flesh, probe her soul with agony. You will know you have been successful when she confesses to this list we have compiled, in pornographic detail, of our fantasies about her.

She will say she has copulated with the Devil and that his

member is made of ice and is painful to her. She will confess to
having copulated with the Devil in the form of a goat and to having lusted endlessly after abominations. She will admit to loving
animals, that she speaks with them. She will admit to loving the
trees and dancing around them. She will confess that she loves the
night wind and gives herself to it, flying over the houses of sober
men. She will confess that she has used these ungodly forces of nature to heal the sick and that her knowledge of healing is from her
love of these beings, and not from the books we have written, and
is therefore unlawful.

This handbook is called the *Hammer of Witches,* and it goes
out far and wide to the churchmen and judges of Europe. Soon
women will begin to confess to the icy member, the goat, the flying, the knowing, the whole list. Soon women will be screaming
in torment, begging for mercy, going up in smoke. When they are
done, when the smoke clears, there will be no healers left, no midwives, whole villages without women. When they are done, our
wisdom will be unlawful, the book-learning of educated and
wealthy men official and exclusive. Today, with copies of the prac-
titioner's guide to torture just beginning to appear in the studies
of powerful men, it is only here and there, now and then. The curandera still gathers her herbs without fear. But for what is coming, she has no remedy. For what is coming, she will find no cure.
From what is coming to her, I, her daughter, centuries later, still
have not healed.

1490: Stolen Women

> *In the fall of 1493, two Arawak women, kidnapped by*
> *Caribs, will ask Columbus to take them home and will*
> *guide him to Boriken.*

It is true on every continent. It happens in every war. It happens
in the street and at the marketplace. Women are traded for salt

or corn, traded for bronze or ivory, sold for gold or elephants, exchanged for horses or iron. Women are stolen. Taken as war booty. Women are slaves. Women travel from people to people, are passed from hand to hand.

The widowed Ts'ai Yen of central China is captured by the Huns and taken to the north. Made concubine to a chieftain, she bears him two sons. Years pass, then she is ransomed by the warlord Ts'ao Ts'ao and must leave her children behind her. He marries her to one of his officers. She writes *The Eighteen Laments* to ease her many-layered losses. Malintsin of the Tabascans is sold to Moctezuma of the Aztecas, who gives her to the Spaniard Cortés. She translates for him and bears him two children. When he is done with her, he gives her to one of his captains.

The women of Middle Africa are sold to Muslim traders who sell them in turn in North Africa, Arabia, Persia, and deep into Asia and Europe. Syrian women are taken by Frankish crusaders. Arawak women are taken by Caribs of the eastern islands. Small tribes around the world bring in new blood by stealing themselves wives and concubines. Invading armies rape their way through the villages of the conquered. The English in Ireland. The Mongols in India. The Cossacks among the Jews. Whoever they want to keep, they take with them.

Stolen women are raped, married off, made domestic slaves, field slaves, captive craftswomen; bear children to their captors and have no rights to them. In this year, in this place called Boriken, as new invaders wait just over the curving horizon, the raping, stealing, and bartering of women is not news.

Bad Dreams: The Prophets Speak—The Americas

From the altiplano of the Incas to the Amazonian web of riverbanks; from the sea of grass west of the Mississippi, where horse-riding peoples pull houses of skin from campfire to campfire, to the volcanic slopes and green valleys of the dispersed Mayas and the city-lake of Tenochtitlan; from the reedy marshes, fragrant meadows, and tall forests where the coast people leave shell mounds around the great bay of the Sacramento River to the pastel deserts veined with dry creek-beds where mud bakes into stone and the Hopi keep the old calendar of changing worlds; from the glowing string of green and golden islands that stretch between Aruba and the Florida Keys to the jagged icy rocks of the seal hunters that flank the coast from Seattle to Yakutat Bay . . . in kivas and hammocks, longhouses and cliffhouses, under roofs of stone and palm leaf, grass and stars, the shamans toss and turn in their sleep. One dreams of white sails like the flapping wings of albino birds of prey, stooping over the villages. Another sees a huge dark wave from the east that will wash over the people and leave them moaning and shaking with fever, covered with sores. Another says, Evil men wearing clothing all over their bodies will come and eat our hearts.

From the four sacred directions the cries of the prophets split the air: *The corn will wither on the stalk. The buffalo will disappear. The rivers will run with poison. We will starve in the shadow of grey houses. The song will be silenced. The cooking pot of the grandmothers will be broken. Our children will be stolen. The people will be scattered and enslaved.* Those who listen to the heart of the earth and the voices of the dead go into the sacred smoke, enter the clear place of the fast, climb and descend to the spirit worlds, call on the ancestors to send them dreams. They return shivering and speak the bad news: the wheel is turning, the world will shatter, we cannot stop what is coming. While the people continue to plant and harvest the yuca and squash, potatoes and pecans, peppers and sweet potatoes and corn, the healers gather herbs for wounds and fevers, and the prophets stand with shadowed eyes looking eastward to the end of the known worlds.

1490: Guabancex Stirs the Pot—Boriken

Guabancex, whose skirts are the swirling winds of hurricanes, is cooking up a mother of all storms. It is springing up in the crowded, disease-ridden streets of Sevilla and Lisbon, Liverpool and Marseilles. It is gathering speed down the coast of Africa, knocking down branches in Canarias, gusting over Elmina, shaking the great trees of the Kongo. It drags the birds of Africa out to sea and throws them on the beaches of Brazil. It strips the leaves from the wide Amazonian canopy, whips through the grasslands of the Orinoco, blows dust into the sky over Tenochtitlan. The splay-fingered leaves of the papaya have begun to quiver. Any time now the storm will break on the islands. Guabancex stirs the great blue pot of the Atlantic until the bitter saltwater breaks on all its shores.

Calendars

In the reckoning of the Hopi calendar, it is the beginning of the new cycle of nine hells. This cycle of the fifth world will last for nearly five hundred years, after which will come a time of purification, and then a cycle of thirteen heavens. In the calendar of the Jews, it is the year 5253 from the creation of the world by Yahweh. The Jews are being forced to leave Hispania at sword's point, forsake their faith, or burn at the stake, and still the Messiah does not come. In Islam, the year is 870 counting from the Hijira of Mohammad, and the faithful are at war against the infidel. For the keepers of the Mayan calendar, the date is 11.13.13.10.2 in the Long Count, interlocking cycles of time that have been revolving since the beginning, four thousand six hundred and six years ago last August. For Christians it is 1492 Anno Domini, the Year of Our Lord, nearly fifteen hundred years since the Son of God was born human. Some believe his return is imminent, when the dead will rise and all beings will face judgment. In the village of Okango it is the eighteenth year since the big flood. It is the Ming dynasty, the Ottoman Empire, the Tudor Period, a generation after Pachacuti Inca Yupanqui began the conquest of the Andes, the last year of the last Sunni of Songhay. It is the Strawberry Moon, the rainy season, the time to move to winter grazing, the return of the great sea turtles who come ashore to nest.

Everywhere people mark time. We count the movements of the stars, the return of the sun, the coming of the rains, the swelling and wasting of the moon and tides. Time is a snake, swallowing its tail. Time is a narrow road climbing forever toward heaven. Time is a wheel of rebirth, spiraling into enlightenment. Time is the movement of gears in a celestial machine. Time is an illusion, our days and nights, infancy and age all side by side in an endless moment that neither begins nor ends.

To tell this story we will use the calendar of the invaders. Their account books are full of our treasures and our labors, their chronicles filled with our deaths and defiances. In the name of trade they have entered all ports, and everywhere they do business according to their own rules. Their calculations have measured the years of our common story. So we will call this year 1492.

But we will not call it Anno Domini, because only a small part of humanity has taken the Crucified for Lord. We do not say Christian Era, because the age belongs to all who live in it. We call this season, two dozen generations ago, 1492 of the Euro-Christian Calendar. But just to remind ourselves that many stories meet here, from time to time we will speak another language and tell the years by other names.

✌ DISCOVERY

The wounding and the healing of nations are not different from the wounding and healing of individuals. As a child I was the captive of a group of cruel men. I experienced and witnessed horrors I could not speak of to anyone.

Unable to betray fear or grief or rage without endangering myself, my body transformed my reactions into a kind of residue of withheld cries, a sediment of silence layered within me that made me allergic to foods and other substances, broke my sleep, and made my bones and muscles ache. Unable to tolerate what was hidden there, I evacuated much of my own body.

As I embarked on my recovery, I re-entered and explored those conquered lands, finding pockets of resistance, sites of massacres, ruins of childhood trust, brave gardens. The bedrock of history is sedimentary, too. Layers of silence and forbidden memory; rage withheld and grief smothered; buried remains of ancient courage and faith kept. There is no distance between conquest and abuse, battering and war. The journey of healing is the same. In the violated places of my body I find the voices of the conquered of my island. When I seek their voices among the yellowed manuscripts, I find my own bad dreams. In a time of personal nightmares and hours spent in archives I wrote these words to break both silences and embarked on the work of a people's historian, a wounded healer. I thank the spirits of the invaded who accompanied me.

I

It begins with terrifying dreams,
and then there is pain.
The dream body,
the real body that was hidden
begins to speak to me.

I am not sure, at first,
how far it extends into the twilight
what mountain ranges
valleys, rivers, plains endure
after so much ravaging,

how the forests kept breathing
all those years since the invasion.

We saw the lights as they rose and fell on the waves
and prepared ourselves for a raid from the islands

but in the morning we saw their strange canoas hung with cloth
their red white faces and hairy bodies, heard their harsh voices shouting.

We saw how they walked heavily on the earth
and at first we were intrigued by their oddness,
but the bohiques cried out to us from nightmares of desolation
and soon enough we realized they were a calamity,
but who among us could believe in the end of the world,
that these were the ones who would take everything?

who among us could conceive of a place as empty and tormented
as the hearts of these men?

2

I take hold of the thread of my breath like a rope,
and go down into the cramped places of memory,
the knowledge each strand of muscle holds like a weapon,
where no blood has passed for years upon years,
and study the archaeology of fear.

This ruined room
was once the granary
(no one in this body can remember
when bread was simple food:
each time teeth sink into crust,
trust shatters again, terror tightens the gut,
hands twist and ache,
diarrhea doubles us up and centuries of weariness
settle like a fine dust) here blood and corn,
iron and wheat, the helpless urination
of those who cringed against these walls, mingle
into a biting odor of rust and death, arthritis caking the hinges
of what was abandoned in haste.

3

She was blindfolded.
She was drugged.
She was an infant crowing at the sky
while they sharpened their knives.
They could not see her growing.
They could not see how this afternoon
her eyes rooted out the source of bird song,
her fingers reached for the mosquito that hovered.
And the other one, the mother, tired at nightfall,
irritated at the neighbors' noise or singing softly sometimes
as she washed the tiny dresses—

they had no way to think of them
the mother and daughter, females
in their own lives.

There was nothing to see,
in their eyes. No one there:
emptiness filling itself
with torture.

All the inhabitants
could be taken away to Castile or made slaves.
With fifty men, exulted the Admiral,
we could subjugate them all and make them do
whatever we want.

This was what they wanted:
agony repeated, endlessly reenacted,
never fulfilling their tortured hopes,
never draining away the pus and gangrene
of their own broken and festering hearts.

There was nothing to see,
in their eyes. No world.
Only their rules and rituals,
only the ache to see fear,
only the terrified wielding of death
that they imagined was power over life.

Because they could not see me,
some of me got away.
In their eyes I was nothing
but the shape of a frightened girl.

They saw the fear, and it pleased them,
it made them hungry for more.

They did not imagine me here
studying that fear, listening to nightmares,
inviting my pain to speak,
following its tracks, until I could see
by the light a body sheds
everything they so carefully hid from me.

They did not imagine
I would ever write a word of what
they said they would slit my throat
and the throats of my family
for even whispering.

They never saw my resistance.
They never saw or imagined
me.

4
My eyes have seen these acts
so foreign to human nature, and now
I tremble as I write.
Years later, the priest,
worn out with testifying to horrors
that had become usual and customary,
with being the only one present
with a conscience . . .
From 1494 to 1508
over three million people
had perished from war, slavery, and the mines.

And *who,* agonized Bartolomé de Las Casas,
Who in later generations will believe this?

Are you sure, she asks, my friend of decades,
are you sure you remember this? I imagine
that I am a survivor of a war that is declared
or at least the citizen of a country from which
traumatized people are known to escape.

My friend imagines I am too normal
for such things to have taken place.
Surely, if it had really happened, I would rave,
drool, steal, use drugs, say things that make no sense,
I would wear the glassy eyes and sudden rages
that mark the places where brutality has been.

By a grace I do not understand, I tell her,
I was able to continue.

5
If they can hurt it, it must not be mine.
So like my Russian many times great-grandmother
I throw things to the wolves: I give them sexuality and digestion,
I give them uterus, vagina, clitoris, intestines, stomach,
I give them sleep and posture, I give them agility and stamina and
    athletics.
I give them all the energy I can give up without dying.
I am hoping to stay alive.

This chieftain Agüeybana was a good person and obedient
to his mother; and she was a good woman,
and as she was mature she had news of what happened

in the conquest and pacification of Hispaniola,
and like a prudent person, continually told and counseled her son
and the other Indians, to be good friends of Christians
if they did not wish to all die at their hands.

And so, because of this advice,
Agüeybana went with Captain Juan Ponce
and gave him a sister of his as a mistress
and he took him to the north shore of that island
and showed him gold-bearing rivers.
Captain Juan Ponce took away much gold,
and left Christians there, living peaceably
and in friendly fashion with the Indians
who gather the gold for them, and bring them casabe.

I give them the lowlands and flee to the heights.
I give them the croplands. I give them
cleanliness, order, beautiful clothing,
the banners of aliveness. I am as discreet as possible
about my survival.

In 1570 these Indians, those few remaining who had been freed
by the end of the encomienda, *moved*
farther and farther away from the Christians
until they reached the bitterest heights of the sierra
and in this year of 1777 there are nearly two thousand
of pure blood, and many more who have married
with both Christians and Africans
and their neighbors call the place Indiera.

In the high, rainy places,
where the next downpour can send the harvest

halfway to the coast
I cultivate what I can: the alphabet, the persistent
beauties of this earth, the storyteller's
sacred craft of memory.

6

The name they gave me was *jíbara*
which, in the language of the greedy,
means countrified, malleable, *we could make them do anything*
and in the language of the stolen,
means *she who runs away and is free*

As a child, I cut my hands
on the shards of their cooking pots,
and learned about secrecy
from the same bloodstained teachers who schooled them,
on the same land.

Afternoons in the mud-colored schoolhouse
the buzzing of blood in my ears
I watched his hand cast shadows on the blackboard
and waited for it to become a claw.
White as bone, the chalk traced
traps of long division for us to wander into
and I would stare at the numbers, unable to think
beyond the smell of slaughter he carried,
my calculations forever thrown off
by the discovery of cruelty.

7

There are people in this world
so terrified that they hunger, night and day,
for the fear of others.

There are people in this world
who can show their wounds only by inflicting them,
and the story of my body
is also the map of their unspeakable pain.

Here it is. I study it in the light of history.
It leads me to the place they forbade me to ever visit again,
this ruined land, this scorched beauty,
this earth that refuses to stop being,
this América that keeps flowering in winter,
that plants its seeds
with black fertilizer of its own blood,
this body, this ground that speaks.

❧ HURACÁN: 1492–1600

❧ Bitters

Eat bitterness. Eat bitterness and speak bitterness and share
bitter herbs upon your bread, for in bitterness we empty
ourselves of poison. Bitterness cools the boiling blood, dries the
festering wound, tightens, reduces, expels, rejects, empties the
toxic wastes that cruelty deposits on our souls. These are the
stories to be taken with horseradish on dry, unleavened bread;
with gentian root, six drops of tincture in a glass of water, a dash
of angostura in your orange juice; a tea of goldenseal and sage.
Without bitters you will sicken from them. Your liver will ache.
Your belly will bloat, your head will throb, your joints will swell,
and you will be unable to eat from nausea. But if you take these
stories as bitters, your own pain will dissolve into the larger
stream of pain and you will find comfort with these women, for
the poison they suffered and died from is the same poison, and if
you eat bitters, drink bitters, speak bitterness with them, you
will be cleansed. You will be healed.

1492: Penetration

Crack open the new land, split the flowering tree with the blade of
an ax, bind the arms and backs of free people to your labor, but first
and last and always rape the women. Hold down the mothers and
daughters of the people and force their legs apart. Turn the wand
of pleasure to a branding iron, a torture blade, a spear through the

womb and heart. Mark the conquered through this act until you believe you have erased their humanness, then you may rape them forever without bad dreams. Some of them will fight back, scratch and bite and kick until you have beaten them and you will tell each other it's just like breaking a mare—the spirited ones give the best ride. Some of them will die in their blood from your invasions. That's war, you will say, some of them always die. Some of their bellies will swell, unwilling, and bear unbearable fruit and you will congratulate each other on the good crop—all the more hands to work.

Rape rides with you into all the ancient lands you say you have discovered. With rape and killing and elaborate signatures on deeds of ownership you repaint the maps to make these places empty so you can inhabit them. Rape stands beside you on the deck as you scour the coasts of the islands taking captives. Rape makes anchor in the bays where you disembark in Lucayas, Boriken, Haytí, Cuba, all the places and women you rename. Rape gallops by your side into the valley of Mexico, the cities of Maya, the villages of Costa Rica, Colombia, Panama. Rape is the story you keep telling like a moral tale of courage—America, the beautiful bride, ravished by gallant soldiers. America, the blushing maiden, stripped naked at the point of a sword. America, the dark-eyed beauty, surrendering in admiration to your greed. You sing it to the accompaniment of guitars as if it were a love song. You embroider it on your flag like the image of a saint. You call the trail of devastation the road to enlightenment and on the aching, violated bodies of women, build your houses of conquest and furnish them with legends of your nobility.

But under the polished floors is an underground river of weeping, a poisoned well of rage. It seeps into your walls and stains your carpets. You wash in it every night and the servants bring it to you each morning in a china cup. It is eating your heart away and you don't even know it. It will devour every possibility of love and leave you barren, not knowing that when you raped the women, you murdered joy.

1492: Lamento sefardita—Spain

> *"I am like that man who carried a brick to show the world what his house was like."* — BERTOLT BRECHT

"Adio, adio querida . . ." the songs and the weeping drift across the water as the ships pull away from the shore, echo against the hills as wagons wind across the border into Portugal. The candle is not extinguished, it only dips and flutters in the wind as the Jews of Spain look back upon ancient olive trees, vineyards, stone houses where they have lived for centuries, the abandoned synagogues of Sefarad, so long the beloved home. As the Jews pull away, roots twelve hundred years deep tear from the soil, and great clumps of earth go with them: the resourcefulness, the culture, the creativity, the knowledge and expertise of the Sephardim. In Constantinople and Amsterdam, in Salonika and Antwerp, Venice and Ferrara, Alexandria and Dubrovnik, Cairo and Marrakech they will transplant the cuttings of romero they took from gardens now owned by others. They will pass on to their children, and their children's children, the treasures of memory, the hope of return, the small iron witness to injustice, worn on a chain around the neck: keys to their stolen houses, held in trust for a future that may never come.

℅ ROMERO

Fragrant rosemary seasons the food of the Mediterranean, opens your nose, pierces your heart, and pulls out treasures from the coffers of memory. Romero commands you to remember the orange you ate with your best friend when you were six, sitting on a hot rock in the sun, and restores the taste of that juice to the underside of your tongue. Romero reminds you of the afternoon when you were eleven, and the rain streamed down the glass windows of a house no longer standing. Romero gives you back the absentminded scratching of your grandmother's fingernails on the skin above your knee as she tells you stories about when she was eighteen. Romero says everything is present, everyone is here. That which is lost is not lost after all. All that we have loved, all that we have experienced, all that we have lived is here and alive. Neither time nor distance can erase the moment when you heard the news and your heart nearly stopped, the smell of steam rising from the baked earth of your abandoned and long since overgrown garden, the taste of your lover's lips that first night as you left the brightly lit rooms together, the candlelight on your daughter's serious face as you welcomed the Sabbath bride together in the darkened house. Romero returns you to every joy and pain, saying, Taste it, taste it again. This is your wealth, this is your name, this is the life that is yours.

1493 to 1511: Leyendas—Puerto Rico

When I was a child in the public schools of Yauco, where this story unfolds, I was given a book of legends to study, written by a descendant of hacendados and men of privilege and power. In this book, the cacica Guanina appeared as a "beautiful Indian maiden" in love with a noble and handsome Spaniard, their story a simple one of star-crossed lovers. In the end, fragrant and cultured white lilies and wild scentless red poppies sprang from their common grave and entwined there in witness to their enduring love. But like Pocahontas, Guanina was no "maiden." She was a woman of rank and influence, charting a course through dangerous waters, and I cannot believe she did so unthinkingly. This story is my answer to Don Cayetano, the story he never thought to look for, a story repeated a thousand times across the length and breadth of conquered America.

I was a girl of six when my sister Guanina was born. It was at sunset and when we first saw her, she was wet and golden, so our grandmother named her after the *guanín*, the golden spirit images we wear. We knew she would be beautiful.

It was that same year that the strangers came to Boriken for the first time. We had seen their heavy, white-winged canoes traveling along our coasts, and we had heard rumors from Haytí. The strangers waded into the rivers looking for gold in the sand. They broke open many rocks to find it. All they asked about, in signs, and then in words as they learned to speak, was gold. What did they want it for? They didn't beat it into thin sheets and use it to gild sacred objects. They didn't shape it into the faces of gods or the bodies of animals or even simple rings and ornaments. They melted it into flat and ugly bars, stacked it up in a hut, and set guards around it. This is what our relatives in Haytí told us.

That rainy season they brought one of their canoes into a bay on the west, and landed for a little while, but they didn't stay. Still, it made us all uneasy. Two women from the Yagüesa valley had been taken by raiding bands from the south and had met the strangers there. Somehow they had managed to explain to these men that they came from a big island in the north and that there was gold to be found here. They were taken aboard the canoes and brought back to Boriken. The women landed a half day's walk from here, so we didn't see this ourselves, but I remember a few days later, when a messenger came. That was when the talking began.

My grandmother once took me out in a storm and showed me how the trees all move differently with the wind. She showed me how the stiffest trees, the ones that seemed made of iron, would shake and eventually shatter, their branches torn off, their trunks broken; others seemed to twist and dance, bending over with each gust, leaves flying. If their roots were shallow, like palms, they might be uprooted, but they rarely broke. After the storm we saw that those trees whose roots went deep into the earth and gripped it tightly, but who bent and turned with the wind no matter how often it changed direction, those trees had lost only a few leaves and twigs. But the stiff proud caciques of the forest, the ones who refused to give, lay splintered and twisted on the ground. This is how my grandmother led the people.

The talking began, and it lasted for years. Because this dry season or next, or half a lifetime from now, we knew that the strangers would come for our gold. They would eat our casabe, build their bohíos by the rivers, and force us to work for them. So we listened to all the stories travelers brought us and watched for signs and looked across the water toward Haytí, where they had built a settlement and were already making trouble.

In most ways, life went on as usual. Babies were born and named. Yuca was planted and harvested. Cotton was picked and spun, dyed and woven. Fish were caught, casabe made, maví brewed. There was ceremony and work, rest and celebration, illness and bad weather, in all the ordinary amounts. I grew up and became a woman, skilled at herbs and healing, often making medicines for our family. And Guanina followed me into womanhood. I see her now, at fifteen maybe, smooth brown skin, sparkling eyes, and hair that made a person think of the heavy rains of autumn.

The news from Haytí grew worse and worse. The new people, they call themselves Cristianos, after their chief god, or Hispanioles, after their far away country, came and went in their canoes, taking away gold and often slaves. The bohiques, the shamans, entered the ritual of the cohobo and returned with solemn faces. Some spoke of the end of the world.

Hatuey was dead, tied to a piece of wood and burned to death because he would not agree to be ruled by them. Already bound and with the torches crackling, they asked him if he would accept their god so he could go to their land of the dead, which they call heaven, and which they believe is in the sky, instead of to the place our own people go. They told him if he did not, that he would continue to burn after he was dead in a place called Infierno. He asked them (we smelled the smoke when we heard the story) if Spaniards went to this heaven of theirs, and when they said, "Yes, of course!" he spat on them and said in that case he would rather burn.

Many people came to us now from Haytí, running away from the smoke and blood in the west. The bohiques said Guabancex had entered the world of people and sent us a hurricane of crazy men.

My brother Guaybana was the leader of many of the young warriors. They liked to strut around talking about what they would do when the Spaniards came for *us*. They didn't listen much to our grandmother, even though she was the most important cacica of Boriken. Even my uncle, Agüeybana, high cacique over all the others, always listened to her counsel, but the young warriors were too full of blood and wanted to spill some. They said women didn't make good caciques. They said the new ways of some of the caciques were good and right; that a wife should be sent into death with her husband, not left to trouble the counsels of her nephews and sons. Their voices were the ones most often raised in shouting, as we tried to plan ahead for what was coming.

But it was my grandmother who called a council meeting when we heard of the death of Anacaona. She was a cacica and our kinswoman. She had ruled with her husband and then her brother. After their deaths she ruled alone. The Spaniards had made agreements with her. Promises of friendship and cooperation. Then they had invited her to a feast. There they had taken her prisoner and hanged her, and burned all her companions inside the feasting house. My grandmother said it was clear that ordinary rules of behavior didn't mean anything to these people. We did not understand them, or they us. She said we must either find a way to make a binding alliance with them, or we must try to kill

them all—which was impossible—or we should prepare ourselves for death.

Guaybana's warriors were angry at this. They said this was
what came of women's rule. They argued that we should make war
on the Spaniards, killing as many as we could. The rest would run
away. Hadn't we been given Boriken for our own land? Then why
shouldn't we defend it? Some of them muttered that grandmother
should have been sacrificed when her husband died, instead of remaining as a cacica in her own right and giving bad advice to
Agüeybana. My grandmother answered them that the best time to
fight is when you have a chance of winning. We had no evidence,
she said, that the Spaniards would run away. Didn't they see how
each year more of their canoas came following the wind, or drifting up from the south? If we began with bloodshed, we would end
in bloodshed, dying as Anacaona and Hatuey and many others
had died. Not all the people were in a hurry to enter the land of
spirits in the west. If we want to live, she said, we will have to give
them part of what they want. Maybe we can adopt them. Maybe
we can keep them content while we study them. Maybe, if we have
children with them, they will come to see us as kin. Maybe, she
said, we can work something out. Maybe we can bend.

But all of us, even my grandmother, were worried. How do you
make friends with tiburón when you're swimming just in front of
her sharp teeth? How do you claim kinship with the hurricane?
What if there was no way to please them and no way to destroy
them? What if the only path was toward certain death? Then why
not fight, and enter the afterlife knowing, like Hatuey, that we had
said "No" to our enemies?

Guanina was a grown woman now, with full, plump breasts, a
round belly, and hands swift and skillful at the loom. She loved to
weave, and her patterns were rare and beautiful. She would walk
in the hills for hours looking for new plant dyes for her cotton
thread, and the ceremonial clothing she made was the richest and

most striking. She made a special length of cloth for our uncle, with zig-zag patterns like the backs of storm clouds or iguanas as a sign of Iguanaboina, the cave from which all weathers come. Between the zig-zags she painted the spiral sign of Guabancex, the storm mother, to keep him safe and powerful no matter what blew our way.

Yes, we prayed to Guabancex who uproots old trees, so that new ones can spring up. We who had grown up in the shade of very old trees and were trying to plant seedlings against the storm. Meanwhile Guaybana grumbled and said we women shouldn't meddle with questions of war and rulership. I wondered what would happen to us when he succeeded my uncle. Clearly, he would not be calling us to council as uncle did with his mother and sisters and nieces. Often a small group of the women met by ourselves, near a spring, a ways uphill from the village. We prayed and argued and made our plans in secret.

Then one sunny afternoon a runner came panting into the settlement to say that three of the big canoas full of Spaniards had come into a bay to the west. Uncle had not decided on what course to take, but he had made it clear to Guaynaba that he'd better keep his young bloods under control. Wearing our best ceremonial clothing, we set out to meet them. In our whitest naguas, with feathers, polished stones and shells, with golden ornaments and flowers in our hair we went to welcome the invaders as if they were visiting caciques. Meanwhile, the naborías prepared a great feast for them with carey and crabs, piles of casabe and corn and steamed beans, mountains of batatas, and plenty of maví and other good things to drink.

I stood between my grandmother and my husband, Caoney, on the beach that day. I remember they were stranger to look at than I had expected. It was a hot day, but they had covered themselves all over with cloth. Their skin was the color of a fruit that grows in the mountains, red and white, and their noses were long and narrow as if they had been pinched. Their hair was very odd, too. One of them had it in a cloud around his head, like cotton. Some of them had hair the color of sand or orange river mud and some had an ordinary color, but it was wrinkled and rough like coconut fiber. There were no women at all.

Our aunt Bayaguex stood beside uncle as he greeted their leader. Through an interpreter, he spoke to us in our own language, although poorly. He said his name was Juan Ponce de León and my uncle begged to be allowed to exchange names with him, as if he were a brave opponent who had earned this honor. Juan Ponce asked to be taken to where there was gold.

My uncle promised to show him the best gold-bearing rivers, the ones that run to the north coast. Then he told Juan Ponce that Bayaguax would be honored to be his wife. In this way, by honoring him as if he were a respected leader, we hoped to begin in friendship. Juan Ponce asked something of the interpreter and laughed, and agreed to accept her. But he did not offer any gifts, and we wondered if he had not understood, or whether his people simply lacked all civilized manners. Still, customs vary. That night Bayaguax went with him to the large bohío we had made ready for them. In the morning when the women gathered eagerly by the spring, she told us his lovemaking was odd and surprisingly brief, but not unpleasant.

Rainy season and dry, and then rainy again, and Bayaguax gave birth to a daughter. Juan Ponce and his men went everywhere, ordering caciques to give them gold, to bring food, to build houses for them. Those who refused were killed, with weapons from across the sea that we hadn't seen before. Each of the Spanish caciques under Juan Ponce took part of our land and set himself to rule over nitaínos and naborías alike. To our own yucayeque they sent Cristobal de Sotomayor, an arrogant young man who believed himself better than even our Uncle. Then one of the things we had feared happened. The next winter, grandmother and uncle both died and Guaynaba became the high cacique.

Guanina and I spoke often about the way things were going. She was sure that grandmother had been right, and just as sure that Guaybana and his group of hotheads were going to start breaking bones and bring down a massacre. There were all kinds of arguments among us at that time. Many of us were worried about the way we were being kept from the counsels. We knew that this new custom of sending wives into the afterlife with their husbands was just another, more permanent way to close our mouths. Why shouldn't a woman take another lover if she wanted to, or take none at all, and continue to rule? But some of the women thought it was better to let the men, the warriors decide. They said we were thinking like old-fashioned naborías instead of cacicas. They said a cacica must uphold the power of her cacique and that when her husband died, she must accompany him to the place of the dead, to uphold him there. Our cousin Guaorama was the most forceful of these. She thought a dead cacica was more useful, and certainly more dignified, than a living naboría.

Guanina snorted in their faces. And one night she sought out young Sotomayor's bed. She wouldn't say much about what happened. "He doesn't understand us at all," she said, "but maybe I can teach him." The warriors grew more and more angry under the cruelties of the Spanish. The Christian men forced women to have sex with them and beat us, women and men alike, saying we were lazy, even though we were forced to work all day and past dark. They killed those who resisted them and even those who did not, but still only in ones and twos. We had not yet seen massacres like those in Haytí. More and more it felt like the air just before a heavy rain, a silence filled with waiting.

It was in the third year after the Cristianos came that waiting ended and the young men acted. One afternoon Guanina came running to my house. Caoney was away with a work gang, digging in the rivers for gold, and I was home preparing casabe. "They are going to kill Cristobal and as many as they can of the Spanish men," she cried. "I can't stop them!" We knew that once it was open war, the bloodshed wouldn't stop until we or they were broken. "Maybe," she said slowly," I should kill him myself." I stared at her.

I knew she hated him for his arrogance, and yet he had sometimes been tender with her as well. I knew she hoped for a child who might cement the bond of cacica and señor. Her eyes filled with tears. She knew there was no way to stop this war. Looking away from me, she said sadly, "Maybe if I warn Cristobal, he will pay attention for once, and the killing won't begin yet."

I know what happened, because I followed her. He laughed in her face, told her she was foolish, said not to worry, that he was more than a match for a few rowdy indios. Then he marched away with his little band, straight into the spears of Guaynaba. Guanina went after him. I heard the conch shells blowing after the ambush and ran towards the place. I was afraid for her. The dead Spaniards lay like a fallen forest. Guanina sat beside Sotomayor, tears running down her face. "Where's Guaynaba?" I asked. "I don't know. The strutting young cock went off to celebrate his victory somewhere. Doesn't he know how completely these deaths will be avenged?" Then she bowed her head over the body of the Spanish leader and sobbed. I turned quickly and went to look for Guaynaba. At least the overconfident fools should prepare for retaliation. If I had stayed, perhaps I would have seen the interpreter creep down out of the tree where he had hidden and make his way swiftly across country, towards Caparra. If I had stopped him, we would have had more time. If I had stopped him, Guaorama would not have found Guanina alone, weeping over a dead man. I was halfway down the valley when I heard her scream.

Guaybana told everyone that Guanina, a proud cacica, had chosen to die with her lover, but I had the truth from Guaorama, still spitting and cursing, knife in hand, when I arrived, out of breath, at Guanina's side. "A good cacica does her duty, and follows her mate into death," she hissed at me. "Your grandmother spoiled you both with her teachings."

Retaliation was swift. They came from Caparra with their swords sharpened and they killed and killed and killed. Those who were left were enslaved, and many were sent away to other islands and even to their distant country, Hispania. The leaders were scattered and no longer had authority. But in secret places by the springs, we women continued to meet, naborías and cacicas and some of the many slaves they brought, from the islands and the mainland, and soon there were others that they brought from across the ocean.

We never found a way to negotiate peace with the invaders. But in time we made new kin. Not with the conquistadores, as we had thought to do, but among their servants and slaves. The naborías became our leaders. Having lived at our command, they knew more than we did about being devious. We taught our new relatives the ways of Boriken, the land, the food, the medicines and rituals, and they shared their own. Together we made a rooting magic, a magic of survival, of many-colored children.

I have a granddaughter whose hair is the same black cotton as her father's, but her eyes are like my sister's. Sometimes when I watch her deftly twisting maguey fibers into rope, the brown threads tangling into something stronger, I think it is Guanina, come visiting from the spirit land. Then I hear my sister's voice speaking in my ear. "Sometimes," she says, "the forest is destroyed by the storm. Sometimes neither bending nor breaking can save it. After such a storm, gather firewood. Twist rope. Use what you have to make what you can." Then she raises a hand to brush away mosquitoes and I see that she is Guanina Nkele, my granddaughter, our heir, the first of a new people. And I go back to my pilón, pounding the bark of fallen trees into medicine.

1509 to 1521: La Marcaida—Cuba and Mexico

I read a story just like this one in the papers last week. I read it the week before. I heard about it in the marketplace in Marrakech, on the muelles of Sevilla, in a park in Philadelphia, in a supermarket in Santurce, on the evening news. Sources close to Hernan Cortés denied today that he was in any way responsible. . .

I remember the Xuarez sisters came to Cuba in 1509 with their widowed mother and a brother, in search of rich husbands. Their last stop had been in Santo Domingo, in the entourage of the wealthy aristocrat María de Toledo. Poor, ambitious, and very beautiful, they circulated through the islands that had become places of magical transformation—for here ordinary soldiers could become, overnight, as rich and powerful as lords. When they did, they needed suitable wives, and decent young women, Christian, Spanish, and single, were harder to come by than gold or slaves.

I don't remember which fortune-teller it was who told Catalina that she was destined to become a great lady, a woman of wealth and position. Such fortunes were told every day to the hopeful adventurers who came on every ship. No matter. Catalina believed in her fortune and pursued it with determination and energy. The sisters dined in all the Spanish homes and were courted with gifts of fine cloth, flowers and fruit, and handfuls of golden ornaments. The governor of Cuba, Diego Velasquez, fell in love with Catalina's sister—I can't remember her name. And Catalina caught the eye of that hard man and expert seducer Hernán Cortés.

Now if it hadn't been for the governor being sweet on the sister,

Hernán would have had his fling and gone his way, and there never would have been a wedding. After a few months in Catalina's arms he was ready to move on. But Catalina went to the governor, who was more than happy to help any of his sweetheart's sisters. Hernán was had up for breach of promise, then jailed, and finally threatened with hanging, so he must have held out for some time, but finally he agreed to marry her. Once it was settled, he even said he was as happy to do so as if she had been the daughter of a duke, because she was honest and well-bred, which was more than could be said of him, let me tell you.

And well-connected. She used her influence with the governor on her husband's behalf now. Hernán became the mayor of Santiago de Cuba and was given crowds of slaves. And when it was decided to send an expedition off to attack Mexico, Catalina pulled strings and got the job for Hernán. She packed up his clothing and provisions and saw him off, and that was the last she heard of him for a couple of years except for one letter that came with some pottery and gold jewelry, spoils of conquest.

But eventually, when he had won enough battles to set up his court and begin establishing himself as one of the new nobility, he sent for her. She traveled from la Habana to Mexico City with a company of soldiers to guard her and at each stop along the way was greeted with ceremony. She was the official first lady of Mexico. The real first lady was the Tabascan princess, slave and interpreter Malintzin, renamed Doña Marina, or the Tongue of Cortés, who traveled and slept by his side and had born him two mestizo children. Not to mention all the other ladies who had done likewise. But to Catalina, this was her destiny, her good fortune come true. She was a great lady.

Until the night, three months later, when she was found strangled in her own bed, with the marks of cords around her throat and the half dozen women of the house all swearing it was her husband who had killed her. Can you imagine a jury of his peers, men who had raped and pillaged their way across Mexico, ambitious men whose commander he was, convicting him of the death of a woman? The charges, of course, were dismissed.

His next wife, Juana de Arellano de Zúñiga, was an aristocrat, and her connections were even better.

1514: Manikongo Affonso's School for Bakongo Girls— Kongo, West Africa

It is two dozen years since the Portuguese came to the city of Mbanza Kongo, and the manikongo adopted the religion and name of the Portuguese king. Now his son King Affonso is infatuated with their ways. Mbanza Kongo has been renamed São Salvador and filled with churches. The Portuguese want slaves, so Affonso raids Ndongo for slaves. The Portuguese have dukes and earls and counts, and so Affonso has dukes and earls and counts. Now the manikongo's sister is placed in charge of a school for girls, to teach them Christian and European ways. To teach them to be worthy of colonialism.

Meanwhile, Portuguese missionaries are becoming dealers in flesh as well as souls, and Bakongo girls, along with women, boys, and men, are learning Christian ways in the holds of slave ships, in the cane fields of Brazil, in the slave markets and plazas of La Guaira and Maracaibo, Hispaniola, and San Juan Bautista. During the long hard days of intense work and perpetual, aching hunger, side by side with enslaved Americans, with relatives and enemies from hundreds of African nations, they trade words and habits, strategies and songs. Together they become American, they make America African.

Just as in years to come, Puerto Rican children will salute the United States flag and chant together, "Good Morning, Meesee," Puerto Rican women will clean the houses of rich, white ladies and learn to say, "Jess, m'am," sew the clothing of United States citizens, and learn the jargon of the sweatshop. Just as Puerto Rican girls, punished for speaking Spanish, mocked for mispronouncing the language of the invaders, taught that they are barely worthy of domination, will trade cultures, take up scraps of Yiddish, pray with an Irish accent, love Central Park, stand in the crowd listening to Malcolm X speak, teach huelga in exchange for strike, and Puerto Ricanize everything they touch, until neighbors from Harlem, from Odessa, from Sicily and County Cork have learned our stories, joined our tenant strike, buy plátano on their own, and dance the cha cha cha with Tito Puente. The enslaved always conspire together; the slave always changes the master.

1515: Toa

On the wide fertile lands that spread beside the River Toa, the Crown has established the Hacienda Real, where Spanish administrators grow rich, squabbling over who owns the labor of how many women and men of this island. They try to grow wheat, try to force this island to be Spain, but the seed just rots. They bring sheep, who collapse from the heat and stop growing thick wool. They plant imported bananas, mangos, native papaya and long for grapes, olives, peaches. They get used to casabe.

Outside in the sunlight, Arawak women and men are forced to work until they drop to the ground, broken with fatigue. They must gather and wash gold from the rivers, grow much more yuca than they need, wash and cook for the invaders. Over and over again, the former caciques protest the harsh labor and continual sexual abuse. Our people are beaten for being sick. Our people are raped at will. Our people are dying from your brutality and from despair. But there is no relief.

"Maria" is a child of five, niece of the cacique Caguas. Repartamiento is the word they use when they share out among themselves the labor of indigenous people, their name for the constant dividing and redistributing of lives. Maria, with all her kin, has been shuffled and dealt to Juan Ponce de Leon, so now she lives at Toa. This year the records show she was given a cotton skirt.

When she is nine, her uncle will die and, as his sister's daughter, she will inherit his title, becoming the last cacica of Boriken. Still nominally in charge of her own hereditary work force, she will be exploited by one unscrupulous mayordomo after another, her people ruthlessly worked to death and her body used to satisfy their lusts. Or so the records say. Who can tell at such a distance, her life recorded in the testimonies of so many alien men, whether she was the captive girl child victimized by men without conscience, or whether her own sexuality was so incomprehensible to the men who eventually sought to protect her that her own choices became invisible?

All we have left is their conversations about her, how the bishop removed her to the custody of a respectable married man, how he negotiated her own marriage to the last of those mayordomos, who had to be bribed with land and privileges to enter such a legally binding contract. How she felt, what she thought about, what stirred in her heart, holding each of her three children as they were born, we do not know.

On those rich lands beside the Toa, now called the Plata, towns have risen, settled by my ancestors. There are fields of sugar cane, tobacco, hillside plots of coffee, pastures of dairy cattle, even patches of rice. Along Route 2 the trucks roar across the river, carrying pipes and lumber, imported foods and cement. The bodies of those who fell to the insatiable greed of the first hacendados have long since been compressed into limestone and clay. But the last cacica's bones are not here in the red soil. They lie deep in the Atlantic. In 1548, Maria and her children, embarking for a visit to her husband's family in Spain, were taken into the rough embrace of the hurricane and drowned.

1515: Piñones

I don't remember what they called me, María or Isabel, or whether
I ever spoke my grandmother's secret African name for me out
loud. But I remember the ship moving out on the afternoon tide
from Sevilla and the relief it was to leave those smelly streets and
the tiny room behind. I remember the weeks at sea, eating stale
bread and salt pork. And I remember my first glimpse of the island
of San Juan, late afternoon again, a palm-swept beach and behind
it a mountain crowned with thunder clouds, a place of gods.

I was the first African woman to set foot here, so they tell me.
Francisco and I built a house by the coast, not far from that first
beach. There was water. Fish. Clams and crab. The other criados
bought supplies from the Spanish and paid from their share in the
gold dust for barrels of pork, sacks of flour and corn meal, now and
then some wine and oil. They got casabe from the Indians. But I
grew or caught most of our food, and Francisco saved his grains of
gold in his own name. After a few years we sent for chickens from
Hispaniola and a little dog to guard them. I planted corn enough
to feed them and us, and we had plenty of fruit and greens and the
sweet, hot peppers they use here to flavor their stews that reminded
me of my grandmother. I planted guingambó and sent my sons up
palms to shake down coconuts. We did well, and both my sons
were strong. They lived to be men and to sail off to Tierra Firme
with new masters and new names, but the place where I farmed
and birthed my babies, grated yuca and coconut, pulled the weeds
that grew as fast as I chopped them, is still called after us.

Almost five centuries later, it's as if I never had a personal name.
Francisco Piñon, they write, and his wife. And yet if it weren't for
me, Francisco would have been just another of the African criados, single men all, who came and went. There are no towns
named after them. But they still call that place along the north
coast Piñones, because I was there, planting roots and bearing
children. Leaving a mark. I planted that soil with his name.

1515: Piñon Shopping List

In 1515 the Piñon family sent to Hispaniola for the following supplies:

Cotton shirts made by forced indigenous labor. Made from the traditional island cotton, originally imported from Central America, where the Mayans and other peoples grew, spun, dyed, and wove it into clothing, blankets, hammocks, and other goods.

Hens and chicks. The Spanish imported poultry from Europe and bred them for meat and eggs. The Piñons sent for fifty-eight hens and chicks, breeding stock that would let them supply their own needs, instead of buying from the Spanish colonists.

Corn. The Piñons bought three and a half fanegas of corn, another American product that was a staple food from Peru to New England and formed part of the indigenous diet of Boriken and Haytí. The colonists learned to grow it from the Arawak people. Ground into meal, they made it into porridge or cornbread.

A small dog. Bought to protect the chickens from predators.

1515: Plátano

Would you believe there was a time when we had no tostones? Plátano didn't start out being Puerto Rican any more than spaghetti was originally Italian! Marco Polo brought spaghetti home from China and plátano went from Malaysia to East Africa with the Indonesians and to West Africa with the Portuguese, and when they found out how many slaves you could feed just enough to keep them going on guineo verde and plátano . . . ¡mija! Se lo trajeron enseguida. Fíjate. One of those traveling priests brought the first plátano to the banks of the Toa in 1515. You know, they still grow plenty of it in the hills around Toa Alta, Orocovis, Naranjito. So who invented the first tostón? Slaves, por supuesto. The patrón throws down a sack of guineos y plátanos and says, "This is your food for the week." So the first day it's boiled. The second day it's boiled and mashed. The third day . . . boiled. One of the women says, Basta ya! Gets a little grease from somewhere, throws in a bit of garlic, and fries it up—but the inside stays too raw, so she slams it with the palm of her hand, throws it back in the pot, y en un dos por tres everyone's eating tostones. On Saturday, the patrón brings them some salt pork for Sunday and someone invents mofongo. Soon they have a whole cuisine going. It doesn't win any prizes for good nutrition, because that's not a slaveholder thing, but making sabrosura out of empty calories is an act of resistance, and soul food is damn good medicine.

1515: Naborías—The Names of the Captives

They were not cacicas.
They were not heirs to yuca fields.
There were no concessions made to their status.
They were not "queens."

Their names are recorded in the lists of work gangs
sent to the mines, the conucos, the kitchens, the laundries
of the Spanish invaders.
    Macaney, field hand.
    Francisquilla, cook.
    Ana, baker.
    Catalina, pig woman.

They were the working women of Boriken.
They were called out of their names.
Casually recorded under the names of Catholic saints,

or the queens of the myriad kingdoms of Spain, renamed
after little sisters or mothers left behind in Estremadura,
Navarra, Castilla, Sevilla, León
or a favorite prostitute from a port town,
or a beauty out of some ballad of the old land.
They were not born Catalina, Ana, Francisquilla.

They were brought here from the islands, captive.
The account books of the governor say *herrose*—
branded on this day—was Elvira Arumaita
from the island of Guadalupe
with a son they called Juanico.

herrose, a Carib called Beatriz, and her son, Juanico.
herrose a Carib, Juana Cabarotaxa, from the island of Santa Cruz,
and *herrose,* a little girl called Anita, Carib,
from the aforementioned island
which we now call Guadalupe, and *herrose,*
also from Guadalupe, Magdalena Guavrama,
Carib, and her child.

They were already here, enslaved, escaped,
and to their great misfortune, recaptured
and branded this day by Captain Juan Ponce de León,
 Ana Taguas, Violante Ateyba
 Leonor Yayguana written down as belonging
 to the rebel cacique Abey,
 and Isabel Guayuca with her son, once again Juanico,
 once owing loyalty to the collaborator Cayey.
They were women under two masters,
the crumbling authority of the caciques
and the new and violent usage of the señores.

At night, after the work was done, what did they say among themselves
speaking the soft sounding languages of the islands?
How did they find consolation? What did they hope for
sitting in the warm evening, watching the stars fall into the sea?

1519: The Speckled Death—
Central America and the Caribbean

First there is swelling in our throats and armpits and groin, then
fever and weakness, then spots cover our bodies, oozing pus and
blood. There is terrible pain, as if we were being torn apart, then
our spirits wander into dreams and we cry out at things no one else
can see, and then we die.

The sickness runs among the people like an invisible jaguar,
and we fall without ever seeing its claws. It spreads like fire in the
grasslands. In the morning one person falls ill. By evening two
hundred have died. The sickness has come with the Spanish across
the ocean, but once ashore, it doesn't wait for them. It races along
trade routes, seeking out villages and tribes, bands and nations
who have only heard rumors of the invaders. Long before they ride
up the roads with their iron swords, the people have lost a hundred
battles and are weary and full of grief. There is no one to tend the
crops, so those who survive the plague go hungry. The healers and
their apprentices burn with the same fever. So many of us die at
once, it is as if the threads had been torn by the handful from the
loom of our lives and the bright cloth unraveled.

The sickness has taken wings from the bird of death. Like a vul-
ture it has flown across the country of volcanoes and fallen upon
all the peoples. There is weeping in Mayan, Nahuatl, Xinca-
Lencan, cries for mercy in Zapoteca, Popoloca, Aruaca. Death has
crossed the water and runs with its tongue hanging out through
the towns of Haytí, and half the people of the yucayeques lie scattered and stiff like branches after a storm.

Three days later it has leaped the channel to Boriken, and the marks appear on our skin. One in three of us die in a matter of days. She who tended a sick relative last night is herself dead by this morning. Those of us who are left are stunned. Everywhere we look there is someone missing. We are filled with ghosts. We try to remember our lives, but there is so much that is broken. Like the burning of the Mayan Codices, like the burning of the women of Europe, like the burning of the Jews, almost everything we know and love has blown away in smoke. When we begin, slowly, stiffly, to live again, it is a different kind of life, made of little things, made of fragments, made in mourning. We have lost wholeness. But we take a step at a time, pull yuca, nurse babies, go fishing. Life does, after all, continue.

ꝯALEGRÍA

Joy springs from the smallest moist crevice, the tiniest pocket of damp soil sheltered from the harsh sun. Life is not easily defeated. In the cracked trunk of the great fallen tree, small ferns and orchids take root, minuscule patches of moss. The morning after the massacre, birds still sing. From the prison window, one can sometimes see a star. The tiniest fragment of beauty, the most distant gleam of light, the most fleeting look of recognition from another human being can save us from despair.

These plants seem so fragile, with their crisp translucent stems and thin, scentless flowers. They are cut in great swathes by the macheteros. They wilt in the hot sun. They cannot be gathered. They are not medicinal. But see how they cover the hillside, in the dim light below the shade trees of the cafetal. They fill the shadows, iridescent petals shimmering with color, delicate and persistent as hope.

1525: Snakeskin—Mexico

Malinali, Malintzin, Malinche, Marina, you are the skin-changer, the snake mother, the many times forked tongue, lightning striking in the space between worlds. We who are stripped of everything, torn from the places and people who know our names and thrown to the wild winds, we who see every mirror shattered that could have shown us our familiar faces: we must learn to be shapeshifters or die.

The snake people learn to adapt, to be what is needed, to speak many tongues fluently, to wear and shed skins. Malinali, Malintzin, Malinche, Marina was born royal in Tabasco to a mother who wanted everything for her son. She was sold into slavery by her own mother and that was the first skin. Malinali, Malintzin, Malinche, Marina, she of many names learned Nahuatl, belonged to Moctezuma, Lord of Tenochtitlan. Belonged to him meaning he chose what her life could be and could put her to death whenever it pleased him. Said, you will go here, go there, lie with me, lie with that other, go away, come back. Captivity was the second skin, a skin she changed over and over again, being what was needed, hiding her heart under the diamond patterns of the rattlesnake.

When calamity swept in from the sea upon the Aztec empire, when destruction swept among the peoples, when Moctezuma presented her as a gift to that hard and greedy man Hernan Cortes, she was already old in calamity, ready for change, slipping out of her skin, ready to be what was needed: his mistress, his symbol of conquest, his voice in the land. Conquest was the third skin. Malinali, Malintzin, Malinche, Marina learned Spanish, lay under Cortes at night, walked forth in his name, the translator, the shapeshifter, blood in the space between worlds, subtly changing intonations, telling more than she was told to tell, owning and not owning her own voice, captive to the conqueror of her captors, balanced between vengeance and mercy, helplessness and influence, shedding scales.

Malinali, Malintzin, Malinche, Marina, her tongue as forked as an oak tree beneath which her people sheltered from a storm too great to withstand, forgave her mother and brother, now so much less powerful than she who was cast out. Bore sons with the stride, the nose, the jaw bone of their father and a smoky darkness in their eyes that was her own. This was the fourth skin.

Then the man who murdered his first wife, married another, an aristocrat. The man who scattered children everywhere had need for legitimate heirs to his stolen kingdom. Malinali, Malintzin, Malinche, Marina was given in marriage to one of the captains, given away again. Shed another skin and held her children close. Lost them to the Empire, these illegitimate sons sent to Spain, into the service of his heirs, the light boy and the dark, with the same name. Lost them to the shame they were taught to feel toward her, the contempt they learned to feel for her presence in themselves. Knew that generations of sons would follow them, cursing her name, considering themselves betrayed because they came from her. The fifth skin and the sixth lie curled underfoot, and when she paces her room at night, they make a dry, rustling sound as she passes out of history and into our dreams.

This is all you have left us, your face in the margins of the codices, half turned away. The aggrieved voices of the bastard sons, collaborators without the courage of their lack of convictions, using your name to define their condition, calling every betrayal Malinche linche linche. The pile of empty snake skins, faintly marked, lying on the garbage heap of history like a challenge.

1526: Conejo's Brothel—San Juan, Puerto Rico

The world is divided into women you can and women you can't. Into those who are vessels for your heirs, who must be kept uncontaminated by any other man's sperm, so that only your own real actual biological sons will inherit your loot; and those whose progeny don't matter, the ones who are available to many, the wicked ones, the ones who get cash per service or a bed and meals instead of marriage settlements. The governors of the empire are worried about you sowing too many creamy brown babies, too many people who don't fit easily into the either/or of conquered and conqueror, servants who look too much like their masters, dark children whose fathers may allow them to inherit, confusing even further the simple plan of who is to be who.

There is another problem, too. The women don't always stay where they are supposed to, one side of the line or the other. The mistresses and whores may become citizens of standing, if they are not tightly controlled by rules and regulations and heavily taxed for the glory and profit of the crown. The wives and daughters meant for monopoly sometimes have ideas and desires of their own. They take lovers, have affairs, behave so scandalously that you become confused and offer them illicit pleasures meant only for the other kind, which makes trouble with the men who supposedly own them.

Conferring among themselves, the governors agree that you can't help it. If there are not enough whores, you will be led by your very manhood and by the wiles of women into offending against the property of others. So King Carlos grants a license to Bartolomé Conejo, profits to be shared as agreed. To protect, he says, the honesty of the city, to safeguard the honor of married women, what San Juan needs is a house with doors, a door with locks, a clear set of instructions about who you can screw. Welcome to the grand opening of Conejo's brothel, where you can do your part for chastity, uphold the colonial order, and have a good time, too.

1534: Slave Mothers—Puerto Rico

You who are our descendants, do not forget us. You who call yourselves by names we do not recognize, we were your grandmothers. We were from people whose names for themselves are lost. The names of the places we were taken from are not on your maps. But the places are still there, and we did live, and you are our children.

We came from the small islands: Dominica, St. Kitts, Guadalupe. We came from the Yucatan and all the shores of the curving sea from all the varied beaches of what you call Mexico, through the long since decimated forests of Central America, around the oil-stained lake of Maracaibo, past the swampy mouths of the Orinoco and the ghosts of rainforests where the desert sugar cane lands of Northeast Brazil erode under the sun, as far south as the great delta of the mother river itself. We came from the sandy, swampy Gulf Coast of North America, from the mouths of the Sabine and the Mississippi, the Alabama and the Apalachicola, and out of bays and inlets and islands from the Florida cays to Cape Hatteras.

We are your Indian grandmothers from Eastern America, stolen from our homes and shipped to wherever they needed our work. From Tierra Firme to the islands. From one island to another. From this side to that, each colony raiding for its own supply, to use or to sell across the sea. They have lists of names of the passengers who came west over the ocean to settle our lands, but our names are not recorded, although the ships from Europe did not go back empty. Some of us died so far from home, we couldn't even imagine the way back: Cherokee in Italy, Tupi in Portugal, Inuit in Denmark.

Many of us were fed into the insatiable yuca fields, sugar mills, and gold mines of el imperio alongside the people of your island, and they called us simply indias. But we were as different from one another as Kongo from Wolof, Italian from Dane. We spoke as many languages, came from as many worlds as las Africanas.

How we remember them with love, las Yelofes and Berbesías, the fierce desert people who the slaveholders would never buy more than one of, because two was a conspiracy. Las Mbundus and Bakongas with their magic and their recipes and their singing back and forth, voice to voice as they worked. All of us uprooted, lonely, angry, sad, captives on this island, eating casabe together at the end of the day.

We are the ancestors of whom no record has been kept. We are trace elements in your bodies, minerals coloring your eyes, residue in your fingernails. You were not named for us. You don't know the places where our bones are, but *we* are in *your* bones. Because of us, you have relatives among the many tribes. You have cousins on the reservations. Do not forget how wide your roots are in this America. Do not forget.

1547: Limpieza—The Spanish Empire

The laws of Hispania say the blood of some people is dirty, that of others clean. It can be soiled by an ancestor who was not Christian. It can be soiled by any of the Sephardim, the Jews of Iberia. It can be soiled by Arab or Berber. It is clean only if you are able to demonstrate with clear records that generation upon generation your family did not intermarry with any of its neighbors who did not also worship Christ. Few of the Southern nobility qualify, but they can afford to forge papers and bribe clerks. If you qualify, one way or another, for a certificate of limpieza, of clean, sparkling, one-hundred-percent-Christian blood, you can hold Church offices, offices for the Crown. You can go to America and get land and Indians and Africans. You can melt down the treasures of the Inca and put them in your account in Seville. You can stop worrying about the competition, those other merchants with business ties in the East. Only you are clean, licensed, legally entitled to work this market. Thus the new regime purges the old and makes monopolies from the repossessed warehouses, orchards, and storehouses of the exiled Muslims and Jews.

1550: **Conversas at the Stake—Lorca, Spain**

There have been Jews in Spain since the days of the Babylonian exile, fifteen hundred years ago. But now, according to law, the Jews are gone. Those who once were Jews are now New Christians and must be watched closely. Do they eat pork? Have you seen her eat pork? Does she treat Saturday as special in any way? When she lights the household candles at dusk, do her lips move? Could her lips be forming the name of Adonai?

A New Christian who secretly practices the rituals of her faith is a judaizer, an enemy of God, tainting the true religion. She is more dangerous to Christian purity than an open Jew, because she may confuse true Christians and lead them astray. It is the duty of every Christian, old or new, to denounce them.

If she repents, after torture, she is given penance and a second chance. If she will not confess, if she declares, in defiance, her loyalty to the Hebrew faith, she is "relaxed," strange code word for being tightly bound to a wooden stake, heaped with fuel, and set on fire. If, at the last moment, with agonizing pain only moments away, she falters, and will confess to sin, she is offered the mercy of having her throat cut first. Otherwise, she will burn to death for however long it takes.

The Inquisition is good business in this world and the next. The Pope wants a monopoly of souls and orders all copies of the Talmud, sacred text of the Jews, to be publicly burned. Christian merchants and tradespeople want a monopoly of commerce and publicly burn even the most Catholic descendants of Jews. Priest and merchant alike know who holds and carries the faith that binds this people together, know who holds these webs of kinship and mutual aid intact, know who will most willingly die sooner than forsake it. The granddaughters and great-granddaughters of openly Jewish women conceal their rituals in the daily routines of women's work. As they have been for centuries, they are still the midwives, wine-makers, fruit-growers, cloak-makers, importers of spice, domestic servants, button-makers, bakers. Now, in a frenzy of greed, their neighbors denounce them. Torn from their homes, they are accused of poisoning the wells of Christianity with their loyalty to age-old ways.

In the town of Lorca, the conversos maintain their networks of kinship and trade. The expulsion order did not break them. Secretly, they keep faith. The licenciado Quevedo is eager to shatter their associations and take over their businesses. He also wants Ribellas, a young married conversa. Her mother-in-law, Magdalena López, complains about the seduction of her son's wife. She follows Quevedo, cursing him, through the streets. She is a nuisance, but a very convenient one. Quevedo denounces her as a heretic and a secret Jew. He persuades her daughters-in-law, two women of her family with whom she has quarreled, and one slave to testify that she is a judaizer. She is imprisoned and tortured until she will confess to everything he asks of her.

Tormented by guilt, one of her daughters-in-law repents of her testimony. She travels to a nearby monastery and confesses to the friar there that she has born false witness. The friar who hears her confession is also the rabbi of a community of secret Jews and her confession brings him under investigation. Unwittingly, the guilty daughter-in-law has exposed them all. Two hundred are jailed. Sixty put to death. The trade partnerships of the conversos are broken. Licenciado Quevedo and the other carrion crows grow fat on the pickings of Jewish bones.

Those who survive grow more secret. Those who survive take ships to far away places, fleeing the stench of charred skin. Those who survive become hidden, kindle the tiniest of flames in silence, remembering mothers and sisters consumed. Saying kaddish in their hearts, without words, without movement, without dangerous tears.

ᏬᏬCALENDULA

Marigolds the color of dying embers at the place where they died. Marigolds to name the ancestors whose names must never be spoken aloud. Marigolds in November when the common people still offer food and drink and fragrant petals to the powerful spirits of the dead. Marigolds for the living. A paste of mashed petals and stems, sticky with the healing sap, soaked in olive oil, and gently swabbed onto burned skin. Marigolds for blackened, blistered, oozing places where fire has touched us. Where fire has blazed up and caught us: the spilled cauldron, the torched home, the candles extinguished in haste, the auto de fé in the plaza, the skirts and hair on fire at the stake. Calendula soaks deep into the burning places, cooling, soothing, making new skin.

1560: Jigonsaseh—New York State

Here is cool water to bathe our wounds. Here is cool counsel for raging tempers. Here is Jigonsaseh, of the Seneca nation, who welcomed and fed warriors and shared, with relish, in their stories of bloodshed and burning.

Praise her, who was the first to listen when Deganawida, the Huron mystic and prophet, came south with his vision of peace among the nations. Speak her name with loving respect, because when she looked in her heart and saw she had taken part in something wrong, she set out to mend the world and went from tribe to tribe, persuading the people to join in confederacy and end the fighting.

But praise her most of all because of this: When all the tribes had agreed but one, when only the Onandaga refused, when the powerful sorcerer Tadodaho, holding tight to his influence and prestige, said the Onandaga would lose face and become less than they were by the bargain, it was Jigonsaseh who said, Then we will trade importance for peace. It was Jigonsaseh who said: Let the council of the Iroquois Confederacy always have more Onandagas than any other nation. Let the chief of the council always be an Onandaga, from this day on. There are things more precious than the place of honor.

Because of her insight the Iroquois Confederacy was made and the Great Law of Peace established. Jigonsaseh made a hearth where everyone could sit. Jigonsaseh made a longhouse where the five nations could gather. She opened a path through hard places. She made unbending sticks into a circle.

At Ganondagan, just south of Rochester, New York, on the banks of a small river, all the quarrelsome peoples of the earth may come to the sacred place where a war-loving woman became the Mother of Nations and was buried in a cloak of freshwater pearls because her heart was like pure water.

1563: Indiera

Jigonsaseh dissolved barriers of stone with water for the thirsty, but here in the mountains it is earth that is abundant enough to hold a circle of freedom. The runaway indias and indios of Boriken weave a village of bohíos in the cool places that are hung with rain. Some are survivors of the encomienda, released by its abolition twenty years ago. Some are from Tierra Firme and have followed the pathways of their native kin to these heights, far above San Germán. Many are children of the storm, the mixing and matching of tribes, called mestiza, mulata, zamba, lora, parda depending on the whims and prejudices of the record-keepers. But up here, no one keeps such records. They cultivate their root crops and cultivate peace, far from the priests and the soldiers. They tend the forest like a mother and plant memory in the red soil. They do not need to put this village on any map, but its name, in the mouths of neighbors, is Indiera.

1569: Dona Gracia—Europe and the Ottoman Empire

All her life, she fought fire with fire. Now, in the early fall of 1569, the Jewish world goes into mourning for Gracia Nasi, called Queen of the Jews. They sing her praises in Constantinople, where she has lived for many years, dispensing money where needed, building communities, advocating with the Sultan. They grieve and pray in the settlement she built near Tiberias, for which she paid a yearly sum to the authorities. Here she had planned to live out her old age and lie at last at rest in the Holy Land. In the cities of Venice, Ferrara, and Ancona, those who knew her tell stories of her Italian years. Associates from the long ago days in Antwerp gather crowds with their reminiscences. And even in Lisbon and in ancient Aragon, in the secret hearts of the conversos of Portugal and Spain, her name is whispered.

Once she was known to Portuguese society as Beatrice de Luna, daughter of the royal physician Miguez, conversos once of Aragon, but in the privacy of her home she was called Gracia of the ancient house of Nasi. At eighteen she married into the Mendes family, wealthy converso merchants. Then at twenty-six her husband died, and with her brother in-law she became the administrator of immense fortunes and a trading empire. It was in that year that the Inquisition came to Portugal. With many others, Gracia moved her family to the spice-trading center of Antwerp, and the Mendes's became the leading spice merchants of Europe.

But more than spices traveled south under their label. Jews from Spain and Portugal, Jews in danger anywhere, were smuggled to safety in Turkey, Italy, Greece. The fortunes of wealthy Jews were secreted among the packets of pepper, to keep them from the hands of the Inquisitors. The spice company of the heirs of Francisco Mendes paid bribes in all directions to grease the wheels. When her brother-in-law was arrested for helping a conversa escape her husband and flee into Turkey, Gracia secured his release, but then came the mass arrests of 1540. The burghers of Antwerp, torn between religious fervor and the profits of the spice trade, hesitated. Antwerp was becoming too dangerous.

Gracia established a defense fund, and she and her brother-in-law began making preparations to leave. And at that moment her brother in-law died suddenly, leaving her to answer charges against him that could allow the crown to seize everything they owned. Fighting fire with fire, she gathered evidence, paid bribes, and got the charges dropped in exchange for a large loan to the emperor. But now her rich and lovely daughters became the targets of old Christian lords seeking profitable marriages, and one night Gracia and her daughters fled to Venice. The agents of her spice empire were scattered throughout the Mediterranean, so she went from Venice to Ferrara, from there to Constantinople where at last she openly professed her Jewish faith. Everywhere she went, she helped other Jews with gifts of money and her influence with sultans and merchant kings.

Fire with fire. In the old port city of Ancona, Jews had flourished for centuries, exempt from oppressive regulations. The converso community upheld the government with loans, and Ancona became a city of refuge for Spanish Jews. But in the year 1555, Giovanni Pietro Caraffa, a virulent anti-Semite, became Pope. Soon ghettos sprang up in town after town and the Vatican began actively persecuting Jews. In Ancona itself, the Inquisition held a series of auto de fés, and two dozen Jewish citizens were burned in the public square.

When news of this betrayal reached Gracia, she was outraged. Many of those who died were known to her. Many were Turkish subjects, legally under the jurisdiction of the Ottoman Sultan and not the Pope. At her urging, the Sultan demanded the release of the remaining prisoners. The grand vizier sent for the consul of Ancona and threatened reprisals. But Gracia herself organized her own retaliation. Sending messages to all her commercial contacts, she persuaded other Jewish and converso merchants throughout the Mediterranean world to boycott the port of Ancona and transfer all business to the neighboring and friendly city of Pesaro, and merchant after merchant in Ancona went bankrupt. Eventually the boycott broke, pressured by retaliations against other Italian Jews, weakened by the fears of some commercial houses that they might have too much to lose. But the boycott of Ancona, set by the sparking heart of Gracia Nasi, was the one fire set by Jews in all those years of flames.

1575: Teresa de Avila Counts Demons

Teresa of Jesus is a cool breeze amidst all too much smoke. In these counter-reformation days the Devil is a seducer and all women are said to be his weak and willing prey. Fifty years ago the heterodoxas gathered in their kitchens to read the New Testament, and religious movements sprang up everywhere, with women visible, powerful, having visions and working miracles. But for a long time now the visions of women have been suspect. It was not that long ago in memory that Magdalena de la Cruz was visited by an angel of light, but entertained an amorous devil by night, deceiving many with her fraudulent stories. Magdalena had served only ten years of her sentence of perpetual silence and imprisonment when Teresa de Jesus began hearing voices and having rapturous visions of Christ.

Teresa skillfully navigates between dangers, defending the virtue and power of mental prayer, the good things that come from women's contemplation of God. God, she holds, is more powerful than the Devil, who always appears with all his demons as hideous tormentors, not potential lovers. Teresa writes that humility is the virtue that protects those who practice mental prayer from the Devil's snare of false pride. But dares to write, as well, that the Devil turns humility itself into a trap, bringing the souls of the faithful to despair. False humility, she says, is disrespectful to God, disdaining the intelligence He bestowed on His creation. Ordered by her confessors to make obscene gestures to her visions, she asks Christ to forgive her since it is He who chose to make such men His priests.

When she has founded her own order, she instructs the nuns that the Devil gains more by frightening women away from arduous thought and prayer than by any errors they may commit. She reassures them that the fear of being too fond of one's confessor, a danger of sexual feeling constantly referred to by the church authorities, that fear itself is but a Devil's temptation. Why should they not love those who tend to their souls? Such love is pure.

When the nuns have visions and miracles to report, she asks if they have slept enough, suggests a break from fasting and endless prayer, counsels them not to be carried away by feverish imagination. But she does not send for the priest to exorcise them. Teresa of Avila clears smoke with her steady, sensible gaze. The women she knows do not crave the Devil's caress. She does not believe their souls are constant prey to demons who possess them. She confidently tells them of the Interior Castle of their spirits, where surely mystical treasures will be bestowed as much on God's daughters as on His sons.

1592: Flames—Puerto Rico

The colony of San Juan de Puerto Rico is an island haunted, in its early years, by memories of fire and smoke. The treasurer Blas de Villasante is the grandson of Medina the Jew, burned in Sevilla. Bailiff Miguel Diaz is the son of conversos from Aragon. Bartolomé de las Casas may be related to those other Casas and Cases whose names are inscribed in the rolls of the Inquisition. The islands are full of next of kin.

It is not only Jews who must watch their steps. Along the north coast people have been accused of harboring shipwrecked Lutherans, dangerous salvage that could infect whole populations with heresy. From charms and medicines to banned religions, anyone who practices in secret the rites of her grandmothers could be denounced. Of the accused, some are reprimanded. Some are sent to the stake.

It has never been as bad as Mexico back in the twenties when the entire Carvajal family, parents and children, sisters and brothers and many of their friends were fed to the flames, one after another, year after year, some weeping, some proud, some reciting poetry praising the name of Adonai. Puerto Rico is a backwater, with fewer interests to defend. It has never been like Lima or Toledo or Sevilla. But there is tinder, and from time to time the inquisitor of the moment decides to strike the match.

This is one of those times. This year two women and a man are burned. They are West Africans. They are slaves. Their names are not remembered, not even their slave names. They sacrificed a goat. Perhaps to open the way. Perhaps for Elegguá. No one in power knows about the orishas. The bishop has never heard of the sacred rites of the Yoruba. They are accused of worshiping the devil. Out under the stars they sought solace and strength from gods who had never blessed their enslavement. For this crime they are tied among piles of sticks and set on fire.

Seventy years ago, when they burned the woman named Morales, suspected of being a secret Jew; they accused her and her brother of hanging a cross on the wall and then whipping it. No one remembers her name or the exact date of her death. Only that under torture she confessed what they asked her to confess. Only that she is the sister of Gonzalo, or maybe his name was Francisco, Morales who fled Puerto Rico for Mexico, only to die there at the same hands. I do not know if she left children. I do not know if she was my aunt or grandmother or cousin. The secret foremother of hacendado patriarchs and immigrant seamstresses.

On my altar I have shells for Yemayá and my grandmother's shabbos candlesticks. I say blessings in many names, on rain and food and children. I kiss earth and trees and skin. I am a Jew. I am a pagan. I am likely to harbor the shipwrecked. If I had been there, if someone had told on me, I would have burned. You would never have known my name.

❧ JENJIBRE: 1600–1699

1600: Catalina Steals Away—Spain and Panama

In a convent in Vizcaya, Catalina Erauso plots an escape from the narrow constraints of girlhood. She has never believed that version of herself, and now she reshapes her life to match the fighting man inside her. From the age of four she has lived with the nuns, in the convent where her aunt is prioress. Her elder brother is long gone into the wars in America, but Catalina must mend clothing, say prayers, be modest.

On the afternoon of March 18th she has one more fight with a nun, and this one slaps her. That night she wraps some food in a cloth, steals the keys while the sisters are at matins, and lets herself out of the convent gates. In the darkness she pulls on the men's clothing she has stolen and throws her dress away. At last she can walk like a soldier.

What does it mean to be a man? It means to carry weapons and ride horses. Catalina makes for Vitoria and becomes page to first one then another señor. Restless in their service, she moves on from Vitoria to Valladolid, from Valladolid to Bilbao, to Estella, to San Sebastián. After three years she makes her way where most restless men go, to Sevilla, to Cádiz, to a ship bound for the Indies.

From the deck of Captain Egiños ship she first sees America: they sail past the Cumaná peninsula of Venezuela to the great port of Cartagena de Indias, point of entry to the riches of the continent. After Cartagena, Nombre de Diós in Panamá. Catalina breathes the air and smells smoke and cornmeal and mules. She

decides to jump ship. Not only will she be a man, she will be a conquistador! She tells the guard she has an errand ashore for the captain. With the five hundred pesos she has stolen from Eguiño and
bravado like a knife between her teeth, she steps ashore and disappears into the tropical American night.

1605: A Seed Falls in Pernambuco—Brazil

In another part of the forest, the same tropical night hides a
different kind of courage. In the rainforests of Pernambuco, a seed
falls on fertile ground. Made from the pollen dust of a dozen African peoples, it will sprout into a strong tree, thick of root and
broad of trunk and nearly a century tall. Such seedlings are springing up everywhere—in Bahia, Matto Grosso, wherever slaves
meet forest. African women become leaders of mixed African and
American tribes who live in fortified villages just barely outside
the slaveholders' reach. But the quilombos are wiped out as
quickly as they appear. Only this one grows so large and strong. It
springs from the wild heart of Brazil and casts its shadow all the
way to the governor's palace. For in the secret state of Palmares, Africans rule themselves.

Or are ruled by other Africans. Here in the country of escaped
slaves, although he is elected, there is a king in a palace and there
are slaves. There are chiefs and warriors and there are wives. Any
slave who escapes to Palmares becomes freed by that act, but those
who are taken in raids remain in bondage until they capture someone else to take their place.

Quilombos, town after stockaded town, rise in the forest, defended by walls of sharpened sticks like a jaguar's teeth. They cluster along the left bank of the river Gurungumba, six leagues from
where it joins the Paraiba. They nestle in the mountains of Bar-
riga, thirty leagues from Santo Amaro.

The Portuguese say the people are from Guiné or they call
them Angolas. Africa is one place to them. But among the run-

aways, all the peoples of the slave coast and the forests behind are found. Quilombo is a Jaga word and it means "war camp" or else it means "to be arrayed for battle." Many Jaga have been taken in the wars of Angola where they sometimes fight the Portuguese and sometimes the Mbundu. The Mbundu also are here, taken in the same wars, and the settlements are also called mocambos, which in Mbundu means hideout. The names of the towns are in Jaga and Mbundu, but they are also in Loango, Kisama, Kwango, Zande, Banguila, Yombe, and in the tongues of the forest people of Northwestern Brazil.

For now, they are out of reach of the moradores, the planters. They are a rumor, disturbing the sleep of both slaver and slave. In the forests they build African towns. The Palmarista women plant grain and yams. Together, the people build houses and store-houses, irrigate their fields, and pay informants to warn them of armed men headed their way. They settle in for the long haul.

1606: Caribes

Indians appear and disappear according to the needs of the hacendados. When they want license to import more slaves, then there are no Indians left to exploit. When they want tax relief, Indians have been attacking them. When the encomienda ended, legally freeing the remaining Arawaks, the vecinos could only enslave those who made war upon them. Suddenly every planter had an Indian raid to report. Whoever attacks is called Carib. The Caribs are known to be wild and fierce, sensationally documented cannibals. When the crown orders the governor to teach Indians the Christian faith, once again there are no indios to indoctrinate.

But this is true. Four years ago a fleet of eighteen canoas, using sails for the first time, invaded Loiza, driving out estancieros and destroying sugar mills. Who they were, what they hoped for, where they went sailing home to at the end of the smoky day, we don't know. Last week it happened again, twenty canoas this time, carrying five hundred warriors. Once again a sugar mill was the target, but the estancieros were prepared and drove them away. The vecinos don't know it yet, but that was the last attack, the last massing of the canoas, the end of open warfare. Whether they were the people we are taught to call Carib, or a band of refugees from shattered nations camped together on one of the small islands sharpening their weapons, or in what place they gathered to talk together about the losses of the day, or where their children's children's children walked on this earth, the chronicles of the estancieros do not say.

1607: Wild West

Frontier towns are all the same: cattle thieves, outlaws, runaway slaves, and women who prefer a freer place to breathe. No one documents the history of this wild west. The chroniclers spend their time recording the absence of Spanish vessels in the harbor of San Juan. What good would it do them to write of the crowded bays of Aguada and Guanica, Salinas and Coamo, filled with the ships of smugglers and pirates from Jamaica, Guadalupe, and Curaçao? Instead they complain of the shortages of beef. The vecinos of San German cannot be bothered to supply them, when hides are so much more profitable and ginger is worth even more.

The herds run wild without brands of ownership, and if the cimarrones and buccaneers help themselves to beef, it's not the end of the world. In the far-off royal court of Spain, the authorities want records, titles, deeds. The orderly accounting that will make it easier to tax. But in San German the vecinos worship in a church of straw so flimsy that nothing of value is ever left there. They gather more often to fend off pirate raids, pursue escaped slaves, tend the sick in the latest epidemic, and repair the damages of hurricanes. And in the mountains above the town, the free people, the mixed-blood farmers, the jíbaras of the cordillera, bring down their surplus to exchange and disappear again into cool, rainy heights.

1608: Gingerbread—
San Juan de Puerto Rico and England

The working people of England eat gingerbread for their suppers. The apothecaries prescribe the root as a tonic. Those who can afford it eat candied ginger for dessert, and the old Queen Elizabeth used to have her baker fashion ginger cookies in the shape of human figures, decorated with faces for her amusement and the delight of her guests.

In the hills of western San Juan Bautista, the lush plants flourish, their spicy roots pushing up through the moist red clay. Ginger is not sugar. You don't need a hundred acres of flat ground to make a profit. You don't need slaves. You can plant it, dig it, cut it by hand, wrap the fragrant roots in a sack and carry them down to the bay where the smugglers' ships come in to trade. You can be a small farmer, with a little plot of land. You can be a woman raising kids on your own.

The trading ships cruise the coasts looking to fill their holds with ginger, hides, and forest woods. They sail to England, Spain, the Low Countries, where the ginger is sliced, preserved, dried, ground, made up into packets. The English baker puts a measure into his coarse sweet loaves, and a young girl on her way home buys a penny's worth for supper.

ꙮGINGER

> Ginger is ferocity and stubbornness. Ginger is aggressive and sharp. Ginger is the friend who drags you out of bed and makes you get up and face the morning. Ginger loosens your cramp against the difficult. Ginger stokes up the fires of digestion so

you can assimilate what you can't stand the thought of having swallowed. Ginger grabs you by the chest when you feel weak and helpless with congestion, weepy and aching with flu, and burns into your surrender, blowing trumpets.

Ginger is the one at the meeting who cuts through all the pointless arguments to say the short sharp thing that brings us back to purpose. Ginger clears fog from the brain. Ginger is the lover who looks at your malaise of self-doubt and insecurity and tells you to stop indulging yourself with reruns of the past, when your present is strong and sweet and spicy. Though ginger may burn your throat, its intention is never to be harsh. It's just that ginger knows exactly what is needed and can't help acting on everything it knows. With its flowers like sex and its roots like firm hands with a grasp of the essential, there is no better friend. Cultivate ginger! Keep it in stock. Fill up your kitchen. Fill up your garden. Add it to everything. Drink it and chew it and sniff it and carry a chunk of it candied in your purse to keep you safe from distractions.

1618: Nzinga's Stool—Angola

History is told from the point of view of the rulers, those who sit. In their stories, we servants always love them and would happily break our backs for them. But I have my own stories.

Royalty is ruthless. When the queen's brother Mbandi became the new Ngola, he murdered his young brother and the queen's son. Now he is afraid of the Portuguese and summons Queen Nzinga to do his negotiating for him. She is willing, and so all of us, her attendants, must go with her, to the palace of the governor. João Correa de Souza expects her humble, the pleading representative of the defeated Mbundu. His audience room has only one chair, his throne. Whoever comes must stand before him.

Queen Nzinga sends musicians playing instruments before her and walks in surrounded by her servants. She sees that solitary seat of power and she is angry, but anger never interferes with her cunning. She summons me with a gesture, and before the astonished eyes of the Portuguese officials I fall upon hands and knees, making of my body a throne for Nzinga. Balanced on my ribs, she meets the governor face to face, as his equal.

My knees press into the stone floor, as the governor asks that all the prisoners we have taken in the years of fighting be returned. Nzinga rocks gently and my hips creak. Smiling, she agrees to return prisoners if the governor will return all the Mbundus who have been carried off by slavers to Brazil.

Nzinga makes deals with the Devil. By the time my wrists and knees are drained of blood, Nzinga has agreed to supply the slavers, return the prisoners, and join with the Portuguese in fighting the fierce Jaga. The governor will recognize her brother as ruler of Ndongo and withdraw his armies. Her ruthlessness buys us time. Soon she will execute her brother and his young son and take over the leadership of the Mbundus. She will marry the Jaga chief and fight the Portuguese again. She has bought us time to survive into the next century. She did it with the lives of the enslaved. She did it on my back.

1618: Witches' Stool—Western Europe

The witches' stool is not made from aching muscles, but of iron, to hold the heat. The inventors are men. The accused are women. Strapped into the spiked chair, they scream for mercy. The men of God build fires that turn the metal red and slowly burn away the women's thighs and buttocks and genitals.

In the villages of France and the Holy Roman Empire women are accused. That they fly through the air, that they change into animals, that they cause their own children to die, that when their husbands mistreat them, they take the Devil to bed and he leaves a mark upon their bodies. At first the woman deny that they are witches. The babies died of smallpox. They do not know how to fly. But the secular courts have all the power. The trials are held in secret. The accused has no lawyer. She does not know who has accused her. There is no cross-examination. She is assumed to be guilty. She is tortured until she has confessed to exactly what the judges have already decided she has done and until she names other victims for them to pursue.

The women are stretched on the ladder and their legs are crushed in the Spanish boots. They are torn with hot pincers and every crevice of their bodies searched for the Devil's mark. One woman scratches her wounds open in the hope that she will bleed to death. Another tries to poison herself by eating her own feces. The families of the accused must pay the expenses of the torturers and also the executioner. For every step in the trial there is a fee, and the judges become rich from the plunder of their victims. And each one, dying, names others, until whole villages are empty of women's voices and there is only the stifled breathing of their children and the smoke drifting across the sky.

1623: Ana de Mendoza Unpacks—
San Juan de Puerto Rico

Ana de Mendoza, wife to the new governor Juan de Haro, has brought with her two cedar chests filled with white clothing. She has two tables, one of *caoba* wood, another captured from ingleses. Her dishes, jars, and candelabras are of silver. Her brother-in-law, the bishop, writes in his diary that they never lack delicacies for the table, for if beef is sometimes scarce, there are always carey, and tender chickens, and fresh eggs. The de Haro family eats bread made of fine wheat flour, cornbread and casabe, and imported rice. They eat of all the rich fruits and vegetables the island produces. Their food is cooked with olive oil from the south of Spain and they wash it down with Canary Islands wine.

The slaves of the de Haro family keep no diaries. Like most slaves, like most of the "free" poor, they probably eat once a day.

They live on green bananas and plantains, casabe and cornmeal. Once a week, they are given a small piece of dried fish or salt pork. They have one garment, of rough cotton. No one makes clothing on this forsaken island colony. Few ships come from Sevilla. Smugglers, however, infest all the waters and crowd into the harbors of the south and west, peddling used skirts and blouses, shirts and trousers from the cities of Europe. The poor wear secondhand clothes or rough garments of leather. The slaves wear less. Even the soldiers at the garrison have to skip mass because they have nothing with which to cover their nakedness before God.

In Ana de Haro's wardrobe are a suit and jacket embellished with cloth of gold, two silk capes, a jacket lined with black taffeta, two green mantillas decorated with gold, two more jackets decorated with gold and also with bronze buttons, two black overdresses, another of Castile color with decorations, and six more outfits of damask with gold or silver ornaments on them. She has another chest full of lengths of fine cloth, including China silk, damask, and other finery. There are bed hangings of blue damask and a bedspread of the same material, a velvet coverlet embroidered with gold and silk, and three more chests, one filled with worked silver, one containing 6,000 reales of gold, and one of jewels. Also, fourteen slaves to swell the ranks of the hungry.

1625: S/he—Latin America

That night in Panamá was only another step in a wild life. No job holds Catalina Erauso for long. S/he hires on with a merchant in Peru, and her/his ship sinks. S/he swims ashore and continues her/his journey. Butcher than butch, s/he fights at the drop of a hat. When the man in the seat in front of her/him at the theater is rude and threatens her/him, s/he seeks him out and attacks him with a knife. Over and over s/he is forced to seek sanctuary in churches. S/he kills a man and must flee for Lima. In Lima s/he fights again, over a woman.

Soldiers are wanted for an expedition into Chile, and s/he signs on. But the Mapuche cannot be dislodged from their land of cold water and rocky forests. There is neither loot nor glory here, only endless demoralizing defeat. Returning north to Concepción, s/he serves under her/his brother Miguel, but they fall out over a woman. Onward to Paicabí, fighting the conqueror's wars, building manhood on the bloodstained ruins of villages. When the commanding officer is killed, s/he replaces him. Mysteriously, this wo/man with the distinctive face is never recognized by her/his relations. Her/his brother never knew who served under him. The ship's captain who brought her/him to America never recognized his own niece. Now in the midst of a brilliant military career, s/he fights a duel over a woman and kills her/his opponent, once again neither recognizing nor being recognized by her/his brother Miguel.

Crossing the Andes to Tucumán, in Argentina, s/he travels on to Potosí of the silver mines and is someone's aide. In La Plata s/he knifes a man over a woman. In Charcas s/he nearly kills another over a gambling dispute. In La Paz s/he does kill a criado of the corregidor Barraza and this time is sentenced to death. Just before the execution s/he asks to confess and when s/he is given communion, s/he takes the host from her/his mouth and places it in her/his hand. (Her/his confessor in prison has suggested this trick.) The attending priests are in an uproar, washing and purifying her/his hand, rushing about, and when s/he is left unguarded for a moment, s/he escapes on a mule given to her/him by her/his friends, the monks.

Cuzco and Lima and Cuzco again. Another gambling fight and this time, injured, s/he confesses her/his sex before it is discovered. The priest keeps her/his secret while s/he heals. Off to Huamanga, then Huancavelica, always on the run because everywhere there are warrants for her/his arrest. Returning to Huamanga s/he is recognized and finally arrested. With sword and pistol s/he fights back and escapes, but three days later a group of guards surround and try to take her/him. The bishop hears the noise, investigates, and decides to take her/him into his custody. S/he decides it's time to be female again and confesses to the bishop. He doesn't believe her/him, but two matrons come to examine her/him and report to the bishop that s/he is both female and virgin. What is this charm s/he holds for the clergy? The Bishop takes her/him under his protection and s/he puts on a nun's habit. Curious crowds wait to see her/him pass as s/he goes to the convent in Lima. There s/he is received by the archbishop and the viceroy. After two years lying low in the convent, s/he puts on men's clothing once more and leaves America for Spain. Wouldn't you know it, on the ship from Cartagena s/he gets into a gambling fight. S/he is thirty-nine.

1629: Manahatta—Mouth of the Hudson River

Long centuries before Harlem had a renaissance or the Barrio had música, there were gente here. Lenape means "real people," and the Munsee of the lower Hudson were the Lenape. Manhattan was where the Manates hung out. The Canarsie had Brooklyn, the Matinecooks were in Flushing, and the Rockaways lived in Queens. Newcomers, though, these Iroquoian-Huron tipos, compared to the old Algonquians. Only four hundred years in the neighborhood, and really pushing their weight around. The last of the Algonques were the Mahicans, way out by Yonkers. Wouldn't you know they'd be the first to be wiped out by smallpox. Not to mention that the newest of the new, those Holandeses who wanted to take home the skin of every beaver in North America, kept selling muskets and powder to the Iroquois, which was bad news for everyone else. Yeah, they had gente killing gente back then, too.

The real gente ate beans just like us. They made sancochos from meat and fish and root vegetables simmered with beans in a big clay pot. They had their parcelitas of corn and calabaza and to-bacco and they liked to go fishing with milkweed nets, dig for clams and oysters, make budin de maiz with maple sugar, and dance up a storm. They traded upriver with the Oneida and the Onondaga and sold fur and fancy beaded leatherwork and good food. It was garment work, colmaditos, and comida criolla even then.

So hace veinte años viene este tipo Henry Hudson, trying to find Asian spice, not knowing he needs to wait several hundred years for those shops to open up so he can get some canela and pimienta in this neighborhood. All he finds are the gente, happily eating asopao de almejas. His bosses back at the East India Company are not pleased. But they figure, What the heck, let's claim the place anyway. The fur traders like the good harbor, and that big river goes deep inland to where there are still plenty of animalitos that haven't lost their scalps yet. So de repente, about six years ago, aparecen a hundred Dutch Protestant neighbors with their farm animals and seeds and tools, looking like your tía Luci that time she left her husband and showed up with all those suitcases, ready to start a new life out of the best bedroom. A los dos años, they got an engineer planning and a bunch of Africanas y Africanos sweating to put up a fort, so you know they intended to defend something.

Only 1629, and already el pastor was talking about these Angola slave women being thievish, lazy, useless trash, when you know who got that fancy shirt of his so white, and who he also didn't mind using out behind the church shed anytime after dark. Anyway, that was the beginning of landlords and cops and the dissing of the gente. And way back before any of us had danced in the park or taken over a building, the old gente of Manhattan were in la lucha, using homemade paint on the whitewashed walls of the Dutch to write "Basta ya" in Huron and Algonquian for "Pa'lante."

1630: The Weavers of Dean—England

In the English forest of Dean the weavers have always gathered
bark and vines, birds and venison, fruit and firewood to supple-
ment their earnings at the loom. But now the lords of England are
enclosing the common lands, vying for options on the oak and
beech woods, purchasing their rights to timber from the king and
not the cloth makers of Dean.

This year the harvest of grain has failed and while those who
farm have something to feed their children, the craftswomen and
men who fill the holds of trading ships with bolts of broadcloth
have neither garden plots nor the wild green woods from which to
fill their bellies, and the coins they earn at the shuttle cannot buy
them food that is not for sale.

So the weavers of Dean and the other forest villagers of England take, rioting, to the roads, break open the storehouses, in-
vade the ships tied up at the wharves, and demand to be fed.
Meanwhile, the cloth they have woven travels far and wide; is
crafted into shirts and jackets, skirts and trousers; is worn and bar-
tered; and makes its way at last to the distant coasts of the Caribbean, where food is plentiful but clothing is not, and cotton not
worth growing when you can sell sugar and ginger, fresh meat and
vegetables, leather and hardwood, and the endless supply of
slaves.

1635: Playa Boquerón

Late at night after we have sold our sacks of ginger roots and bundles of hides, after we have bought iron tools, bottles of oil, items
of woven cloth, then we dance on the beach with the sailors. The
sweet, sharp cries of their pipes and whistles call to us above the
crash of waves, and we lift our skirts, laughing, hook arms, and
twirl on the sand. Sailors are our kind of people, forced into service by press gangs or by hunger, and no friends of authority.
Around the fire they tell us news in the savory trade language

blended of Spanish, English, French, Carib, Portuguese, Yoruba, Dutch. It is from sailors we hear the rumors of an African country hidden in the forests of Brazil, rumors that run like whispers of fire through the slave markets of Cartagena; of Algonquian sabotage in New Amsterdam, of the burning of secret Jews in Mexico, of indenture and servitude, of fevers and pirates and loved ones lost far beyond the horizon. Many a criolla goes home humming horn-pipes and jigs. In her sack she carries back a sharp new knife, a powerful story, a haunting melody. And who can blame her if sometimes she finds she has brought home more than she intended: a few loose shells in her pockets, a strand of seaweed in her hair, a red-headed child in her belly?

1636: I Believe It Is No Sin—Galicia

In the green hills of Galicia, women inherit land and independence. Marriage is not the only road and many don't bother. There are not so many men to marry anyway. Most of them are away with the fishing fleet or working somewhere in Castile. The only men who stay put are the priests. Gallega women know how to work the tiny plots of stony soil that the men reject as unprofitable. What do they need with husbands when a lover is so much easier to dismiss. Gallega women often live with lovers, bear children to different men, try out their fiancés for several years before the wedding, and, if they part, demand support for babies, not a wedding ring.

The Inquisition worries that old Christians of the north do not take doctrine seriously enough and come to Galicia to discover who does not believe the pronouncements of the Church. Since words and thoughts have more power to corrupt than deeds, those denounced for simple fornication, for sex between the single, are the ones who talk with neighbors. Brought to the table of the inquisitors, Ysabel de Paco says she didn't know sex between single men and women was a sin, and Marina de Cedeyra, a servant of eighteen, believes it cannot be a sin, since they can always marry later. Alberta Rodriguez, a servant in Santiago, says it's only half a sin, a fraction not recognized by the authorities. Margarida Alonso, overheard discussing a young couple, says the sin is not so very big.

The women of Galicia fail to make sense of the priorities of the Church. Ana Fernandez, who lives next door to a battered wife, says it is better to be a concubine of a decent man than be unhappily married because at least people pray for those in mortal sin, but the wife has no one to intercede on her behalf. María de Fiscal agrees. She was denounced for bursting into tears and declaring she'd rather be someone's mistress, and only sin from time to time, than be wed as she was, which did no service to the Lord. María Rodriguez, with a husband twenty-six years gone to America, said at least a woman with a lover could stop sinning when she wished, while *her* lonely misery was endless. María Afonso, the nineteen-year-old wife of a tailor, told her neighbors that she had been the unwed lover of a man for a year and a half and in the service of God, but now she saw that her marriage served only the Devil.

Unabashed, these women stand before the robed men of the Inquisition, declaring they would rather see their daughters the concubines of priests than married to ruinous men, sooner the friend of a cleric than an unhappy wife. In the wild lands of Galicia, the power of patriarchy has not yet invaded every dream. They stand on the land their mothers gave them and, laughing, speak the old refrain: Men count for nothing where we women are.

1640: Paula de Eguiluz—Colombia

In Cartagena de Indias the inquisitors beg to be excused. If they were to arrest every person known to practice magic, spells, unlawful healing, there would be over four thousand prisoners in the first roundup. The entire country is steeped in spiritual practices declared to be witchcraft and sorcery by the Inquisition. Paula de Eguiluz has been had up before the authorities before. She practices herbal medicine, blesses her patients, uses all the varied lore of her mulata mestiza heritage. This time they cannot afford to release her. They must not be lenient. But Paula has attended the inquisitors' wives in childbed, doctored their children through fevers, prescribed the perfect remedy for their own headaches.

The law is clear. Paula de Eguiluz is condemned to imprisonment for life. But each morning she sheds the garments of penitence and goes forth in a cloak with a golden hem, carried through the streets in a litter as she attends her patients. She is richly paid and before returning each night to her prison cell and the black hood of a penitente, she purchases fresh foods, delicious treats, every imaginable comfort for her prison-mates and herself.

1647: Stuyvesant—New Amsterdam

Que mal hombre, this Stuyvesant, this new jefe of New Amsterdam! What bad news all around. He tortures the Quakers and begs to expel the newly arrived Brazilian Jews. He wants to be el gran dictador and is pretty pissed when the king grants the citizens a government. So much loot to be had here. He wants the looting organized to serve him best. He's swimming against the tide, though, with so many other hungry fishes in the pond. He tries to make everyone pray exactly as he thinks they should, but he only manages to make everybody mad. Slaves he welcomes, as long as they stay slaves, but twenty-three Jewish merchants from the West Indies he thinks will pollute his town. Oh Stuyvesant, you bad, bad man, what a nightmare it would be if you could only see ahead. Did you have dreams sometimes that woke you in a cold sweat, of all those multicolored, many-languaged, all-religions people you can't stand, filling the streets of a city that is long gone out of your hands?

1648: The House of Peace

The men of San Juan Bautista complain that there are not enough husbands for women of good families to marry and that fathers are unduly burdened with the endless support of unmarried daughters who have nothing suitable to occupy their time. They need a religious house to which they can donate their surplus girls.

Ana de Lanzós was not a surplus girl. She married well, but her husband has recently died and the young widow turns one of the houses she has inherited into a house of peace for her sister, her neighbor, and herself. With her wealth she endows the first convent on the island, and the three women become Carmelite nuns. They need not ever marry again, now that they have become brides of Christ. Within the cool walls of the convent, they study and pray, garden and sew, have hours of silence in which their thoughts are their own, uninterrupted by husbands or children, neighbors or visitors. Each evening as they come together for prayer, gratitude rises heartfelt from the little chapel like the scent of goodness rising from new baked bread.

1650: On the Road to Veracruz—Mexico

On the road to Veracruz, a famous soldier has fallen ill and lies, delirious, on the bed. Catalina Erauso has worn so many names since his birth, sixty-five years ago, in the Basque lands. In his fever, he wanders again. Once more, she is leaving America, casting off the nun's robes. Once more he visits Cadiz, Sevilla, Madrid, sets off to Rome to petition the pope for his jubilee and is arrested crossing France, suspected as a spy. In her dreams she is writing the memorial of her services to the crown, all the battles she has fought for the Empire that will entitle her to a pension of eight hundred escudos. Eight hundred escudos and recognition that he has earned a soldier's gender in exchange for a lifetime of slaughter.

Or, no, he is traveling. Where is it this time? Once again to Rome, by way of Barcelona? She tosses and turns, wrestles with the servant attending her, because she thinks that she is again being assaulted on the road to Barcelona, left destitute, forced to beg until he can get a message to one of his high-ranking friends. The servant wipes his forehead with a damp cloth, but the fever rages. He tries to get the dying soldier to take a sip of wine.

Ahhh, I remember. Catalina becomes gracious. She is being received by the King, telling him the story of her travels, and with the money he has given her, at last she is in Rome. She is quieter now and the servant breathes a sigh of relief. The old warrior is no joke to handle in a delirium. But in his mind he is not fighting at the moment. He is dining with princes and cardinals, being received by Pope Urban VIII. Writing his memoirs in the careful hand taught to her by the nuns, standing at a window in Naples, sitting for her portrait in the studio of Pacheco in Sevilla.

And now in the dimming light the faces of women appear: Beatriz and Carmen, Isabel and Leonor, María Inocencia and María Luisa. It is summer, and he is returning to America in the fleet of Miguel de Echazarreta, and on the deck beside her is the lovely young woman she has been hired to escort to the home of her parents in Mexico, in time for her wedding. It has been twenty years, but Catalina still remembers her laughing eyes, the way the wind blew her hair, the taste of her lips. By the time they reach Mexico, the bride no longer wants her bridegroom. In his fever, Catalina reaches for his missing sword. He is restrained, as he was then, when powerful friends of her sweetheart's parents prevented the duel . . .

But it's time to get up. Mules and crew have rested long enough. Hit the road again and get this load to Veracruz. She sighs and goes out into the dazzling sun to see to the horses. The servants look at one another, approach cautiously. Yes, one of them says, he's gone. Catalina Erauso has run off again, down a long road without end.

1663: Nzinga, the Warrior Queen—Angola

In a rock by the Cuanza River there is an ancient footprint. It was made thousands of years ago, but people say it is her footprint, as if the sole of her foot could melt rock. For forty-five years she has maneuvered her forces, keeping her people out of the jaws of Portugal. She has fought beside the ferocious Jaga, inspired the Manikongo of Kongo to fight his former allies, joined forces with the Dutch against their rivals. She has been baptized more than once in the interests of peace. She has ordered the death of her treacherous brother and poisoned his son. She has had many husbands, among them the chief of the Jaga. The Portuguese have killed thousands of her people. They have strangled one sister and held the other captive for eleven years. The Jaga got out of hand, the Manikongo backed down, and the Dutch were defeated, but she has continued to fight a guerrilla war from the heights of Matamba.

In these mountains, she has built a new country, where even some Jagas give up eating human flesh and settle down in peace. She has led her own troops into battle, dressed as a king. For many years she kept a harem of young men dressed as women for her "wives." She has corresponded with the Pope. Her last husband is one of the youngest "wives." She has released the rest. Nearing death, she still has the power to install her sister as ruler after her, marrying her to the general of the armies to secure her position. In December of this year, Queen Nzinga of the Mbundu will die. Matamba will remain in African hands for a few more generations, then fall, like Ndongo, to the Portuguese, who will call their colony Angola.

But more than three hundred years from this day, her descendants will rise up against the Portuguese, driving them out of this land with the same guerrilla warfare she used against the same enemy, singing Nzinga as they fight. And African women from Bahia to Harlem will look into the cold, mean eyes of whoever would crush them, and they will touch her name to their lips and fight.

1664: Decree

Folks at the top just can't resist doing each other a bad turn, even if it accidentally does some good to us. The Spanish, the French, the English, the Danes, the Portuguese, and the Dutch are all over the map, seizing islands and coastlines from each other, sinking ships, sending out pirates, burning towns, and trying to cut each other out of deals. When four slaves, three women and a man, escape from St. Thomas and make their way to the coast of San Juan Bautista, the local officers who recapture them are all for a quick sale in the marketplace and some coins for the town treasury. But thanks to the governor's farsighted malice, the sale is interrupted. What if, says the governor, we let all *their* runaway slaves who come here remain free? Sniggering in his sleeve, he imagines depleting the sugar mills of his rivals as their labor pool slips away in stolen boats. He barely sees the four captives as he promises them their freedom and a bit of land in exchange for baptism as Catholics and allegiance to the crown. He thinks of them as a living taunt, as a sneaky piece of policy, as a feather in his cap. As the new libertas make their way to the edges of the swamp, prudently aiming for "out of sight and out of mind," the governor is already thinking of his next move. So certain of his pawns, he never imagines they will make their own moves or ever feel more loyalty to his own runaway slaves, hidden, fed, and passed on, than they do to him.

1694: The Death of Palmares—Brazil

After nearly a century of defiance and strength, after twenty years of invasions, one after another, by the Portuguese and the Dutch, after the government of Brazil is stopped from granting diplomatic recognition to this hardy transplanted nation when local planters cry out for blood, after all this, death is finally at hand.

Indigenous trackers have spent two years and many, many lives bringing an army to this place where a dozen townships flourish behind wooden stockades. One month of siege, and although Palmares is reduced to a single, fortified stronghold, the invaders must send to the capital of Pernambuco for a new army of four thousand men.

Finally, defeat does come. Two hundred Palmaristas hurl themselves from a high rock rather than accept enslavement. Those who are captured alive, many of them women and children, are shackled and sent to market like so many wild cattle. Instructions are to sell no more than one in any one location, so fearful are the captors of their prey. So the legacy of Palmares scatters far and wide, carried on the breath of those born free within the legendary realm.

The authorities are satisfied that they have stamped the dangerous example out. Palmares will not rise again. But more than two hundred years later, in the village of Alagoas where a township of Palmares once stood, the descendants of that moment resurrect their freedom in an annual passion play. There in the plaza, they perform once more the last battle for the kingdom of the unenslaved and touch the soil that once was liberated land.

⚘LLANTÉN

Llantén has the power to suck the ugliness from a putrid wound, reach down to the place that violence never touched, and draw the good, uninjured body toward the sun. Llantén knows there is bedrock underneath the eroded surface of the hills, a place where cancer has not penetrated yet, that sap still flows within the mutilated tree. Llantén is the quiet certainty beyond defeat, the roadside herb lifting its humble spikes from the dust of passing traffic, spreading its leaves where anyone can tread, always underfoot, always somewhere in the landscape, unnoticed until the time of need. Look to the ground, you who are wounded to what feels like the blue-lipped edge of death. There is more than desolation in the wastelands and the empty lots where we suffer. There is plantago, plantain, llantén, common as breath that continues when the heart is choked with anguish. Common as day that disappears and comes again.

1695: News of Sor Juana—Mexico

Juana de Asbaje is an illegitimate child, born in a village near Mexico City. But she has found a place for herself at the Viceroy's court. She is intelligent and beautiful. Reading and writing by the age of three, at eleven she debates with philosophers and mathematicians, physicists and musicologists and is a favorite with the Viceroy's family. At eighteen she is especially and passionately attached to the Viceroy's wife. There are no diaries, no snapshots taken together, no friends to be interviewed about this passion.

At nineteen she joins a convent, first the Barefoot Carmelites, which she finds too severe, and then, when she is twenty-one, the Order of St. Jerome. There she becomes Sor Juana Inés de la Cruz. Her library, the most extensive in the Americas, has four thousand volumes, and her cell is full of scientific equipment with which she conducts experiments. She is an acclaimed poet. She writes *hombres necios que acusais a la mujer sin razón*—"Stupid men who accuse woman without cause . . ." Men who seduce women and then blame us for being loose, who say they want us to be pure and chaste as lilies and then hit on us.

The Bishop of Puebla, writing as Sor Filotea, condemns her

unwomanly interest in science and literature and her presumption in seeking to know about the world. In a brilliantly argued essay, Juana turns the very same biblical authorities he cites against him, with deceptive humility, in unabashed and skillful defense of the right of women to think. In 1693 *Reply to Sor Filotea* becomes the first feminist essay published in the Americas. Copies appear throughout the Spanish empire. Perhaps, late in the year 1694, a copy comes to San Juan, to the Carmelite convent, and the nuns gather around it and whisper and frown and question and maybe a few eyes sparkle with excitement. Maybe one of the nuns undertakes to write to her illustrious sister, but the letter takes many months to compose and many more to find its way to Mexico. Meanwhile, there has been yet another epidemic, and Sor Juana, who has sold her books and equipment, as ordered, to help the poor, has been tending the sick and fallen ill herself, and, at the age of forty-seven, has died. Maybe, in the delirium of her deathbed, she imagined you—brown-skinned, poor, female, sitting in a college classroom, reading about her, choosing among books, picking up a pen. Then her spirit flew into the sky over Mexico, bursting into hundreds of fragments of brilliant light, and became a new constellation.

1696: The Weavers of Tayasal—Guatemala

Tayasal is the last stronghold of the Mayan warriors, and now it has been overrun by Spanish troops. But a people's strength is not in strongholds. Not only here, but throughout the wide lands of the Maya, women weave and reweave the world, a map of the cosmos, recreated daily in garments worn under the very noses of priests and soldiers who would eradicate all memory of it if they could. Memory persists in their hands from Tazumal to Chichen Itza, from Palenque to Pusilhá, as the provinces of Spanish empire rise and shift and fall, as countries emerge on the ruins, women of Guatemala, Mexico, Honduras, Belize, El Salvador hold processions to honor the goddess of weavers as a Christian saint and keep remaking the world.

In this year, say the books, the Mayans were finally defeated. Three hundred years later, they will still be making the same endlessly hopeful and premature announcement of conquerors everywhere: order has been established. Meanwhile, Quiché-speaking armies of the poor battle soldiers in Guatemala, the Mayan Zapatistas of Chiapas declare war on Mexico, and unthinking tourists, dazzled by the brilliant colors, scramble to buy the weavings in which the universe that conquest shattered is remembered whole.

❧ PARTERAS: 1700–1798

1700: The Forests Sail East—New England

White pine and red pine, Douglas fir and spruce, the forests of the great north are cut down, stripped, and stacked. Ten thousand trees leave Boston harbor in one day, headed for the shipyards of Liverpool. They will return as masts and decks, as the hulls and booms of clipper ships and slavers, of traders in sugar and tea. Where once birds sang and deer moved through dappled shadows, there are desolations of stumps, rooted up for plowed fields. Soon no one will remember that these meadows were once tall groves of sap-scented shadow and rooted calm. That once the forests reached, rank upon rank of trunks wider than our arms can stretch and farther than any eye could see, thousands upon thousands of miles from the heart of the Midwest to where the ice cap twinkles under the northern lights, from the edge of the prairie to the sandy shoals of Georgia and the craggy coast of Maine.

The forests of America lie stacked like the corpses of civilians in a ruthless war, piled into mountains of wood to feed the ravenous commerce of the Atlantic. Do any of the sailors, themselves grist for the same harsh mill, look down in pity at the once-living logs that lie, a wound in the heart of the landscape, oozing their sap into the sunlit sky?

❧ WHITE PINE

Grief is in the chest, and white pine goes there, sharp and bracing as the forest air, tangy with resin and snow. White pine pierces

the thick mucus of hopelessness, dissolves it from the walls of
our lungs, and lets us cough it up and spit it out. White pine,
astringent needles puckering the mouth, reaches into
the most protected places of our brains, scouring out the
unnecessary, the self-indulgent, the poison of self-pity. White
pine shouts, "Wake up!" Clean and empty and cold as a wind
out of Canada in winter, white pine looks the world in the face
and refuses to close its eyes. White pine always takes one more
exhilarating breath as the blade of the axe flashes in the sun.
Who knows but that this morning out of a thousand, the logger
may smell the forest and put the axe away. And if he does not,
white pine will drink the earthy water till the last instant of life,
and even after it falls, the yellow resin will fill the air and cling
to his clothes and keep on speaking its unrelenting truth.

1701: The Country of Women

Not all histories are written in books. Sometimes memory is a
smooth river stone, a cooking pot, a rocking chair handed down
through many years. In the mountains around Utuado, Pedro
Matos tells a story that has lost its name. In some year long before
the coming of roads and newspapers, word comes to the cordillera
on foot and mule of a great discovery of gold, away to the south.
The mountains empty of men, especially white men, as young and
old leave their plots of yuca and plátano and walk to the coast to
find ships. From the shape of the journey, we can name the desti-
nation. The place in the south that draws and devours the men of
the cordillera is Ouro Preto, a huge hole in the heart of Brazil,
where gold is mined, stolen, smuggled, and fought over night and
day. Into that hole they vanish and do not return.

Utuado is a cluster of houses nestled in the green arms of the
forest. In the surrounding mountains, each farmer burns a little
clearing and plants malanga, batata, yautía, plátano, greens. A
few rainy seasons and she moves on, letting the vines and seed-

lings take back her tiny farm. In this forgotten year, the cordillera becomes a country of women and children. Mothers, sisters, grandmothers, aunts lead mule teams loaded with cattle hides and ginger, fresh produce and forest woods to trade along the coast for iron hoes and cookpots, machetes and needles, clothing and oil. For a generation, until their sons are grown, the brown-skinned women of Utuado, negra, mulata, parda, mestiza, control the economy of the interior. At night, sitting together on their porches, talking, smoking a pipe under the sweet-smelling branches of the forest, the women look out under the leaves toward the sea, talking quietly, telling stories, laughing among themselves.

Fourteen generations of children have grown and gone away since then, and the sons have long since recaptured that world for the fathers. The municipal histories are about hacendados, mayors, and militiamen and do not mention anyone else. But like the worn handle of a well-used hoe, this story still passes from hand to hand, smooth from the touch of many palms, and continues to turn the earth.

1706: Beatrice of Kongo—Central Africa

She has shaken the very foundations of the colonizing church. Kimpa Vita, priestess of the cult of Marinda, daughter of the aristocracy, has had a vision of St. Anthony, beloved of the missionary priests. But this Anthony is African, and he has announced the rebirth of Kongo, now crushed under two hundred years of slave raids and factional wars into poverty and despair. There have been prophetesses and prophets before her. The Virgin Mary appeared to a woman of the villages and spoke of her anger at the destruction. An old woman, Ma-Futa, claimed to have the disfigured head of Christ, in the form of a stone from the Ambriz river. But Dona Beatrice, as she is now known, has awakened the people with a vision of hope and pride.

She has seized the gospel and made it African. Kongo, she proclaims, is the Holy Land of the Bible, Christ was born in São Salvador, and the apostles were Africans. Her followers shed their European clothing and return to the bark cloth of their ancestors. She tells them polygamy is not a sin in the African church. She prophesies that São Salvador will be repopulated, and believers flock to the city in search of miracles. Lords of the city offer her the ends of their capes as tablecloths for her to eat from, and wherever she goes, noble women walk before her to clear the way. Now she has given birth to a child she claims was immaculately conceived.

The Capuchin missionaries are in a cold sweat. Among the many manikongos fighting each other for control, they choose one to silence Beatrice. Shortly after the Child is born, Beatrice is arrested. The manikongo wants to send her to the bishop in Luanda. He tries to wash his hands of her. But the priests want her death and that of the infant son. In the public square, the mouth of the manikongo speaks the sentence of the Church. She is to be burned at the stake. Afraid now, she tries to recant, but the crowd is in an uproar, and the prophetess and her child are heaped with wood and burned. In the morning, the missionaries come again and burn their bones, so there will be nothing but ash. Still, the believers come and comb through the grey dust with restless fingers, looking for the woman who, for a while, gave them back their faces.

1714: Cangrejos

In the swamps to the south and west of the capital a village has been growing for half a century. The settlers were once slaves, or their parents and grandparents were. There are African children living here two full generations from bondage. They came in canoas, in stolen fishing boats, on homemade rafts. They are still coming. From St. Croix and St. Thomas, Tortola, and even Jamaica. In the marshes crabs are plentiful, and there are plots of vegetables where the land is dry. This year freedwomen and men petition the governor for title to this land and found their own town, which they call Cangrejos, after the crabs that stew up so nicely with ají and guingambó.

Much later the muckety-muck Santurce will come and build a tower or a church or some other public building and officials will decide to name the town Santurce as a gesture of appreciation, but under the bustling streets are buried beams of wood, rusted cook-pots, fossilized palm leaves in the mud of long-drained marshes, piles of crab shells buried by the kitchen door, long ago, when Cangrejos meant freedom.

1720: Cecilia Ortiz

Eight generations before my birth, Cecilia Ortiz is the earliest abuela for whom I have a name. I come from her childbearing by many threads of blood. Her granddaughter María de Gracia will give me no less than three direct ancestors, as cousin after cousin marries inside the family, binding the web of kinship with land and houses, titles and deeds. Further than this the records do not go. The parish did not register the day or hour of her birth, the moment of her baptism, whether she was widowed young or died in childbirth, whether she was a poor relation or had ample wealth and lands.

The women of my family love to detect microscopic evidence of kinship in the bones, eyes, and habits of the children of the clan. Bad temper, they claim, came in through Jose María Hernandez, a Spanish soldier who married Cecilia's great-grand-daughter Isabel. The Moraleses are responsible for "morra," the inability to wake up quickly or cheerfully. Our square heads are a legacy of intermarriage among Canarios, and Morales inbreeding gave us thyroid disease and a sense of confirmed entitlement. I am said to look like one of my remote cousins whom I've never seen, and every time I visit, my aunts remark on it again.

Any momentary pause in conversation is likely to be broken by a musing speculation on whether my eyes are more like the eyes of this relative or that, whether it's the corner of my mouth or the curve of my chin that most clearly proclaims the Díaz in me.

But Cecilia is too remote for such questions. It is only I who wonder about the mysteries of descent over so many generations. Three of her grandchildren gave birth to my great-grandparents. Surely, some concentration of her essence remains. There is no portrait, no photograph, no evidence by which to find her shadow in my cheekbone or the crook of my little finger. But I imagine her sometimes, as I move to the rhythms of my woman's work, the turning of my wrists to clean a pot, the long, repeated strokes as I brush my daughter's hair. Imagine that something common to us both, some echo of her gestures, of the way she breathed this air, remains.

1728: Nannytown—Jamaica

In the encampments of the Windward maroons, high in the blue mountains of Jamaica, the obeah woman Nanny provides medicine and bravery, bandages and spiritual counsel to this community of former slaves, living in open rebellion. When the English offer to leave them be if they will return any future escapees, the Leeward maroons agree, but Nanny and the Windwards refuse. Nannytown is what they call this place, although she is not the military leader. Stories of her powers will long survive her, slave-quarter tales of how, naked, she drove off an enemy armed to the teeth with the power of her African woman's body, catching his bullets between the brown, muscular globes of her buttocks and farting them back into the redcoat ranks, to watch soldier after soldier fall. Long after she is hunted down and killed and the band is broken apart, the spirit of Nanny visits the cramped rooms where her congregation sleeps, and passes through their dreams like a memory of freedom, shaking her breasts, her sex, her butt in the face of death.

1736: The First Cafeto

It is a beautiful, slender plant. Long shining leaves of dark green. Clusters of fragrant white flowers with the scent of gardenias. It comes from the highlands of Ethiopia, but in Haiti the enslaved children of Africa harvest its red berries, wash them, shell them, dry them, roast them, and load them onto ships for the sons of France. So far, it has put down few roots in the hills above Yauco, but this is good coffee country. For now, the plantations of far-away Ceylon and neighboring Ste. Domingue supply the growing thirst for coffee. The forests of Río Prieto stand undisturbed.

But the plantations of Ceylon will go under, and the haciendas of Ste. Domingue will fall to the torches and machetes of slave insurrection. Haitian mulatos, skilled coffee farmers and producers, will flee the smoke and ruin and settle in these foothills. Mallorcans and Corsicans well-supplied with credit and eager to plant cash crops will follow on their heels.

It is a hundred years in the future still, but coffee will rule these mountains. Baskets loaded with red and green berries will pull at the backs of thousands of women and children, who will spend twelve-hour days inching along these slopes to fill silver coffee pots in Philadelphia mansions, china cups on Parisian breakfast tables, and flowered urns in Viennese cafes. Arabiga will transform the face of the land. The hacendados will bring shade trees from South America to shelter it, carve the hillsides with roads to reach it, clear the old forests to plant it, and cut down the hardwood to build their houses. Arabiga will transform the lives of the free people, those who settled here long ago to grow their small crops in peace. They will no longer be allowed to move from plot to plot at will through the mountains. Fences and deeds will make them laborers on the land of others. Today a few slender seedlings grace the shade. Tomorrow, the world will change.

1741: Many-Headed Hydra—New York

In the harsh winter of 1741, a conspiracy brews in a tavern by the waterside in New York. Women and men of many colors and conditions, united in rebellion. Listen, now, to the murmur of their voices. Irish, English, Spanish, French, Greek, and Dutch, trade languages and secret tongues of slaves and native tribes. Look back at them gathered on the brink of rising. This much-feared, "many-headed Hydra" of the waterfront.

There were soldiers, sailors and apprentice journeymen, household servants and indentured maids. They did not see themselves divided. They swore to go forth and burn the rich and white, and not even the English thought that white meant them. They burned the governor's mansion, the fort, and the armory, attacked the homes and havens of the ruling class. They were defeated. Seventy-seven transported, twenty-one hanged, and thirteen burned. But this legend persists along the docks of the Hudson, that as the bodies rotted on the open gibbet, a lesson to all who would rebel, nature inverted the lesson to another. For the body of an Irishman turned black, and his hair curled tight, while that of his brother, an African, bleached white as bone.

1748: Escapees—St. Croix

The men are sent out to fish for turtles and other sea creatures for the tables of their masters. They work at the port unloading and loading. They run their hands along the ropes, feel the solidity of the wood, sniff the wind. The women who sell sweets in the square, the women who are hired out as laundresses, the ones who set foot in the street on the master's business every day, listen to the creaking of the wood, see the straining in the anchor rope. Last year nineteen slaves stole a boat and never came back. Tonight, the soft wind is warm and moist. Clouds cover the moon. She leaves her laundry basket in the corner, wraps a few bites of food in a rag, tied to her belt, and slips down to the waterfront. One by one, shadows separate themselves from the walls and creep on board, until there are more than three dozen souls crowded together on the gently rocking deck. Swiftly and silently, ropes are cast off. The fishing vessel slips back from Christianstead quay and flies west on the night wind. Puerto Rico is only forty miles away. When the sun rises, it throws their shadows forward, toward the shore.

1765: The Song of the Forest

Even a few of those big men from the towns are starting to notice that the forest is shrinking. Up here in the mountains trees still stand thick, covered with vines, their crowns high in the cool air of the cordillera. We have to use our blades to cut a path through them when we need to collect medicines: *tuatúa, yerba cangá, sueldaconsuelda, quinino de pobre, maya, gran señora, guayacán.* It takes weeks, with fire and iron, to clear a patch for yuca and plátano, and in a few years, when we move on, the forest takes the land back so fast, often we can't find the place again.

But down on the coast they're cutting faster than anything can grow, *palo mora, guayacán,* loading the wood on ships, *capa blanco,* trading it for shirts and trousers and oil, *capa prieto,* making it into furniture, houses, the masts of sailing ships, fences, *algarrobo, ausubo.* Here we live with the forest, down there they live from its bones. Once it stretched all the way from the cordillera to the beach. All that pasture land was cut and cleared, all those naked hills stripped. It used to be hardwood right to the beaches of Guánica, east past Ponce, west to Cabo Rojo.

I'm an old woman, and I can see things coming. My grandchildren don't believe me when I tell them: the sugar fields will swallow the foothills and devour the streams; coffee will carve itself into the flanks of the mountains. I don't tell them the worst dreams—how they grind up the hills themselves and pave the land so the sweet rain runs into the sea and leaves the earth parched. I tell them, "They will cut down the old trees for their ca-fetales and plant quick-growing softwooded foreign things for shade and the soil will start to wash away." The children laugh and run away to play. *You're dreaming, abuela! How can the earth wash away?*

1777: If Fray Iñigo Had a Sister

The lands near [Yauco] are mostly very rough, of little use, closed in by forests . . . the meadow next to the town is very good for cultivating cane, tobacco, rice, and coffee . . . the rest has abundant and excellent wood which goes to the islands in exchange for clothing. — GEOGRAPHIC, CIVIL, AND NATURAL HISTORY OF THE ISLAND OF SAN JUAN BAUTISTA DE PUERTO RICO. FRAY IÑIGO ABBAD Y LASIERRA, 1778

"I told you . . . that Shakespeare had a sister; but do not look for her in Sir Sydney Lee's life of the poet. She died young— alas, she never wrote a word." — VIRGINIA WOOLF

Maybe her name was Violante, or Cecilia. Maybe it was Teresa. Teresa Abbad y Lasierra. Maybe her mother was a freedwoman, and she herself mulatta, recognized by her father, and educated by the nuns. She came on a ship from Sevilla and for two years she traveled the Indies, writing her own chronicle of the things she saw. The officials of the crown did not escort her. She bought a horse and a pack mule and went off on her own, following moun-tain trails, skirting swamps, visiting all the small towns and settle-ments of San Juan Bautista.

She saw the same city by the bay that her brother saw, but she entered into the poor homes of planks and beams, with palm-thatched roofs, and sat with the women, cooking the evening meal. Crossing the sierra near Humacao, she, like her brother, marveled at the thick trees, the vines, and flowering branches that dimmed the sun, but she also listened to what the country people told her—which plant was good for stomach problems, which one would clear up a cough. While Iñigo preferred the richly pastured towns of the north coast, Teresa liked the arid villages of the south, the small communities among the fruiting trees, where perhaps forty houses cluster round the square.

This was Yauco, where she fished in the Río Vantana. Iñigo, passing through, said the land was no good, too forested, although the valley showed promise for sugar, tobacco, coffee, and rice. He noted with approval the export of wood in exchange for clothing and passed on to praise the ancient noble families of San Germán. But Teresa liked it here and did not follow. One day she rolled up her bedclothes, packed her books and pens into her saddlebag, and, instead, followed the rivers up into the rain-hung hills.

There she disappeared from all knowledge of the literary world. Teresa never read the words her brother wrote, and her chronicles never reached the bookstore shelves. They sat, locked in an iron-bound chest under her bed, volume after volume of sketched birds and plants, recipes and remedies, memoirs of planting and trading, escapes and childbirths that she wrote at a rough-hewn table by the door, that with the passing years were eaten by termites and crumbled into dust.

1786: Párbulos

The poor die from infections of the lungs and from diarrhea, and the young die fastest. In the parrish books of Yauco, the black ink has faded and the pages gone yellow, but the word is written again and again, *párbulo*, child, buried today. Juan, two months old, son of Juana Ramirez. Juana, daughter of Maria Acosta. Sebastian, son of Casimira Quiñones. Guillermo, son of Teresa Rodriguez. Jacinta, daughter of Benita Cordero. Thomas Ramon, newborn son of Cayetana Thorres. Jacob. Five months. Son of Maria de Jesus Feliciano.

Not all the children are lost so young. Some of them flourish for years, grow deep into their mothers' hearts, seem secure. There are no antibiotics. No hospitals. No ambulances. This year the priest said prayers over Alfonsa, two years old, daughter of Micaela Mercado; four-year-old Rita, daughter of Rita Torres; the six-year-old daughter of Paula Machado; Rita, aged eight, daughter of Ursula Ortiz; and Clara Alicia, nineteen, daughter of Bárbara Lopez. No one recorded the age of Manuel, son of Eusebia, slave of Gregorio Rodriguez.

But the worst time is November. Rain falls day after day and those who become chilled can't seem to shake it off. The water rises and no one knows how to keep dead animals and sewage out of the drinking water. Dysentery, cholera, and parasites attack the already weak. The harvest is many weeks away and food is scarce. Undernourished, chilled, damp, the children succumb.

On November 3rd, two-year-old Juan, born in France, the five-year-old slave Juan, son of Ysidora and property of Manuel Pagán, and Jacinta, age fourteen, daughter of Juana Caraballo, are all laid to rest. Slave children do not get doctors. On November 5th the one-year-old child of Ygnacia, slave to Maria Quiñones, dies in the parish. Her name was Maria Antonia. On the 7th the thirteen-year-old daughter of Ana Torres dies, but her name is not recorded. On the 11th another newborn, Manuela, daughter of María Rodriguez. On November 15th Bernarda, Ana Perez's eighteen-year-old daughter, is stricken. The next day it is Bernardina, fourteen, daughter of Lucía Rodriguez, and also Juana Lorenza, the infant daughter of Ynes de los Santos. Nine children in less than two weeks.

How is nationality made? Men make it with declarations and battles, transactions and deeds. But year after year the children are laid into the soil with their mothers' grief and endurance, tying *these* women to *this* ground with cords as thick and red as the muscles of their hearts.

1788: Reverse Slavery—Ste. Domingue

The slaveholder Le Jeune has decided slaves imperil their masters. In a time and place where any white person may commit any atrocity upon the person of an African slave, Le Jeune believes the slaves on his plantation are the dangerous ones and that they are committed to poisoning him. Since slaveholders are nine-tenths of the law, Monsieur Le Jeune vows he will torture the truth of this terrifying conspiracy from these people who hold him captive with apprehension. That it is fear of retribution, the nightmares of a guilty conscience, does not occur to him. He proceeds to torture and murder with such mad ferocity that the slaves undertake to file a legal complaint with the authorities. The law allows such things in punishment, but the slaves say they have not committed any offense against the rules of slavery, that they are being killed for the sake of imaginary ghosts.

The court agrees Le Jeune is out of control, but before they can move to censure him, the white planters of Ste. Domingue are in an uproar. Any constraint upon their powers will make them vulnerable to the blood lust of the slaves, their well-known affinity for violence, their hunger to control. Terrified of the reality of who they have become, the masters grip ever tighter to their power to be cruel, imprisoned, not by their slaves, but by the soul-murdering sickness of enslavement. The charges are dropped, the tortured slaves of Le Jeune abandoned to their fate, and the desperate rage of those in bondage simmers toward a full and scalding boil.

&Anamú

Anamú is a hiss between the teeth of the last resort, the flat eye of
the cornered snake about to strike, the clenched fist of dark wood
that protects at any cost, the metallic taste of revenge under the
tongue. With the deadly humor of those who have almost nothing
to lose, they call it "amansa senhor," or tame the master. Stroke
him, soothe him, calm him, put him to sleep. Anamú is a healing
bath, an easer of unbearable aching, a spell, a tool, a knife that
leaves no trace of itself, a slow grip squeezing the heart of your
enemy. Call it Congo root, Gully root, or Guiné. Whatever
name it wears, it can steal through the house undetected.

Anamú enters the master through the bowl of soup, the cup
of coffee held by the expressionless maid. First he is uneasy,
excitable, unable to sleep, hallucinates eyes of fire and strange
voices in the corners of his bedroom. Soon he becomes dull and
apathetic, then loses all interest in his affairs, no longer capable of
ordering punishment or entering your room at night. The body
servants wash and comb the idiot, who is still technically their
master, with meticulous care. Slowly over the months, as the
household slaves spoon his warm milk into his mouth, he
deteriorates. It is a stealthy poison, too slow to blame on a single
toxic meal. The family considers it a mysterious tropical decline.
It will take nearly a year of those careful feedings before his
throat becomes paralyzed, incapable of any speech, his limbs
rigid and convulsed.

When the final spasm releases him and drops him limp as the
dish rag she wipes her hands on after touching him, his slave
woman will wash him one last time and lay him out. Anamú
cannot give her back her life, only take his. Anamú cannot
restore her freedom, only the solitude of her bed. Anamú does
not lift the load from her back, only lets her shift the weight.
Anamú has no tenderness to offer her, only a narrow, harsh
passage out of despair.

ৡLAZOS: 1800–1898

ৡ MELAO

Molasses is the juice of green sugary fields reduced to blackstrap, a taste of earth and iron. Molasses says do what is necessary, do what you must. This sweetness has passed through the fire that singed away leafiness, the blade that severed stalk from root, the crushing teeth of the trapiche, been extracted from every hiding place, every sweet swollen fiber of the cane, and then boiled for an eternity to the consistency of a tropical night before a storm breaks. Molasses has no sympathy for whining without action, for evasion, for the sick smile of politeness plastered over rage. But if you accept necessity, take responsibility, molasses will back you to the last mile, strengthen your backbone, add red to your blood, give you heart, and carry you through. Melao faces consequences and offers you the power of decision. Dip your finger in the bucket and savor the taste of burnt bridges. The smoke of a dying past.

1804: News from Haiti

Smoke on the western horizon, sweet with the burning of cane fields and the exultant laughter of slaves, pungent with charred lace, mahogany, and rosewood, acrid from the curling, blackened pages of account books. Ste. Domingue is in flames. Who could have imagined it? the frightened landholders exclaim. That they could revolt so completely, with such savagery, against us! Among the rustling, razor-edged leaves of the cane fields of Ponce and

Guayama, the news is whispered, hearts beating faster, lungs open wide to the scented wind. Ste. Domingue is Haiti! Ste. Domingue is Haiti is Black! *¡Vámonos!*

Slaveholders see conspiracies everywhere. The number of small boats missing from the coasts is on the rise. Imagine! In Haiti there are no slaves. In Haiti the perfumed ladies are running away with their jewels hidden in their corsets. In Haiti the Africans have run amuck and are destroying civilization. In Haiti the slave woman slaps her mistress and spits in the master's face. How wonderful! How horrible! It is terror, it is birth, it is destruction, it is freedom, it is humiliation, it is jubilation. In Puerto Rico the hot air hangs still and heavy over the cane fields, over the big white houses, over the palm-thatched huts. There is a muttering of thunder in the air. Haiti is burning in everyone's dreams.

1817: War Widows

While Bolívar and his officers sweep through South America, cutting link after link out of Spain's golden chain of colonies, the widows of Spain's fallen soldiers circulate like dust in a hurricane. From Guayra to Maracaibo, Santo Domingo to Curaçao, Mayagüez to Havana the widows petition for their pensions from the few remaining governments of the Spanish Empire. Juana Tavarez has come from Guayra with four children, one of them already a widow herself. Ana Ordoñe de Alvino, of Cumaná, has four children and slaves. Magdalena de la Torre has five grandchildren, one Black woman slave, one Jewish woman servant, and no money.

The towns of Puerto Rico house women from Colombia, Venezuela, Peru left emptyhanded by the victories of the new republics. The houses, farms, horses, bank accounts of their husbands are no longer theirs. Their only inheritance is human: the slaves come with them and share in their poverty, round and round the Caribbean, asking indifferent Spanish officials in one white-washed colonial headquarters after another for the pensions they were promised. But the money has been eaten up in the Wars of Independence. Mexican silver no longer pays for Puerto Rican garrisons. The last colonies are heavily taxed, and refugees are un-popular. Francisca and Concepción Hurtado are from Santa Marta, Columbia. They have tried their luck in Maracaibo, Coro, Curaçao, Puerto Cabellos, Curaçao again, and Santo Domingo. In Mayagüez they worked as seamstresses for four years, moved to San Juan to petition once again for their pensions, received only six pesos a month, and have applied for permission to leave, this time for Havana.

The widows keep drifting, their hands always busy, selling candy, doing laundry, making dresses, hiring out as cooks, writing again to the officials of a collapsing empire for their promised share, for the price of their husbands' lives. Drift and settle, as it becomes clear that the old order has overdrawn its accounts, that they are on their own, that their lives will be as they make them, one cooking pot, one laundryload, one hand-stitched seam at a time.

✿Yerba Buena

It grows almost anywhere. A sprig will root and take over your garden. It climbs and tangles in the grass, among the ornamental flowers, shade, and sun. It's a hardworking herb. It will settle your stomach, clear your headache away, soothe you to sleep, calm your nerves, stimulate and tone and sweeten the air. You can carry it with you, give cuttings freely, dry it in bunches, steep it in water, breathe it in steam, bottle it in alcohol, pound it into ointments. The good herb, the common mint, the workhorse

of the herbal that carries medicines into your blood. The
seamstress, the laundress, the mother, the cook, the good
neighbor, the reliable friend, the ordinary miracle of the
generous, hardworking heart.

1820: Maestra Cordero

Celestina Cordero has such a heart. She is like a blue-flowering
mint, stubbornly digging in roots in the toughest soil. She was
born of a liberta mother in the hilly neighborhood they call Culo
Prieto, or Black Ass, for all the free and dark-skinned women who
live there, mulata y negra. Her little brother Rafael is the one we
hear about. How his parents taught him to read and write because
no school would admit Black children. How he became an avid
reader. How at the age of twenty he opened a free school in San
Germán for Black and mulatto boys. How he supported himself as
a tabaquero and refused all payment for his vocation of teaching,
later opening a school in San Juan that even some sons of the elite
attend. Because of this, there is actually a portrait of him, with his
students gathered around him. But Celestina came first, began
younger, taught girls.

No one has painted her, standing in a cotton dress, petitioning
the city council for money to support her school, which has one
hundred and sixteen girls and has been going since 1802. No one
has asked her to sit for her portrait surrounded by girls with books.
She was fifteen when she began teaching, and there are no distin-
guished gentlemen among her former students to see to it that she
is recognized. Her brother donates the contributions of civic organizations to charity, refusing the patronage of the wealthy, pre-
serving his independence. Celestina's struggles are not recorded.
Where or how she earned her bread, what encouragement she gave
Rafael, what example she set him, how she prospered or failed.
There is a rumor that in the end, she will go insane, rambling and

frightened, cared for with loving respect by her brother Rafael. He will be the only Cordero remembered and honored with the title of Maestro.

1824: We Treated Them Well

Sitting in the living room of my favorite tía, soaking in all that family love, talk turns to the past. She tells me what she was told, the family legend, the soothing lullaby for guilt, the well-worn lie rubbed smooth by so many fingers touching this place of reassurance. *We were slaveholders, but we treated them well.*

How does one treat a slave well? Slavery is the condition of constant violation, of losing one's life not once but daily, hourly, year after year. Is there such a thing as friendly murder, gentle rape, considerate invasion?

We were the landowners of Toa Alta. The buenas familias. Morales. Díaz. Cabrera. Rivera. Rodriguez. The founders of townships. The commanders of militias. The mayors of municipalities and godparents of the poor. We married among ourselves, daughters to cousins, sons to nieces, braiding the rope of our privilege, joining our lands in childbed. The lands my tía's grandparents owned were a reward from the crown because in 1797, Pepe Díaz fought Lord Cumberland at Martín Peña bridge. On the other side, Braulio Morales, founder of Naranjito, was eleven, his brother Claudio twenty-one. Already they were heirs to their father, Justo, ready to inherit his acreage and the lives of the people he thought he owned. My great-great-grandparents said that the slaves loved us. That they were devoted to the family. I know they did not love us. Lives lived together can beget affection, but coercion cannot breed love.

I look at the faded ink that inscribes their births and deaths in the yellowed pages of the parish registers. I touch their names with my fingertip and I say to Jose, I say to Tomasa and Angela Gracia, to Manuela and Antonio, Maria and Leonardo, Maria and Clemente that I know they did not love us. I tell them I will never forget that their enslavement paid for my inheritance, although by the time I was born, what was left was mostly attitude. That I know it was the work that was wrung from them that allowed my many times great-grandparents to grow up well-fed and shod, playing the piano and dressed in ribbons. I tell them that although they did not choose me as a descendant, I will honor them as ancestors.

Talking in the sultry evening of Guaynabo, my tía tells me the way they spoke about those times, how they said that on their property slaves were never whipped or treated harshly. That in our family slavery was kind. I imagine her, a wide-eyed girl, trying to make sense of the stories, wanting to believe we came through intact.

1794: Rumors from Haiti set fires in Guadaloupe and St. Lucia. 1795: Slaves revolt in Cuba and Venezuela. The slaves of Aguadilla rise up and are crushed. But they were always devoted to us, the hacendados say, bewildered. We always treated them well.

This is slavery in Puerto Rico. Children begin working in the fields when they are eight. Disobedience is punished severely. Slaves are whipped with lashes, must work with heavy weights fastened onto them, are pierced and burned, have their ears cut off, have an overseer cut off a hand or a foot.

Remember the winter of 1812, I whisper. Remembering, the room grows dark. Rumors flew that slavery had been ended, that the whites had tried to hush it up. It spread like wildfire, and everywhere slaves gathered and passed the word, talked of taking up arms to claim what was theirs. Slaves shot for resisting arrest. Fifty lashes for a disrespectful word, for any tool that could be used to fight. A state of marshal law. In Cuba, eight hanged for burning the canefields. Voluntarios de la Patria patrol the countryside in a reign of terror. My great-grandparents believed this: that the slaves *preferred* to stay on the hacienda after abolition. That they liked working for us, so they stayed.

1821: The Marcos Xiorro slave conspiracy is right next door in Bayamon. In Barranquitas, where the Riveras and the Gomezes live, a riot. 1822: Conspiracies in Guayama and Naguabo betrayed by informers. 1826: In Toa Baja and Bayamón, a plan to flee to Haiti, passed from mouth to mouth hidden in the lyrics of a bomba, and betrayed by a child. The actions speak so much louder than the words.

The Morales ancestors say nothing about the slaves they held. On that side there is only silence. But I say to María de los Santos and her infant son José, to the other José, brought from St. Croix, and his parents, Guincel and Yini, to Tomasa and her daughter Angela Gracia, that I don't know if they liked where they lived, but that I know they did not love working for us. I say to Manuela and Antonio, María and Leonardo, and to the María whose son Clemente died young, to María Barbanera, Patricio and María Silveria that I do not think it was a pleasure to be Morales family slaves.

1828: Uprising in Guayama. 1831: Uprising in Vega Baja. 1833: Uprising in Ponce and again in 1835. 1838: Disturbances in Vega Baja. 1839: Ponce reports disturbances. 1841 and 1842, conspiracies in Ponce are betrayed. It goes on. Isabela, Naguabo, Toa Baja, Vega Baja. Speaking together in the dim light of the living room, we see shadows cross the walls. We are modern Puerto Rican women, long past that cruel time. We live with other cruelties. But the same choices swirl around us in the dark. We are the heirs of these stories, both the polished stories of complacency and the jagged stories of blood on the lash, desperate whispers, rope and flame.

1824: Runaways

The new law provides harsh penalties for those who shelter runaways. The slave who flees her master, the wife who leaves her husband, or any women who choose to live without men. The slave must be returned to slavery, the wife to marriage, the free woman to the domination of father, brother, guardian, to so-called protector. None of these persons can be permitted to walk freely down the street, choose which way to turn at the corner, none of them exist as human beings under the law.

But someone must be sheltering them, or why would the lawmakers make this law? Somebody must be opening the back door, beckoning silently, handing out blankets, pieces of bread, hot coffee to steady the trembling hands of the refugee. Slaves still escape. Unmarried women continue to leave home without permission. And wives lie awake at night, plotting how to run away from their husbands, counting the coins they have hidden away against the price of children's shoes and food, and silently blessing the name of the friend who will offer a bed when the day comes.

1825: Flora Tristan Reads in Bed—Paris, France

Flora Tristan is such a wife. Her aristocratic Peruvian father died when she was only five, leaving his daughter and his French wife destitute in Paris. She was seventeen when, at her mother's urging, she married Chazal, the printer, and for five long years she has endured his violent abuse. At twenty-three Flora is recovering from the birth of her daughter, her third child. Propped up on pillows, she reads the passionate prose of Mary Wollstonecraft, who once lived here in Paris and died in childbirth years ago.

"But what have women to do in society? I may be asked, but to glitter with easy grace . . . Women might certainly study the art of healing and be physicians as well as nurses. They might also study politics, and settle their benevolence on the broadest basis . . . Business of various kinds they might likewise pursue, if they were educated in a more orderly manner, which might save many from common and legal prostitution. Women would not then marry for a support . . ."

Eagerly, Flora turns the page with one hand and cradles her daughter Aline to her breast with the other. She has been captive for so long, married to a violent man in exchange for food and shelter and the respectable name of wife. "How many women thus waste life away, the prey of discontent, who might have practiced as physicians, regulated a farm, managed a shop, and stood erect, supported by their own industry . . . nay, I doubt whether pity and love are so near akin as poets feign, for I have seldom seen much compassion excited by the helplessness of females, unless they were fair; then perhaps it was the soft handmaid of love, or the harbinger of lust." She lays her sleeping infant down beside her and listens to the soft sound of her breathing. Then taking up *Vindication of the Rights of Woman* in her hands, she turns the pages long into the night, plotting her escape.

1833: María Bibiana Writes

María Bibiana is the daughter of a criollo officer, child of a rising class of native wealth beginning to flex its wings. She writes *La ninfa de Puerto Rico* to celebrate Puerto Rico's acquisition of its own court of law. Her voice wavers, flickering. She is a loyal, longing daughter of her king. She is a proud woman of Mayagüez, petitioning for the freedom of the unjustly imprisoned. She is a woman refusing to be courted by fickle men. She is the first published poet to speak in a Puerto Rican voice, a criolla voice. Twelve years later, a group of young students in Spain will publish a collection that scholars will praise as the first breath of a national literature, but this is 1833, and María Bibiana's poems appear in the newspapers of the island, recalling the defeat of the English in 1797, singing praise of the golden land. She is a daughter of privilege and sees only what privilege allows. She writes of flowers and butterflies, of flags and fortresses, of the hardships faced by free white men. Sitting at her desk, she reaches absently for the cup of coffee handed to her by her slave and never sees the woman's shadow fall, leaving no trace, across the page.

1833: Voyages—Peru

Two ships sail along the Pacific coast of South America. In each one a clear and observant intelligence watches the world and takes copious notes. Each will write a famous book. One looks at the wings of finches, the other at the burdens of slaves. One studies iguanas, the other the corruption of the new republics. One develops a theory to explain where humanity has come from and how it came. The other asks herself where humanity will go and how it will get there.

The *Beagle* and the *Mexicain* stitch across each other's wakes. While Charles Darwin stops at the Galapagos and asks questions about isolated populations of fauna, Flora Tristán asks for her inheritance and finds she has been cheated by her uncle, that her relatives in Arequipa will not help her, that in the new Peru, gilded palaces are still built on the broken backs of the Indians, and that always, everywhere, the most downtrodden man can still abuse a woman.

Charles Darwin wonders about the extinction of species, but not about the lives and deaths of "natives." He writes, in *The Voyage of the Beagle*, about all the fascinating processes of nature he has seen and returns to England to present a controversial paper to the scientific societies about the origins of species. Polite society is horrified at the thought that we may be descended from apes.

Flora Tristán writes all the way back across the Atlantic about the cruel things she has seen, and her notes become *The Peregrinations of a Pariah*. She declares, "From now on, my country will be all of humanity." When she visits London, she converses with socialists and dresses in men's clothing to listen to debates of Parliament. The Bishop of Arequipa burns her book in the public square. Marx plagiarizes from her writings the opening paragraphs of his *Communist Manifesto*.

Darwin asks himself how species will continue to evolve, what forces will change the shape of a butterfly's wing. Flora Tristán wants to know how society will evolve, what forces will change the consciousness of working women and men, release them from passivity, and turn them toward revolution. Darwin continues to study and conduct experiments. Tristán takes to the roads, conducting her own experiment, talking with workers, writing essays, arguing about the future and the rights of women, barely escaping from her husband's murderous attacks, going out again and again, hastening the day.

1833: María Barbanera

The slave women of the Morales brothers are having babies. On the darkened pages of the parish register the elegant hand of the priest has recorded the names of Marta and Juana Lucía, Eugenia and Silveria, Manuela and Paula and María Barbanera, *slave of Don Claudio, slave of Don Braulio*, and their infants, also slaves. It has recorded the names of godparents—usually other slaves or the recently freed. The stories lie in the spaces between the curled letters. In the phrase that leaves so much to the imagination. Why was Silveria's newborn daughter freed at birth by Don Claudio? *Did she look like him? Did Silveria leave me cousins somewhere?*

María Barbanera's first girl is Eleuteria; the father is Patricio, liberto. The register says Eleuteria was born in May of 1830. But four years later, when Antonina is born, also in May, the priest records her mother as María Barbanera Morales, *liberta*. How did they do it? Patricio earned wages, or perhaps profit from a little plot of land. Did he take on all the extra work he could, hoarding coins to purchase his family? Did María Barbanera get permission to hire herself out, to do laundry, cooking, sewing, take on extra tasks, after hours, and manage to keep a few pesetas for herself? What of Eleuteria, the slave-born child? The register has no reason to record whether she was also bought free, or if she remained enslaved, the firstborn in bondage, her little sister free.

As I read those silences, I savor the bare fact of her freedom, this woman whose labor kept the founders of Naranjito comfortable and well-heeled. Somewhere in Puerto Rico or its far-flung diaspora her descendants breathe, and perhaps still carry the name I also bear, related to me not by blood, but by the sweat Maria Barbanera shed and my ancestors put in the bank. And related to me by the name "liberta," because reaching that hard for freedom still takes everything we've got.

1834: Autos de Anti-Fé—Spain

Some people write *libros de cocina* full of recipes for housewives, with instructions for concocting rosewater candies or making gelatin from the tails of fish. Others write books with exact recipes for virtue that tell the people what God expects of them and measure the worth of their lives. For centuries the Church has burned those who do not follow instructions. They call this burning the auto de fé, the act of faith. Now the people reciprocate. All across Spain the peasants, the poor, the hungry, the exploited set fire to faith and demand solutions, not prayers. They break down the doors of monasteries and convents, churches and parish houses, set flames among the altar cloths, and cry out for salvation here on earth, for bread more filling than communion wafers, for labor that provides a living, for modesty and humility among the powerful, for simplicity and charity among the clergy, for purity among the corrupt, for honesty, generosity, and justice in a world where the meek inherent only crusts and rags.

❧Yellow Dock

I dream of iron, but I am so weary, so breathless, so aching. To get out of bed in the dark of pre-dawn, I imagine teams of oxen like the ones that haul the sugar carts along the coast. They drag me out to fetch wood, haul my hands to strike flint and start the fire, dip water from the bucket, make the coffee and the cornmeal.

The clay of the cafetal is red, and the ripe coffee is red, but my blood is pale and my heart aches from the struggle of trying to do more with less. All the endless day, picking plump red berries from the thin branches, it seems as if the coffee fruit sucks all the color from my cheeks, all the sweet, juicy life, all the energy from my limbs, and men pour it into sacks, load it onto mules, lead it away toward the coast and the waiting ships.

Oh, for a medicine that could bring it back! A deep yellow root, bitter and strong. I would fetch water straight from where the Rio Prieto trickles out of the mountain. I would crush the yellow root into the water and watch it stain. I would let it simmer until the steam filled my lungs, till it filled the hut and made the rusty knives turn bright. Then when the brew was strong and dark, I would stir in molasses, black as my children's eyes, and take my medicine from an iron spoon.

I would rise up from this hammock, my face rosy, my eyes bright, and stride down the hill to the patio of the patrón. When he saw me coming, he would fade and shrink into his rocking chair. Tres pesos, I would say sternly. Three pesos a week to pick your coffee, and fresh meat in the pot for my children and me! I would take his money and buy meat and milk and chicken's eggs and come home and put up the soup. Then I'd make myself a cup of cafe con leche, strong and sweet and creamy. I can almost smell it as I lie here, eyes closed, drifting farther and farther away from the sound of my children crying and my aching body, and my face white as bone.

1844: Some Lives Burn Like Quick Flame—France

Flora has swept back and forth across France like grassfire, and like grassfire, consumes herself in flame. Her daughter Aline is a disappointment, a tame girl, married young, to be remembered only as the mother of the painter Gauguin. Her adopted daughter is a spirited young woman who travels with her, from factory town to factory town, as she speaks to the workers. Sometimes they catch fire from her words, but often they distrust her, this woman who will not wait for organizations, parties, rules of order. She has been on the road, ceaseless, for months, and like the crackling heat of summer brush ablaze, collapses suddenly in a roadside inn, burns a few days with fever, and crumbles into ash. I imagine that when she died, she left nothing on the crumpled white sheets, no body, no coals, no residue at all. Some people use themselves to the last grain of substance. Some lives illuminate the dark for a time and burn out like quick flame.

1868: Francisca Brignoni

So here we are at the commemoration of the Grito de Lares once again, and once again everyone is talking about Manolo el Leñero and Betances, the good doctor, and Doña Mariana Bracetti, the Golden Arm, con su brazo de oro, sewing the flag as if she never had anything else to contribute at those meetings. No one mentions the Serrano girls, all those sisters who were the reason these men who were married to them knew each other so well. No one mentions Eduvigis Beauchamp, who wanted to take a gun and go out that day with her brother and her father, but they wouldn't let her. And they sure as hell don't mention me. I always come to these things. Francisca Brignoni, a su servicio.

Those people, they were sincere, tu ves, they wanted to be out from under Spain. All those banker peninsulares were wringing them dry on the interest on their loans. And to get there, some of them were willing to free some slaves, but they weren't sure how much they wanted all of us out from under them. Betances, sí. He used to attend the baptisms of the slave babies, to certify that they were in good health for the patrón, you know, and often he would buy them from the masters and give them back to their mothers, free. Mulato, ese, and true to where he came from. Mariana, too, me cayó bien. We were in jail together, after the uprising failed, and she had a real bad time, lost the child she was carrying.

But normally most of those people wouldn't associate with me. Only to pass in the plaza and buy my candies. Yes, I'm a candy seller. I make the best dulce de coco you can find anywhere. And when I went around inciting, that's what they called it, inciting to revolt, it wasn't the high interest rate on loans that worried me. I wanted abolition, land, a burning pile of passbooks, something a whole lot bigger, deeper, redder, more full of life. I come to Lares every year, moving through the crowds with my candies wrapped in wax paper, calling, "Dulce de coco, guayaba, mango. Dulces del país." I'm waiting to hear if someone mentions my name. I'm waiting for that something bigger that still hasn't come.

1873: The Freedwomen Contract Themselves

In the year of abolition, the old slaveholders try to drag the institution a few tottering steps farther and require every freed slave to contract with an employer for another two years. If they don't, they will be forced to join public works projects. However, the newly freed don't have to work for their former captors. They can choose anyone.

They choose their families. They cross the island in search of parents and children, spouses and grandparents for whom they have longed. They walk for days to find ancestors and babies long divided from them, but never forgotten. They no longer risk the lash or other tortures for a glimpse of kin.

The roots of the family tree go deeper than the cruel reach of slavery. Juana Gutierrez seeks out her granddaughters Josefa (twenty-eight) and Matilde (thirty-two), the first liberated from the establishment of Sucesión Turull, the second from the grip of Teresa Amadeo. Juana Geigel, from Carolina, ex-slave of Teodoro Chevremont, presents herself in San Juan, in order to work for her father, Felix Angulo, "to provide him with the necessities of life." Also from the Chevremont place, Felícita and Guadalupe come looking for their fathers and find them and contract themselves, Felícita as a domestic servant, Guadalupe to help in the fields.

In slavery most children are parted from their parents by the age of eight. By the time they are eleven, only a few live with kin, usually siblings. Now the freedwomen of Puerto Rico go looking for their mothers. The new liberta Francisca, age fifty-four, formerly held by Ruperta Gomez, binds herself to her mother, María Rosario Acosta, in order, she says, to help her in all things. The lost daughters go barefoot along the coast roads, their skirts gathering dust, returning to the women who gave them life.

Eustaquia Amigó works as a candymaker for her mother María Luisa Amigó. Her contract says she does not wish to be paid. Maria Narcisa, freed from Ysidro Cora, Yrene, freed from Rafael Cabrera, and Ventura, freed from Micaela Benisbeitía, fly like swift and hungry birds to their mothers and work for them, provide for them, take up their loads. For the first time in their lives they can choose their labor. They sit down and wash their mothers' hard brown feet and the daughters sing at their work.

1875: Campos de soledad—Galicia, Spain

> *Este vaise i aquel vaise,*
> *e todos, todos se van . . .* —ROSALÍA DE CASTRO

I do not know her name. She lived in the port town of Ferrol, a woman left behind in Galicia with fourteen children while her husband went to America, a medic with the armies of Spain. She was one of the *"vuidas de vivos e mortos"* widows of the living and dead that haunt Rosalía de Castro's poem full of empty fields. I do not know her name. Her eldest son, José Roque, finally went looking for his father. At fourteen, he arrived in Puerto Rico only to learn his father had died days before. Her son also never returned. I do not know her name. When her daughter married without her absent younger brother's consent, that brother, that adolescent boy strutting his manhood as head of a family of far-off women, broke all relations with them, following generations of Gallego men into unknown distances. I do not know her name or anything else of her story. I am descended from the son who left, and it is only his name, José Roque Moure, and his destiny that I know. But I know her longing for the touch of a dear one far beyond reach, how the face of the beloved fades into a memory of a memory until you long for the image itself to return clear so you can feel in that sharp and vivid pain, the relief that you still remember what you lost. I imagine her in the cold and rainy dark of an autumn afternoon, lamps in the windows, looking out at the empty sea that rises and falls and never sends anyone home.

1880: Tortures—Tennessee and Puerto Rico

In Memphis, Ida Wells talks relentlessly about lynching, about the campaign of terror unleashed against the liberty of Negro men, so recently slaves. She dissects the mythology of rape with which this murderous war is justified. While others hedge their language, seek out allies among the liberal whites, and curb their tongues not to offend, Ida Wells ignites the freedwomen and men of her city, of other cities, calling them to act. Miss Ida speaks truth to power and leaves the honey off her tongue.

In San Juan, Lola Rodriguez cuts her hair short and stands up in the tertulia, the place where men gather to talk politics and art, demanding action for the prisoners of Spain, an end to the tortures carried out in the cells of El Morro. One by one, she frees sixteen men from the calabozos with her agitation. She is a journalist, a bold outspoken woman, unafraid of exile, aware of exactly what a prison cell contains. Her pen slashes windows of light and air into those dark holes of horror.

1886: Damas

Las damas de San Juan have formed a Ladies Association for the Instruction of Women, a suffragist league, a host of organizations for reform. They intend to teach working women how to read, so they can improve their moral tone, raise more cultured sons, be more intelligent wives. Confident that they have a better grasp on life than the poor, they strive earnestly, generously, passionately to reach the working women of the island. For themselves, they want the vote, want schools and books and journals, better access to the world, and better legal rights. For their sisters in what they call the lower classes, they define what is needed, education not unions, social services not revolution. Those who cannot read and write are not ready for self-rule. Themselves they see as participants in the world of governance. Cultured women will add compassion and common sense to election years to come. For their sisters they seek only opportunities for self-improvement, so they can strive to earn and someday deserve the same.

1895: Charcas, or the True Story of Cafe au Lait

In the cafes of Paris, philosophers and poets lean back in their chairs and savor their steaming cups of Yauco coffee, the best in the world. Well-dressed ladies serve it from silver coffeepots in Vienna, New York, and Philadelphia. Mrs. J. P. Morgan always special-orders her own personal supply.

In Yauco, in the coffee barrios of Rio Prieto, Rubias, Carrizales, women and children pick the ripened berries for pennies a day. Sometimes there is not enough to buy a loaf of bread. In the warehouses of Yauco, women squat to sort huge mountains of coffee beans, the ripe, the verdimaduro, and the most precious, convoluted bean with the gourmet twist, the caracoleado. Every rainy season a few women die of infections made powerful by hunger, of anemia made deadly by malnutrition and hard work. No one here is studying to be a nurse. No one goes to debutante balls or becomes the Reina de Belleza of San Juan.

Manuel Zeno Gandía writes a novel of liberal outrage, an exposé, a Puerto Rican *Cabaña del tío Tom* about the lives of coffee workers, called *La charca*. Here in the mountains there are many charcas, many dark pools, shaded by the brim of a battered straw hat or a cotton rag, many eyes behind which thoughts are stirring, invisible to the best-intentioned gentleman. They are not as helpless, mute, and doomed as guilt would paint them. They suffer and think about their suffering. Some will die here. Some will starve on piecework wages, sewing embroidered collars for the rich. But in ten years there will be a coffee pickers' union in these mountains. Some of these girls will be reading *Union obrera* in the tobacco sheds. Some of these pools will fill with water from fresh fallen rain and overflow, flooding all the low lying places in these hills.

1897: Luisa in Love

The young Luisa Capetillo used to accompany her mother to work at the house of the Marqués of Arecibo. There she met his son and, at the age of fifteen, became his lover. Luisa is a child of anarchists and believes that the state has no business regulating love and sex. Brought up by her mother, Luisa has read romantic novels and philosophical essays, books on physics and medicine, religious treatises, and political pamphlets. Now she is carrying her first child. Her lover comes when he can. She is the one who cares for the infant daughter. Sometimes he sends money.

Time passes, and a son is born. Luisa notices that her lover is the one who decides when he comes and goes. She only waits. He is jealous and wants her confined to the house when he isn't there. She stays behind her doors with the two children and waits for him to come. He does, and says he adores her, but he does it on his own schedule. His family decide it is time he was married, and he marries. He doesn't think it matters. But Luisa weighs things in the balance and is angry. This man is the love of her life, but she will leave him. She will walk away from this sweet and suffocating place, leave her children in her mother's care, and step out into the tumultuous world where women struggle and shout and move about in the open air.

1895: Mercedes a caballo

My great-great-grandmother is an excellent horsewoman with a fiery temper and an independent spirit. Her cousin Evaristo Izcoa Díaz is forever in trouble, defying the authorities, calling for action, starting newspapers that are closed down within weeks, always out on bail. This time he's in prison in Ponce. Mercedes rides two days across the cordillera, guiding her horse along the narrow mountain trails to see him. She goes every other week, and watches as he wastes away. He will last for six more years, greeting the U.S. invasion with threats of war, trying to raise troops in the mountains above Sabana Grande, hauled off to jail again, and will die, raging at the State, at the age of thirty-six. Mercedes Gomez will remain married to José Roque Moure, a Gallego accountant, who every evening stands outside and reads *La democracia* aloud to all his neighbors who want the liberal point of view, while Mercedes listens and watches airy fires burn and fade across the sunset sky.

1898 to 1900: Guabancex Again

The mother of change shakes her skirts and the heaviest branches go flying. First the price of coffee plummets. Brazil has flooded the market with cheaper beans and no one will pay last year's prices.

Last spring the hacendados were ordering pianos for their wives. This spring they are selling their horses and going on foot, losing their houses, their farms, their shirts.

She stamps her feet and the world turns over. New invaders anchor in Guánica Bay and the old order is quickly defeated. Marines in wide-brimmed hats march through the mountains and the flag of the United States is hoisted up over the castle of El Morro. No one has the same importance as yesterday. The cards are shuffled and new hands dealt.

She spins and the sky whirls around her. The storm they call San Ciriaco blasts along the cordillera and leaves the mountains naked, not a coffee plant or shade tree standing, lifts the roofs off houses, exposing the beds and chairs, floods the streets and living rooms, leaving red mud on the walls.

A drop at a time the water begins to fall, a woman at time leaves the farm and the house behind. First one, then ten, then a hundred, until they are streaming down the roads by the thousands into the tobacco sheds and arrabales of the coastal towns. It's a season of high winds, when things fly through the air and old ways shake loose. The women run together, eddy at street corners, push on. The heavy moisture rises and clouds gather. The women are talking, and not in whispers. They tilt their heads and listen, knowing the rain, the heavy cleansing aguacero, is about to come.

≈ AGUACERO: 1899–1929

1898: Ghost Dancing

This year's debutantes are dancing at the governor's palace in Old San Juan. Daughters and sons of hacendados and merchants, bankers and sugar mill owners dance to the tunes of the new regime.

General Nelson Miles waltzes with the daughters and wives of his new subjects, but among the swirling gauzy skirts there are always other dancers, and the smell of smoke and blood mingles with the sweetness of gardenias. Women in deerhide dresses holding children by the hand weave through the crowd with implacable eyes and red holes in their chests. For thirty years their shadows have followed him. They are the people of the coyote, of the dappled horses, sprung from the green Wallawa Valley of Oregon, hounded by armies, driven from home. Thirty years ago the Nez Perce chose exile over captivity and began walking to Canada. But this man with a heart of gun metal was sent to stop them because those who survive can return. Because those who live free are an open door at the edges of conquered lands.

Only thirty miles from the border, on a day of yellow aspens quivering in the late September air, Nelson Miles sent soldiers into a camp full of women and children and a handful of warrior men. The soldiers were veterans from the civil war, young men taught to burn and pillage in the South, hunger recruits from the farms of Appalachia and the Midwest, the devastated South, the smoky industrial cities of the North. For four days they shot, burned, and stabbed with bayonets until the man renamed Chief Joseph stood rooted to the ground among the bodies of his kin and cried out in anguish, "From where the sun now stands I will fight no more forever." Even now, as General Miles dances in San Juan, on the Colville Reservation in Washington, Thunder Rolling in the Mountains dies slowly under the weight of his broken heart.

But there are others ready to dance for him. Dead warriors with shattered bodies and unwavering eyes. Grandmothers with ashen hair, beating softly on the drums of memory. In the ballroom in Old San Juan, they chant the burden of his bloody past, the leaders he drove down to defeat, the people he scattered. They have followed him for a long time. They chant of the Red River War of the Kiowa and Comanche, singing *Lone Wolf, Satanta, Kicking Bird.* They say to each other, nodding, *Quanah Parker*, and is it the sea outside rising and pounding on the black rocks, or do the spirits beat their muffled drums louder to honor the Pan Indian man who shared the peyote ritual and bound the scattered, war-wounded peoples into one sacred hoop?

Shuffling with a sound no louder than the wind rustling the palm leaves, they dance the honored names of the captives: *Crazy Horse of the Oglala, Lame Deer of the Mincajou, Dull Knife of the Northern Cheyenne.* Crazy Horse dead for resisting orders, Sitting Bull fled to Canada. Branches blow against the windows with a sound strangely like the rattle of a desert snake and the spirits hiss the bitter end of the Apache War, twenty-five long years of resistance. *Geronimo, Nachise, Nana* break free from their captors and Miles is the hunter set to track them. Geronimo is the last to come down from the red mountains and surrender. *We remember*, branches rattling, *how he was sent to the east in chains.* How the citizens of Arizona, *the citizens,* would not allow a single one of the Chiricahua Apache to ever set foot in their own land again. How Comanche and Kiowa offered to share their small reservations and were not allowed to. In the damp southeast where the Apache leaders are held prisoners, a quarter die of tuberculosis, coughing up their lifeblood in the sweltering barracks. The tropical night seems suddenly a little suffocating. Miles loosens his collar, has another sip of rum. In his cell at Fort Sill, Geronimo looks out between iron bars at the same stars.

Out of the corner of his eye, the general sees something that makes his throat tighten. It is only the white suit of a young man he met earlier, the son of shipping company manager, but for a moment it seemed like a shadow out of the Dakotas. It has been only twelve years since Nelson Miles was sent to crush the new religion sweeping through the Lakota, restoring heart to the people Miles and his kind had worked so hard to leave hopeless. The people feel thunder gathering and prepare for the storm to break. Some go to Pine Ridge and hope to weather it, send word to Sitting Bull. *Sitting Bull arrested, shot in a scuffle. Sitting Bull gone.* As the band of Big Foot wend their way toward shelter at Pine Ridge, Miles sends the cavalry to waylay, to divide. Miles tells his superiors that any people treated as these have been are bound to rebel. He names the injustice and, in the same breath, devises the cruelest plans against them, a professional soldier, doing his job and aiming to be the best.

He is commanding from afar when the soldiers catch up with Big Foot's band and surround the camp by Wounded Knee Creek. They set canons at the four corners of the camp, aimed at the families waiting in the snow. *Big Foot slowly dying of pneumonia in the bitter cold.* They rough up the young men, searching for weapons, looking for trouble, manufacturing an incident, and a gun goes off.

As people run for cover, the canons open fire, and a hundred and fifty are dead in moments, left bloody in the snow. For days the soldiers wander through the bodies, stabbing those who still live, stripping them for souvenirs. One month later the last warriors at Pine Ridge surrendered to this man, who now circulates so smoothly among the dancers, his mind already on the next assignment. Then the government of the bankers and railroads, the shipping magnates and merchant kings, declared the Indian Wars over, that there was no "frontier to settlement," that the continent was theirs from sea to shining sea. And they turned their gaze across the waters, to the green islands, just lying there, to the east and west.

1900: Civilization—Europe

Western Civilization is eating up the world, tearing great hunks of it from the bone. The ancient island culture of Hawaii becomes the image of a little girl, grateful to be taken into the home of her attackers. "Little Hawaii has joined the great federation of the United States," announce the heralds. Sitting around a mahogany table cut from other people's forests, the self-declared champions of progress meet for the banquet. They take pen and ink to the map of Africa, dividing the pie into so many railway concessions, mineral rights, acres of hardwood or rubber, so many hands available to be put to work, as if an entire continent of civilizations had been waiting, idle for millennia, for this ultimate moment of fulfillment. In the fantasies of rapists, the ravished are always grateful, and the captains of Empire congratulate themselves on their generosity, their willingness to bestow the benefits of being eaten on primitive peoples who, if they could only understand, would be glad to be finally of use.

1901: The Death Train—Southwestern United States

They leave the countryside of the west, looking for a way to eat. They crowd onto ships that dock at Guánica and Ponce, sent by the sugar companies of Hawaii. They steam away into another life. Docking at New Orleans, they are put on trains. The sugar barons want to break the unions. They try to keep secret this new shipment of cheap hands. The trains run at night along the silver rails. By day they sit, doors shut in the desert, guarded by armed men. Inside the stifling iron boxes of the freight cars, people die of the heat, and infections pass from breath to breath. By night, the guards take the bodies and leave them on the empty platforms of anonymous stations. One family loses seven children along this iron road. A boy of five dies of scarlet fever. The guards take his body from his weeping mother without letting her say goodbye. They want no quarantines. The child's body must be hidden until these laborers are well on their way. The Black trainmen are silent. They tend the trains, and the guards do not notice their watching eyes, the outrage stirring there. In Los Angeles the survivors, sick and sad, are boarded on ships to Honolulu. And the trainmen go and file a report with the coroner of the young boy's death, leaving the only official news of the passing of this train. But in the memories of children grown old in the sugar fields and kitchens of the big island, el tren de la muerte, the death train, still rolls silently through their dreams.

1903: Postcards of Colonialism

The latest colonizers come armed with cameras to drool over their new possession. "She welcomes us with open arms!" they cry. "She surrenders herself graciously to our virile marines! She is well-endowed, she is fruitful, she is docile—little Miss Porto Rico is ours!" They send back stereographs. Placed into viewers, the snapshots give the illusion of depth. Beneath the portrait of a destitute family standing beside a tiny bohío, some Philadelphia employee of the stereograph company has printed, "Be it ever so humble, there's no place like home!" and filed it under Happy Natives. Three young women of the slums are captioned "Dusky Belles of Porto Rico."

Soon the dusky belles will be on strike, marching along these *Roads to Enchantment* through *Scenes of Tropical Beauty.* They are tobacco workers, laundresses, coffee pickers, and needlewomen.

Their unions spread like mildew after rain. Seditious newspapers blow like yagrumo leaves in a high wind. Strikes flare along the coasts. Soon a laundress and the daughter of a laundress will be standing on park benches, shouting to the crowds. Juana Colón is a curandera and the self-taught daughter of slaves, Luisa Capetillo is the well-educated child of French and Basque anarchist immigrants. They dance on Little Miss Porto Rico's grave.

1909: La otra Aurora

She is a servant in my great-grandmother Mercedes' house. Naranjito doesn't offer any more in the way of opportunities than other towns. The pay is modest, and my great-grandfather José Dolores has an eye and a groping hand for a woman. I do not know whether he forced or bribed or seduced her. The story comes in fragments, in the separate broken bits of memory held by my great-aunts.

I know that one day my great-grandmother realizes the young woman is pregnant, and, for whatever reason, whatever bitter knowledge her marriage has brought, she understands that her husband is the cause. Whatever her rage and humiliation, whatever bloody fantasies she entertains lying awake at night, in the end she offers the woman money and tells her never to enter their house again.

No one remembers what happened to her. The baby, my aunt believes, did not survive. We have no unacknowledged cousins living on the wrong side of town. Instead, Mercedes bears a daughter to this man who is laying waste to their inheritance, drinking and dancing, gambling away the future of his children. When this daughter is born on the first day of June, José Dolores chooses to name her Aurora, revenge upon his wife for dismissing his mistress. No one calls her Aurora. They call her Lola after her father, don Lolo. The name lies dormant.

But in 1954, in February, my parents choose it again, for me.

They don't know they have named me for family secrets, for disgraces, for bitter things, for a woman whose face I cannot see. This is my legacy. I carry her name and a hunger for her story. I am descended from that bitter marriage, and from the servant's unwritten life, driven to tell the things we're not supposed to know.

❧RUDA

A sprig of rue seems such a fragile thing to defend against enemies, guard against spells, protect young women from the consequences of fertility. Rue says sometimes intention is enough. Rue says do not surrender to bitter circumstance. Sometimes attitude can carry you through. Sometimes bluffing becomes truth. Fake it till you make it. Rue says walk into that garden where I stand in full daylight and break off a twig. Tuck it jauntily behind your ear, so the leaves watch your back, and set off believing no one can touch you now. Go ahead and steep that tea. Maybe you counted wrong. Maybe your body will change its mind. Maybe this child that will bring so much trouble will dissolve into a stomach ache and disappear. Rue says bravery does count for something. Rue says sheer nerve may carry the day. Rue whispers outrageous options into your ear until you laugh in the face of disaster and let the slammed door creak open just enough to let you squeeze through.

1909: Lessons

In the grade schools of the Yauco countryside, lessons are set by clothing manufacturers in far away Philadelphia. Girls must learn to read instructions, to add stitches, to multiply profits. They embroider flowers and butterflies, make eyelet lace collars, learn to decorate the clothing of socialites. They must turn in piles of homework every day, so many pieces of work to be done that they cannot keep up unless they enlist their mothers, sisters, aunts.

This is not unpaid labor, the superintendents insist. It's education. These girls are being fitted for a useful role in society. When the work is turned in, it is packed away in boxes, and each week the teachers sell it to the companies and pocket the money. It won't be long before eight out of ten homes are workshops for the garment industry. Women and children will sew late into the night for two cents an hour, whole families laboring for just enough to buy a single daily meal of coffee and bread.

In the glittering windows of the department stores, elegant ladies will exclaim over the exquisite needlework. Such tiny stitches, such lovely lace, such delicate embroidery and beaded detail. Accepting compliments at the next dinner party they attend, they will say, "Yes . . . Isn't it just darling, dear . . . and every stitch made by hand!"

1913: Opiniones

Luisa, I dream you sometimes, striding through the night streets of Havana in your suit and tie, stars over head and a good cigar burning a hole in the dark from the shadow of your mouth. I dream you some cool morning at a desk, laying onto thick reams of paper your visions of what could really be, or in blazing afternoon light, arguing with your comrades, putting your thoughts into the air with blunt gestures of your strong hands, keeping them all mesmerized with the force of your character.

One day, one moment, you are writing the latest manifestos for the tobacco workers' union; a few hours later you are crafting an argument that Christian salvation and human liberation are one, the road to paradise to be found in class struggle and the freedom of the workers. Another day you work out a dialogue between two men, arguing about a woman who has taken a lover and the sexual double standard. How is it, you ask in the voice of the enlightened comrade, that sexual experience makes a man more desirable and a woman less so?

I see you in the crowds, stepping onto platforms, speaking your

mind without apology and arousing whole meeting halls full of
patient faces, setting them ablaze. There are many like you and
there is no one like you at all. The male comrades think your views
on sexual freedom mean you will always put out. I watch you reply
with less and less patience to their propositions. You say women
need education not to raise enlightened sons, but to gain financial
independence from men. That every girl needs to learn about sex
so she can hold her own. You're a vegetarian and want women to
exercise more, to take back our bodies. You write for the newspapers and people gather around to hear your words read aloud.

Criss-crossing your path all those same years is Juana Colón,
daughter of slaves, who became a rabble-rouser by a different road.
She was a curandera, healing the illnesses of tobacco workers, and
what she saw of their lives enraged her into action. She agitates just
as fiercely for labor rights, but is an ardent suffragist as well. "Que
revulú" goes the popular refrain, "que alboroto, que Juana Colón
no tiene voto!" What a scandal, what a fuss—that Juana Colón
cannot vote. The battle for the vote is raging all around you, but it
doesn't interest you much. Your only input is that literacy must
not be a requirement for suffrage. You have no great expectation
that elections will change the face of poverty.

Whenever you move through the twilight of my sleep, I recognize you. I recognize you in your man's hat pulled forward to
shade your eyes; in your boundless energy, running from strike
to strike, hopping trains, hopping boats, Tampa, Havana, New
York. In the boarding house full of cigar-makers that you run for
a year or two. Writing impassioned letters to your daughter, being
raised by nuns in the convent school of her father's choice, to make
prayer her own.

We could have used you, Luisa, in this collective and that. We
would have argued with you into the dawn and embraced you
when you left, would have loved your boldness, read your latest
editorials, made you stay for supper before you went to the airport

for a rally in some other time zone. We would have understood every word you said about your lovers, about the man you finally walked away from but couldn't forget. How we would have vied with each other to lure you into bed! Longed to probe your muscular heart with kisses, given you pots of Chinese herbs to drink, and tried to slow you down long enough for you to soak in our tenderness.

When you fell ill, we would have gotten your support team together in a flash. We'd have practice at it these many years. The shifts of people cooking for you, doing your laundry, giving you massages to unravel the tension in your shoulders. We would have taken you to your acupuncture appointments, fixed succulent dishes to strengthen you, been irritated at your bad temper when forced to rest. Luisa, we would not have let you die so young, of something so much easier to beat than cancer and AIDS. We would have loved you back to life again so we could talk with you a little longer. Talked with you through decades you never lived to see, through the thirties and forties and fifties and sixties and, with careful tending, maybe even into the seventies before we let you go, satisfied and celebrated, from this life.

1914: Delmira—Montevideo, Uruguay

She was a poet, full of starry darknesses and fiery songs, full of desires and words. He was her husband. He thought she would put him first. Put babies first. Put his desires before her own. She was a poet first. From the age of ten she had written her dreams onto paper. How could he imagine she would leave such pleasure? How could she have imagined he would want her to? She kept writing, rising from their bed when he wanted her dreaming and sated with sex, going to the table and writing quickly, absorbedly. He saw that she would escape his possession, that she transmuted everything, everything into poetry, used up her whole life and his to fuel that passion into which she escaped from him. He quarreled, stormed, had jealous rages, insisted she be a wife to him. She said no. She filed for divorce. She would not surrender her desires to his, so he raped her. She would not silence herself, smother the flame, choke the life out of herself. So he did.

1917: War Effort

In a building at Parada 17 the ladies of the Red Cross have organized a major campaign to support the war effort. Dozens of women of color work around the clock, while the white ladies supervise their activities and are graciously prepared to accept the gratitude of the nation. The campaign grows and must soon be moved to another facility, a pineapple-canning factory on the road to Carolina. Because of the patriotic nature of the work, the owner donates the facilities, while the patrón of Central Aguirre gives 35,000 pounds of raw materials. Within two months, the women of Puerto Rico will be able to ship out the results of all this activity: twelve and a half tons of guava jelly for the wounded soldiers returning from the battlefields of France.

1918: Lavanderas

With so many men in uniform, somebody must wash their clothes. With so many shirts and pairs of trousers to wash, somebody should make a profit. So reason the managers of Marchan, Sicardo y Compañia. Everyone is in a patriotic fervor, decking themselves out in French and American flags to see the soldiers off. Last month, three hundred women signed a strike petition when their employers wouldn't allow them a reader to keep them abreast of the war news. Everyone has a relative overseas. Why not give the women more clothing to launder and less pay for laundering?

The strike committee is headed by Victoria Lopez, Matilde Pardo, and Julia Torres. They are not taken in. "We know," they write in their statement, "that current conditions are terrible, and all good citizens must aid in the triumph of world democracy. But we, who give our sons for the war, cannot consent to the owners enriching themselves by exploiting our blood." They will wash no more uniforms for the laundry bosses, they declare, but will willingly clean the clothing of the soldiers in metal tubs of steaming water they heat in buckets in their homes. They know that the democracy that fills the emotional speeches of the war-makers stands on the dignity of working people like themselves, who will not surrender their self-respect for a song and a flag.

1918: Vida alegre

The word has come down that moral weakness is undermining the war to end all wars. Gambling, cards games, and cockfights are lowering agricultural production in San Sebastian. But more serious still is the damage done by loose women. Nearly half of all Puerto Rican soldiers have venereal disease. This will make it impossible for them to give their all, life and limb, on the battlefields of Europe. Governor Yager launches a campaign of social hygiene. Soldiers are confined to camp, to keep them uncontaminated, and the forces of cleanliness and godliness go forth to round up prostitutes.

Hundreds of women are jailed, while lawyers protest the loss of civil rights, the continuous abuses and false accusations. Four hundred in Ponce, three hundred in Arecibo, some in every town. Many of the women are infected, and the prisons become hospitals. Judges and newspaper editors are denounced for cooperating with this massive roundup. The military has no interest in what becomes of these women, as long as they are no longer available to enlisted men. The women are simply dirt to be scrubbed off the soiled reputation of war, which is a clean and manly endeavor. But the Ladies Committee demands the right to help them. They enter the jails with pamphlets and speeches about moral education, about goodness and purity. They call these women, who have exchanged the use of their bodies for a few coins, mujeres de vida alegre, women of the joyful, the festive, the happy life.

It is Luisa Capetillo who speaks about sexual harassment on the job, of bosses who use hunger and the fear of joblessness to extort sex from women workers, who says if you want women to stop exchanging their bodies for bread, then give them bread.

✼MAGUEY

Spiky century plant whose thorny leaves reach out from a tender heart and pierce the space around you, who once in a hundred years thrusts up your immense stalk of flowers, green and waxy and smelling like something old and lasting at the edge of memory, enters the places where our flesh was ravaged by use, and washes it clean. You who cannot be casually touched, whose silky inner core is so well-defended, soothe the sores of syphilis from our skins. We have been handled without thought by so many grubby fingers, entered by so many casual lusts. Your sticky substance could erase those other juices spilled here, could lubricate the overburdened valves of our hearts, restore sight to our dimming eyes, and pull us back from unending nightmares of feverish hours, awake when others sleep. Merciful maguey, bright candle against the sky, ease us from the consequences of our losses, from the scars of what this world has forced us to accept. Do not let us go, uncomforted, into the dark.

1919: Lost Bird—Western United States

She was found under the stiff and bloody body of her mother, in the bitter cold of winter on the slaughter fields of Wounded Knee, and from that moment she became a souvenir. The soldiers would not allow her people to retain her, such a luscious little lump of sugar, such a black-eyed trophy, such an adorable symbol of conquest, little Zintka, the Lost Bird of the Lakota.

Leonard Colby was a Brigadier General, with first dibs, a man of devious mind and ruthless appetite. With great fanfare and flag waving, he adopted Zintka and exhibited her to the world. Two thousand paraded by her in the first weeks, until she grew ill from their gazes and their withering breath. Clara Colby, a suffragist and a goodhearted woman, cared for Lost Bird as best she could, but never understood that pit of sorrow within her, full of deerskin and dried blood.

Leonard understood it and relished it. It was for the wound, for the helplessness, that he took her from the frozen ground. It was for the helplessness that he kept her and, as she ripened toward womanhood, would enter her room at night and take the field, and watch a people fall to earth again and again. Separated from Clara, Leonard had all the power. Pregnant, despairing, imprisoned by her father in a boarding school where any disobedience was punished with the leather straightjacket, Zintka gave birth to a stillborn son. Clara, demonstrating beside Emmeline Pankhurst in London for the suffrage of women, never heard her silence until it was too late.

Look at her now, her face distorted by syphilis, a bequest from her husband, Zintka of the Lakota dances in buckskin and beads as the mascot of a sportsman's club offering the illusion of exotic worlds to jaded white men hungry for what they had tried to destroy. Lost Bird, she flies through the silent films as a beautiful "Indian maiden" and into the noise and tobacco smells of Buffalo Bill Cody's Wild West Show. She tries to go home, but her relatives don't know how to claim her, the city girl with flashy ways. Look at her now, on a rainy day in February, gasping for breath as her heart, squeezed tight by the disease of conquest, succumbs to the flu that is killing hundreds of thousands. She is the lost child, the wounded wing, the broken song, the stolen girl, the invaded land. She died of syphilis, she died of grief, she died of contempt, she died of costume, she died of ignorance, she died of theft, she died of her missing name.

1921: Harlem—New York

Harlem swings and struts to the sounds of a spirit that will not die. Harlem eats the blues and spits back jazz, drinks jazz and whispers back blues, twirls a cane and decks its hair with flowers. Harlem is full of poetry and passion. Back to Africa, cry the Garveyites and sell their shares in the Black Star Line to those dazzled by a vision of dignity. There goes Langston, words clear as rain falling on thirsty ground and Zora striding past convention in her big hat. Sweet smoky singing pours from the nightclub doors where illegal liquor passes in back rooms.

"Se buscan mujeres . . ." say the newspaper ads. "Young women wanted to sew ladies' blouses, to sew dresses and suits. Clean rooms, women only, strict supervision, and Spanish-speaking only. Mothers, come inspect our workrooms, we need your daughters' fingers, no experience necessary. We will happily train."

Girls from San Juan and Aguadilla, Ponce and Mayagüez, Yauco and Arecibo go to work sewing clothing. After the long day of stitching, their mothers expect them home. But tired as they are, they linger on the streets to listen. All the big band masters have been to Cuba, have played the casinos in San Juan. The rhythms and riffs blend in the streets of Harlem and set tired feet twitching to something both familiar and breathtakingly new.

1923: Tuberculosis

Malaria kills the cane-worker, and dysentery comes for all the poor, but now, as women crowd into tobacco sheds and sewing shops, tuberculosis stakes its claim. TB invades of the lungs of young, hardworking women. Pale and sweating, they cough up blood and cannot breathe. Day after day they struggle to continue, to earn the food that will bring them back some strength. Those who can take a rest, lie listless, and the doctors prescribe oranges, milk, meat, things they cannot afford.

Luisa has been working herself beyond the point of exhaustion. Always on the move, always with a word to say. But slowly her lungs are filling with congestion, choking her voice, slowing her down. Today tuberculosis took Luisa Capetillo. The streets are full of mourners who call her name. Today tuberculosis took one of the righteous. A woman whose eloquence gave discouraged people hope. She should have been exempt from the death of the downtrodden, they think. She should have lived to be an elder. To be honored when her hair was white. She was only forty-four years old. They stand in the rain to follow her casket. They look at each other, stunned that she is gone.

❧MULLEIN

Silver-grey leaf, soft as fog entering our lungs, slides the heavy viscous matter from our chests. Mullein does not need to shout. It simply says what has to be said, and the heaviness clears. Mullein is the one who explains the reason for the strike, how plain it is that nothing else will work, how reasonable the demands. Mullein does the task that no one else competes for, runs off two thousand fliers on a mimeo machine, explains to the printer why the money will be late, fetches the isolated voters to the polls in the old station wagon, in the rain. Mullein doesn't make extravagant promises, is impatient with fulsome praise, just wants, with every fiber of its being, for things to be the way they are supposed to be.

1927: Pasodoble

Aurora Moure Diaz, still known as Lola, accompanies her father
to the casino of Naranjito. He is still a gambler, a womanizer, a
dashing man, and she adores the ground he treads upon. At the casino, José Dolores stakes his daughter's future on a turn of the
cards, a roll of the dice. While she dances pasodoble with young
men from good families, her father is losing the family store. There
may be one boy she likes better than the others, but his family will
not approve. He'll be packed off to relatives in Nueva York. For
now, she has no thought of such unknown destinations. The steps
of this dance are so familiar, so secure. Unworried by her father's
eager concentration on the dealer's hands, she smiles as she circles
on a young man's arm. When the music stops, she thinks she
knows where she will land.

1929: Journey

Jane Speed is a child of the aristocracy, an Alabama girl descended
from slaveholder wealth but already beginning to catch fire. With
her mother, who is divorced, she takes a walking tour of Austria.
Jane goes to the *gimnasium* to study, and briefly marries and then
divorces a young man before she turns twenty-one.

There is more to see in Austria than the Alps. Over the border
in Germany, young men in brown shirts march in formation and
grow violent. Here in Austria, their sympathizers also march, but
they want violence with an Austrian flavor. They attack the workers' housing co-ops that the socialists have organized, breaking
glass and throwing people and furniture into the streets. The ten-
ants get weapons and fight back. Jane and her mother, Dolly, speak
with people, ask questions, discuss opinions, buy newspapers,
read books. When at last they turn toward home, they are full of
new ideas. On the ship, Jane sits on deck, reading *Every Intelligent
Woman's Guide to Socialism* by George Bernard Shaw.

When at last they wend their way home to Birmingham, she will no longer be interested in tea parties. Dolly will work with the Southern Tenant Farmers' Union and Jane will join the Communist Party. Five years from now, on May Day of 1934, it will be Jane and a Black man who are chosen to address the rally in Montgomery, illegal simply because they are there together. She will be instructed to keep on speaking until she is carried away, and as they lift her into the police wagon, she will still be shouting her encouragements to the crowd. Because she is heir to privilege, because of those tea parties she has refused, they will offer to release her. But her allegiance has changed and that door is no longer open. She will not leave prison without her companion and spends her weeks there, knitting and unraveling her small supply of wool.

1929: Hechos desconocidos

More women die in childbirth than all the deaths from typhoid and diphtheria. Denied knowledge or adequate care, women embark on reproduction as a dangerous voyage into the unknown. The women who have become the voice of healing want female doctors free of harassment, want nurses regulating themselves, not practicing at the prejudiced whim of male physicians. Rosa Gonzalez leads the fight for the nurses. She writes *Los hechos desconocidos,* telling the history of women's part in medicine in Puerto Rico, and makes an impassioned call for more power over our lives.

In Naranjito, the pasodoble is over, and Lola Moure has discovered the end of the dance was unknown after all. The store lost to gaming debts, the inheritance dissipated, her father has told her he can no longer afford her. She must marry. The one she yearned for is gone, lacking the backbone to resist his parents' orders. One of the neighbors, a young man who has been a teacher, comes home and asks for her hand, and before she knows what has happened, she has consented for her family's sake, for the sake of something new, and has stepped onto a boat for New York City, into a different tune.

The suffragist nurses and doctors of Puerto Rico know what women and children die of. While the male doctors continue to defend their privilege and ignore the truth, they strive to lower mortality, fight infection, lower the risk. Do not act on what you know, for you know nothing, say the medical men. Abandon the midwives and come to hospitals, sterile and cold and devoid of comfort or touch. Few and far between, on this island of poor.

Our lives are nothing to the ones who say they are responsible for our safety. Marry him, he wants you, say the relatives. Manhattan will be better, this husband better than the other, you don't have to love him yet. Marriage is a good thing. So many hechos are desconocido. Childbirth after childbirth, ship after ship leaving port, choice after choice made in the dark, struggling to find a lifeboat in the waters, we launch new lives.

✌ DERRUMBE: 1930–1954

1930: El barrio

This is not Naranjito. No mango trees, no banana leaf rustling, no oranges ripe from the tree. My grandfather will spend the next forty years growing philodendrons from cuttings and dark clumps of snake plants until, by the time old age sends my grandparents home, the clumps have become thickets and the philodendrons wind all the way across the ceiling of their last New York apartment and down the other side. But my grandmother Lola sparkles like the mica in the sidewalks, despite the cold, the poverty, the hunger and dinginess. This is not Naranjito. She can walk out in Central Park, talk with the neighbors, the grocer, the salesladies, and no one will tell her mother-in-law, "I saw Lola downtown . . ." with that speculation in her voice. Here there is no surveillance but her husband's jealousy. She will return to Puerto Rico in the end only with reluctance, to be enclosed within the decorative iron gates of his dominance in a suburban urbanización with no public transportation.

But now it is 1930, early November, Manolín out of work, breadlines and rags, down to one single brown dress, and Lola is nursing her first child, my mother, with nothing in the house for her to eat, weak with hunger, feeding her daughter with her own shaky body. This is how people are rescued: someone is promoted from janitor. The little group of Puerto Rican men who know each other gather to decide who to groom for the now-vacant job, and because of that two-month-old infant at my grandmother's breast, they pick Manolín and take him down at night to teach him how to use the industrial vacuum cleaner. In the morning he gets the job and, with his first pay, buys eggs and butter, goes home, cooks scrambled eggs, and holds the spoon for his half-fainting wife. More than half a century from now she will remember the taste of those eggs, that kindness of the compas, how because of it she grew strong again and stayed in New York and lived far away from the snug web of family ties, rode the subways, made friends, found her half-measure of freedom.

1931: Tiempo muerto

Tiempo muerto. The dead season. The sugar cane's gone to market and the workers have been laid off. You can get a dollar twenty-five to weed a cuerda of land, which is a solid week's work. A woman picking coffee gets thirty-six cents, maybe as much as forty-two, for a day's work. A man gets as much as eighty. For sewing, eighteen hours, forty cents.

First you pay for the place where you live, nailed up boards, thatched roof or maybe tin, a dollar a week to keep the rain off your head. Then to the colmado to buy food. Rice is twelve cents a pound. A family of five needs at least five pounds for the week. If you get broken grains, it's cheaper, only nine cents. Beans cost nine cents a pound. A pound of salt cod is eighteen cents for one family meal so you stretch it out as flavoring in bacalaitos. Flour is eight cents a pound, eggs three cents apiece. Oil is a dollar, so you get lard, which is thirty-four cents. Bread is a dime. You fill corners with bread and bacon drippings (bacon at thirty-two cents a pound is a seasoning, not a main course).

You're a mother with three children. There isn't any way to feed them enough and it rains. There are outdoor latrines, droppings from horses, cattle, goats, dead animals in the rivers. The water gets contaminated. Everyone is sick. Cornmeal is six cents a pound, cheaper than rice. The children's eyes are getting too big in their faces. The baby has diarrhea. The oldest never stops coughing. Fresh milk is eight cents, but it spoils so fast. A can of evaporated milk is fifteen cents. A doctor is not even a dream. Months still before the sugar cane is tall and fat with juice.

It's the heavy half of the year, an unrelenting grinding away of hope. Always a few more children wrapped in sacking and laid back into the red earth, always a few exhausted mothers surrendering at last to tuberculosis, malaria, anemia. You give the baby manzanillo and fennel, yerba buena and dill. It begins to recover, but one of your neighbors loses her struggle and you hear her children wailing in the night. You help out with the wake. Second-best quality coffee at thirty-two cents a pound, sugar at ten. The dead woman wore herself out picking that coffee two seasons ago. Her eldest boy cut the cane that the sugar came from.

℘MALANGA

This is the food of emptiness, the starchy handful of bulk that will fill the stomach without nourishing muscles, feeding the blood, energizing the heart. In times of starvation, malanga is a delicacy: the slippery white root tastes better than bark, digests more easily than clay, is more filling than guavas. Malanga root crouches under huge elephant ears of leaves like a tiny, hairy child carrying gigantic umbrellas. Malanga is the foraging jackpot of trespassers slipping quietly into the patron's land in search of supper. Malanga boiled to a bland, pale lump and sprinkled with salt can taste like another chance at life. But the children grow thin, small, stunted. Their bellies swell, their eyes sink, malanga keeps the breath moving in their chests, but it cannot lift them toward the sun.

1933: Pura Belpré—New York

What does lift children into the sun are the stories Pura reads on Sunday afternoons at the library at 115th Street. In all of the New

York Public Library system, she is the only Puerto Rican librarian. When the children come, clutching their mothers' hands, peering out from behind their skirts, she entices them with tales of Juan Bobo. She goes here and there, finding stories to feed them, shelter them, sing them to sleep. She invades the offices of administrators, insisting that they stock the shelves with books that will taste good to immigrants hungry for welcome. She throws parties for their families at Christmas and begins rewriting folk tales of the island for the children of New York. When she leaves the library, it is only to write full time and travel with her jazz musician husband among the heirs of Harlem's renaissance and other circles of Black artists and intellectuals. From her pen, the goats and frogs, tricksters and fools of that faraway tropical homeland crowd onto the passenger ships and erupt into the streets and living rooms of New York City so that the children can grow tall and strong.

1934: Needleworkers

Who clothes the world? Immigrant women, poor women, women underpaid and overworked nearly to death. My mothers stitch through the decades, through strikes and disasters, the changing fabrics passing through their hands. First it's my great-grandmother Leah, her sister Betty, and her husband, Abe, known as Pop, only he's a foreman and they are labor, back around 1909 when young Clara Lemlich stood up in the meeting and shouted out the call for the great garment strike they call the uprising of the twenty thousand.

Both Pop and my bisabuela Rosario make nurses' uniforms. I don't know if the women make shirtwaists or trousers, dresses or suits. On the island women hand-sew in their homes. In New York there are dark rooms full of machines and dust, and bins of cotton, linen, wool. My step-grandfather's sister makes blouses at the Triangle Shirtwaist Company and is one of the dead when the building catches on fire and seamstresses locked into upper rooms burned among the piles of cloth or plunged to their deaths in the streets below.

"Oh, the cloakmaker's union is a no-good union" . . . my father sings this to me when I am a child . . . "it's a company union by the bosses!"

My aunt Eva is in the hatmaker's union, which is much better. "Oh, they preach socialism, while they practice fascism to preserve capitalism by the bosses—Sss." And David Eidelstadt writes a women's lament: *"Tsu gott vel ikh veynen, mit a groys geveyn . . ."* (To God I cry out with a great cry, why was I born to be a seamstress?).

1933. My great-grandmother leads a circle of unemployed women, talking, writing, organizing. She reads to them what she has written about her own grandmother in the old country, the one who "planted the revolutionary spark" in her, the rabbi's wife who wouldn't sit quietly where she belonged. 1948. Lolita Lebrón is only one among thousands of Puerto Rican women who pass from small town island homes, many of them filled with women sewing, into the sweatshops of New York. Only she's the one who picks up a gun. 1956. My grandmother Lola Morales commutes two hours to make bras and girdles, girdles and bras, hour after hour in deafening noise. Go there and look. Women are still sitting in the same rooms, sewing for pennies. Chinese women. Haitian women. Vietnamese, Salvadoran, and Laotian women. New immigrants take the places of the old so the machines won't miss a beat. New languages have replaced the Yiddish and Polish and Italian. But the meaning is the same in their singing and sighing and angry whispers and on the picket signs and leaflets in the streets.

1935: *Bread upon the Waters*

Rose Pesotta has been organizing garment-working women since she was first an immigrant teenager in New York, making shirtwaists and listening to the women talk union. She's worked her way up through the bureaucracy of the International Ladies Garment Workers' Union, shouldered her way through the boys' club at the top, and been in charge of more campaigns than you could count.

Two years ago she went to California and, in spite of lazy union officials and a leadership reluctant to fund her, the membership has skyrocketed. It was the mexicanas, young immigrant women, who were the heart of her militant followers. By September she was ready to take the cloakmakers out on strike. The union leaders asked, Wasn't it a bit late in the season, and wasn't she supposed to be concentrating on the dressmakers instead?

The Mexican cloakmakers and dressmakers, she snapped, would be the backbone of the union in the West. You're as dead as the petrified forests of Arizona, she told them, and went on to win the strike. When las mexicanas filled the jails, singing and shouting, she took the white men from the office down to hear them, so they wouldn't underestimate them again.

In the harsh winter of 1934, she moved on to San Francisco to take on the Chinese sweatshops. She would not report the abuses to immigration, would not see anyone deported. Instead she found ways to talk with Chinese women and teach them what she could, in spite of family employers. She persisted in spite of labor council men who would rather see Chinese women in tiny, underground shops than competing with the white, America-born women in their lives.

In her memoir, *Bread upon the Waters,* her battles against racism are clear. She says plainly that only during World War II did the Chinese workers of California get a fair deal. She says Mexican women were the boldest and most reliable and she put them in charge whenever she could. She has campaigned aggressively for women the union would have left behind. She has been so successful she is now a vice president of the ILGWU. Because of what she has accomplished, they send her to the garment workers of Puerto Rico.

Rose is unprepared for the misery she encounters. The dressmakers of San Juan live in wooden shacks barely lifted above the mud, without plumbing, without electricity. She has never tried to organize people so weakened by parasites, anemia, and malnutrition. When she calls a meeting about the conditions of labor, several women faint from hunger. Rose begins bringing baskets of food to the meetings and information on sanitation, birth control, basic health care. She stops talking about labor laws. The garment workers are afraid to enforce the regulations for fear the shops will move to cheaper islands, leaving them unemployed. What she hears and sees breaks her heart. She fought for the Los Angeles mexicanas, the San Francisco Chinese, but here she cannot think beyond the wounds. She cannot bring herself to challenge these women to risk anything more. Did they remind her of some half-forgotten glimpse of shtetl starvation, some legacy older than her years of organizing, that they haunted her so? She, the fiercest union woman of them all, cast many loaves of bread upon their waters but forgot to teach them how to bake.

1935: Julia in Naranjito

Julia de Burgos is the eldest of thirteen children, a bottomless spring of emotion, a boundless heart full of desires, a beautiful and eloquent woman who generously spills her spirit onto page after page. When the ink dries, poems lie scattered everywhere on her table, crying out for freedom, for love that satisfies, for men who keep faith, for an end to suffering.

Last year she worked at the milk station in Comerío, serving free breakfasts to the hungriest on this hungry island, but the milk station closed. Now she teaches school in Barrio Cerro Arriba in Naranjito. She is newly married but unhappy, and will soon be divorced. Her mother has just been diagnosed with cancer.

Looking out over the rich valley, she writes a love poem to the river of her childhood, the slow and wide river of Loiza. Writes of those ardent blue waters that caress without trying to own her. She closes her eyes to see the floods that wash down from the mountains and hears a great cry of anguish as if the land itself wept. She leans over the page, hand moving swiftly, and writes of a river that will kiss her everywhere, that will turn her body into an ocean licked by continents, fling her into the sky as rain, and let her fall in red torrents down the slick, wet hills. Surrounded by hunger and sorrow, Julia makes love to life and writes of that ever-faithful river on whose sun-warmed surface she drifts.

Putting down the pen at last she imagines herself pulled upward by the heat, dispersed into tiny droplets of steam. Feels herself rising, as mist, into cold high places, blown this way and that by winds she doesn't recognize, drawn far away from the warm places of her heart, so that she falls again as snow on the streets of an immense, anonymous city.

&Naranja

Bitter orange for sadness in the stomach, for queasiness, for too much happening at once. Bitter orange for settling the heaving unsteadiness of lives upset by too much loss, too many changes, too much to figure out. Dark green leaf and orange rind shiny with sharp oils that cut through the swirling doubts, straight into the heart of the one present moment, that say this is all you can do, cut rind, crush leaf, stay in this here and now, and smell.

1937: The Jane Speed Bookstore— Birmingham, Alabama

In this photograph, Jane is standing in the bookstore, a place of gathering she maintains for the Black and white progressive intellectuals of Birmingham. Her knee-length red hair is braided and wound about her head in a crown. She has had lovers, had comrades, had the companionship of her feisty mother who just recently visited the office of the Italian ambassador on the pretext of wanting to take a cruise, and, in her white gloves and elegant hat, proceeded to spill ink all over his desk in protest of Mussolini's invasion of Abyssinia.

She is about to leave Birmingham, although she doesn't yet know it. She's going to a Party training school for organizers, and among the attendees will be a good-looking comrade from Puerto Rico, César Andreu Iglesias. She will decide on marriage this time and, with her mother and the remaining shares of their inheritance of Wesson Oil stock, will pack up and move to San Juan, where there are plenty of battles to take on and the flowers she misses from her old country home will flourish with more abandon than ever before.

1937: Madre patria

"La madre tendida en el lecho. . ." says the great patriot, the small, dark man for whom thousands will hush. Our country is like our mother, stretched on a bed of rape. Our country is courage and sacrifice. Our country is an imprisoned flower in a fist of iron.

Madre patria is the nationalist prayer: part mute mother, part shining inheritance. Now the Nationalists gather up threads of rage and dispossession, knotted toward a single end. Not class, not gender, not race, not all injustice, but a pure and singleminded cry for nationhood, for the share of the cheated younger son. The problem is not the extortions of the native, landholding rich, the debasement of the female, the ransacking of the soil. It is the tyranny of the yanqui. The poor rally round, for nowhere else is the passion for a different future so naked, their hunger for self-respect so simply and fully fed. And women come, finding a place for power, a place for public speech. A place to take weapons up into their hands and fight back against the suffocation that constrains them. They organize and conspire, write poetry, and burn with the vision of republic. But the silent mother remains upon the bed, a symbol to be passed from hand to hand. She has no voice in their manifestos, no presence in their policies. It has never really been her freedom that Don Pedro dreams.

1942: Wartime at the PO—New York

Women of words get the strangest jobs to pay the rent. We cluster around employment that lets us tinker with language even if the language is not our own. I have spent eight hours a day rearranging the resumes of engineers and translating surveys about rape in women's lives. On each job, everyone was a poet, a novelist, a playwright stealing lunchtimes on the IBM Selectrics.

But this is 1944, when typewriters are manual and letters written by hand. The literate women of the barrio pay the landlord and the grocer by censoring the mail of Latina families to their loved ones overseas, and from the soldiers writing home. Loose Lips Sink Ships. Not a hint of anything sensitive must go out. No unwitting help for the enemy in the chisme of the vecindario. That Tata's boy is on such and such an island in the South Pacific may warn the Japanese of our intent. That in spite of ration cards we have no sugar, must not leak out to hearten Hitler's troops. That Miguelito was wounded in a certain part of France, met up with Soviets by a river, is liking the Belgian food or not, could hide the crucial fact that must be hidden. Over and over they read the private mail of their neighbors, Querido Papo. Mi santa madre. Dios quiera, God willing, this letter finds you well. The words they black out remain behind their eyes, the voices of longing fill their dreams. The words they take away, on government orders, stay with them, germinating in the fertile dark like seeds. The words soak into the language of these writers and wait to emerge, wait for peace, for homecomings, for someone to listen, for the empty page.

1943: The Ghetto Comes to the Barrio—New York

In the bitter spring of this year, rumors creep into the barrio from the sparkling eyes of Jewish friends. Tears and embraces. Handshakes and trembling joy. Hitler has taken his first defeat from a handful of starving partisans, a ragged band of Jews. Every Puerto Rican knows someone who has heard of it. In the unions, in the workplaces, in the neighborhoods and the schools.

Jesus Colón, immigrant journalist of the poor, writes columns for the leftist newspapers, communists, socialists, nationalists, anti-fascists. He lives next door to my great aunt Eva Levins, a communist hatmaker, and her husband, Einar, a Norwegian veteran of the mining struggles of Idaho. They talk over the fragments of information smuggled out of Warsaw—how the Nazis have swept across border after border but have not been able to subdue the Warsaw ghetto. How each time they proclaim victory, another Molotov cocktail explodes. How weeks after they say they have exterminated the Jews, someone finds a lit candle, a warm meal hastily abandoned, leaflets.

Jesus writes a column for *Pueblos hispanos* called "The Jewish People and Us," exorting Latinos not to fall for the trick of blaming Jews for the predations of the bosses. In the barrio, many have never before met real live Jews. Didn't they kill our Lord? Aren't they greedy, secretly rich? The children of jíbaros run after effigies of the treacherous Jew, "el juá," the Judas who betrayed our Christ. The hissing of the inquisitors still lingers in Catholic school and parish, and when the new immigrants look around them they don't see the chairmen of boards in the far-off Protestant suburbs. They see Jews who own shops, Jews who are bosses, Jews who control the union and don't listen to las puertorriqueñas. The wedge of class is beginning to divide us. With the world of European Jews in flames, some of their kin take the fantasy road of assimilation and upward mobility, leaving behind friends and neighbors who still struggle to make the rent.

But in the barrio in this year, solidarity is still a strong, bright thread. Militance still holds its own between opportunism and fear. Families have been crafted in union meetings and opposition newspaper offices, in sweatshops and apartment hallways, and on the sidewalks of immigrant neighborhoods. Jesus Colón and my Aunt Eva rejoice together over the news, go arm in arm to meetings, and know the same songs. In the springtime of this bitter year people bend over the war news, exclaiming over the partisans of Warsaw in Spanish, Yiddish, and English. The ghetto enters the barrio and leaves a burning yellow star upon its heart.

1944: Nuestra guerra—New York

In our war, my mother says, one of the things you notice first is that you can't get olive oil, and for sugar you must stand in line twice, once for ration coupons and again at the grocery store. Another thing is that everyone saves the drippings from whatever beef or pork they get, and in my mother's house it's my grandfather who mixes it with lye to make soap. There are men in uniform everywhere, a new set of colors to the landscape. Although no one in the family has been killed, her tío Pepe came back with his hand injured and tucks it into his shirt when he's photographed. Other people's uncles and brothers have come back missing pieces—sometimes legs, sometimes their peace of mind. Some people come home crazy as can be from what they've seen and done. All my mother can find out about what's going on behind the war news is in the stories of her new friends, refugee Jews from Germany or Poland or Czechoslovakia. What they tell her haunts her dreams and makes this piece of history her own forever.

Because the war effort requires everyone to sacrifice, the unions have a hard time fighting back against plans to make the sacrifice belong mostly to workers. They open up their hiring halls and organizing drives to the people most likely to be used against them. That's how my grandfather gets a real job, as an electrician wiring up battleships at the Brooklyn naval shipyard.

In school my mother knits things for soldiers and it's all one big effort for democracy. But when the men come home from England and France, Germany and Italy, the heroes of the liberation are still the colored boys of the Jim Crow U.S.A. They have been used to respect, used to dancing with whomever they please, sitting down to eat in any restaurant. Demobilized into segregation, Puerto Rican soldiers are as angry as their African American comrades. When the war is over, we inherit distant graves, wounded veterans, in-laws from a dozen countries, and a simmering resentment just this side of rage.

1948: Julia Drinks a River of Sorrow—New York

Julia de Burgos, the glowing poet of sensual rivers and waves crashing against sea walls, is drowning slowly in despair. I who am also poeta, puertorriqueña, needing both love and art, fighting political battles by day and demons by night, I have stood at the brink of that river of sorrows, tempted by oblivion. I live in a far more generous life, created for me by the labor of countless women, thirty years of collective agitation, thirty years of wrestling with the culture and consciousness of women and men. I do not face her terrible choices, the punishments meted out to passionate creative women of her day.

I have both love and work and am not forced to choose. My compañero has passed through the hands of many feminist

women. He delights in my brilliance, eggs me on to excel. I have a
wealth of liberated territories: the women's bookstores, the
presses, the magazines, the shelves of feminist books, of Latinas in
print, the conferences, the networks of solidarity and support, the
classrooms where my work is taught.

As I gaze back through years to that cold and merciless time
and watch Julia, with her glass in her hands, drinking to deaden
her pain, I say this prayer in her honor.

May I never take for granted what we built with such effort.
May I remember to be grateful for what struggle has won me.
May I not forget the brilliant women who died of loneliness; the
poets who were silenced and smothered in roses; the passionate
women who loved unworthy men and could find no road out of
despair, who swallowed sorrow until they sickened, whose bright
rage turned to lead because no one could name it back to them,
who went blind from a lack of mirrors, who were pulled by the cur-
rents of their self-medications and went too far from shore.

1950: Threads—New York, Puerto Rico, Illinois
Side by side in their separate cells, Ethel Rosenberg and Rosa Collazo await their sentences in the House of Detention. At night the
prisoners are allowed into the "living room" to talk among themselves. Ethel knits sweaters and hats for her sons. Rosa talks about
the Jewish grocer down the block who is feeding her daughters on
credit. Ethel has the most beautiful voice and sings for the other
prisoners. She is so generous and warm that everyone loves her, but
with an aching at their hearts. The rumors say that she will go to
the chair. When they sit together, they talk mostly of their children. Their imprisoned husbands. The trusted one who betrayed.
Turning fear into motion, the needles twist threads into something colorful and warm.

Threads also twist and bind in the sewing machines of the

clothing manufacturers. Each new immigrant group in turn enters through this vestibule of America, the clattering din, the cotton dust, the long hours in airless buildings. Everyone passes through here, Jews and Puerto Ricans. My great-grandmother and my grandmother. Leah and Rivieka Sackman, Lola Morales and Lolita Lebrón. Women of the island have poured out of small towns, out of the neighborhoods of San Juan, from the coffee barrios of the mountains and the sugarcane flatlands, and landed in the garment workshops of New York. Lolita sees thread turning on thread, binding one thing to another, and imagines an infinite flag, endless stripes flowing from her needle into the streets. Thinking of Rosa Collazo in prison, she does not yet imagine she will spend twenty-five years missing the taste of garlic and her daughter's face from within a cell. Of all the children, it will be Lolita's who will die. When her son drowns, a cruel prison guard will toss her the newspaper—"something of interest for you on the back page. . . ."

One day Ethel asks Rosa whose case looks more serious, hers or that of the Nationalists, because shooting at the president is no small thing. Rosa has read in the papers that most likely both her husband, Oscar, and she will be executed. Both of us, she says, both cases are bad. Ethel worries about her children, her little sons. Rosa about her daughters. Ruth Reynolds, that Gandhian resister from the Black Hills, was raised turning up the bones of old injustices in the South Dakota soil. She came to Harlem to study pacifism and work for the freedom of India when a Puerto Rican minister challenged her to look closer to home. Swept up in the Nationalist cause, now she, too, is in jail, charged with sedition.

Jane Speed is not in jail right now, but she will be. When Lolita and her comrades open fire in Congress, six years from now, and the crackdown comes, Jane will spend six months in jail, crocheting, thinking of her son. The women in jail braid and unbraid their hair, knit sweaters, make doilies, sew gifts for friends, bind things together that are lasting. They do not let life unravel from their hands.

1950: Stories

How do I tell the story of my young mother in the mountains of Indiera? She is a writer, already telling the events in her own voice. She is my mother: her voice shaped me, lives in me, crosses a border from something that is hers into a living part of me. But who knows exactly where?

I came from an almost unbearable density of stories, thick as the red clay of my barrio. People ask me my name and I say my great-grandmother's grandmother was rebel and a rabbi's wife. I say my great-grandfather seduced a servant and his wife cast her out. They ask where I'm from and I say slaveholders and slaves. I open my mouth and spill stories. My mother says the mix was outside her, in the streets and apartment buildings. I say the mix is in my body. I *am* the mix.

My mother says as a girl she felt new, without history, freshly made. A new-minted child of immigrants among all the rest of the New York 1930s kids whose only question was "Where ya from?" and who answered with their parents' countries of origin—Cuban, Italian, Polish, Irish, Puerto Rican, Russian Jew. My grandmother kept recounting the details of that whole matted web of small-town family ties, obligations, and grudges that was her original world, but my mother didn't listen. It was a coin with no currency. It was when they came to Puerto Rico that she says she landed into people's stories, thousands of them.

So whose tale is it, that they arrive and meet Jane Speed and her family, husband, mother, son, that the FBI follows my father's job-seeking steps and closes all doors, that practical Jane says get land so you can eat, and they do? How do I tell about my mother's shyness and courage, the way she and I both remember how it *felt* to do a thing so much better than the thing we did, and forget the facts of our own boldness?

What our parents tell becomes part of our bones, our gestures, our explanations: that my nineteen-year-old communist parents met, fell in love, and were engaged two weeks later after a lecture on the Woman Question. That they went to Peekskill to hear Paul Robeson, my father as one of the guards, my mother as one of the crowd. I don't recall the dates, but I can smell the sweat of the violent bottle-throwing mob, see the tense shoulders of the young people linking arms to make a fence, hear the earth-moving, rolling depths of Robeson's voice.

I know the exact feel of the wooden park bench in Ithaca where they sat, just married, draft-age and the war newly broken out in Korea, pacifists and reds facing unknown consequences. I can smell the unfurling spring around them in the almost-warm air while they discuss the options and decide to go to Puerto Rico, just for a year, to know her country, study and work, see what comes next.

I can't tell you every detail about my father's arrest in the roundups of 1954, although it's a legend of my house. But I can tell you about my father leaping up when the rain started, to rescue all those diapers almost dry on the line, the police sitting him back down, and how the neighbors saw cops taking in our laundry. How Gregorio Plá shook my father's hand as he was led away, and as soon as they were gone the church women came to sit with my mother and, being used to family arrests for numbers-running, calmly tuned her radio to the right frequency for police news.

I grew up saturated with the lore of that little cluster of organizers living in hard times in a place of incredible beauty and poverty. Jane becoming a Tampax sales rep because when she appeared at country women's houses and stated her purpose, the men fled and she could talk with the women about their lives in peace. My mother helping organize the agricultural extension club that brought women out of their homes and taught them to make tin ovens and group decisions. My father drinking unimaginable amounts of coffee while listening to the men's fears about starting a coffee workers' union.

I grew up walking to school each day past that little wooden house, knowing all about how my mother was newly pregnant and just back from studying biology in San Juan when Papi got hepatitis. How he turned white as paper and she got round as a melon, contented with his nearness, while I spun and floated inside her.

I can't tell my mother's stories, only the shape of my listening, my upturned face in the light of a kerosene lamp with the sound of rain on the roof and the sweet sharp chorus of coquis and her musing voice.

Tell me your mother's story, you ask, and I say there was an orange and white dress, flagrant with huge flowers. My mother wore it all my young years and gave it to me when I was a grown girl, and I never knew until yesterday that it was Jane's dress, lent to my mother when she went back to the island to bury her friend, and that she shocked Jane's sister, my shy, bold mother, by showing up at a time of mourning in cotton the color of flame instead of black.

1953: No nascas—Puerto Rico and the United States

In the countryside, women in white uniforms administer the experimental pills, test out the intrauterine devices, encourage the operation. They are the fingertips of an immense hand reaching out to close around the wombs of Puerto Rican women and stop the children from coming. The colony does not need more workers now. It needs fewer mouths to feed, fewer voices clamoring, fewer ideas, fewer Puerto Ricans. The fist of empire clamps around the fallopian tubes of women and says to the tiny sparks of potential life in their ovaries: No nascas.

She has six children living, the oldest only nine. She has two more in the cemetery. She has piles of laundry to scrub by hand, half a dozen small mouths always hungry for more than she has in her rice pot. His touch is sweet fire in the night, but she turns away. She will have no more swelling in her belly, no more little ones crying for what she doesn't have, no more anguish than she already carries in her heart. She can feel his frustration, his hunger for her edging toward a sullen anger, and weeps dry tears, her own desire imprisoned in fear as she counts the days since last she bled, whispering into the dark: No nascas.

One in five women over twenty have had the operation, have had the tiny passageways of life severed and clamped. After a decade of propaganda it will be one in three. They are still testing other methods. The pill sometimes kills the women in these trials. They tinker with the recipe and keep handing them out. The IUDs cause intolerable cramping, especially in the young. No one tells the women that there are such things as diaphragms. An option that fits in the palm of a woman's hand. The population-planners do not trust women to make the right decisions. They will follow primitive instincts, have unscheduled children, forget their own best interests. Surgery is the method of choice. Surgery is permanent. The policy-makers promote surgery. They misinform, bribe, and coerce. It is not imperial greed that causes hunger, according to their reports. It is that the colonized are too numerous. They say to the unborn generations of us: No nascas.

She is eager for the little knife that will free her from the annual babies her mother and sister bore. She enters the white room happily. Two will have to be enough. She is young still, and maybe in a few years she would have had another, but the nurse says it's the only method that is sure. This little incision will change the shape of her life, open doors, relieve her from ever having to worry again. The nurse hands her a paper to sign and she signs as if it were the deed to a house: her womb. No one has told her she could have kept her options open, used other ways to prevent babies, until she was sure. The staff of the clinic are sure. They say to the last kid she might have had when she got out of school, her newfound power of choice: No nascas.

I am the body of this story. I have tried almost every method. Spent ten days a month in an agony of cramping from the IUD, burned from the chemical gels and foams, felt my cervix turn raw and bleeding from the sponge, struggled with the slippery caps and diaphragms, battled over condoms, charted temperatures and mucous endlessly. Raged at the thought that anyone could invent so sadistic a shape as the Dalkon shield. One day I, too, walk into the clinic. I hold the exterminating grip of empire in one hand, centuries of women counting days in the other. I can hardly bear the cheerful woman behind the desk, how unambiguous it is for her. How she can see nothing in this choice but freedom.

There is no provision in this world for the choice to be easy. Either way, we fight to live. I say to the second child I will never have, I would build a joyous entry, make a home here for you if I could. They have made you unaffordable, pressed us to the wall. I listen to all the echoes, clamoring, cascading, changing the sound of my voice when I say to my unborn child, to the children we cannot bear to bear: No nascas.

1953: The Bad Mother—New York

Now, Ethel, you know the answer to that question of three years ago. Rosa is free, and it turns out that yours is by far the worse, the more serious, case. They have decided to kill Julius. You, too, have been found guilty of giving away the secrets of mass destruction.

The judges must decide what to do with you, a woman, a mother of young boys. Their notions of you are at war within them. A wife. A spy. A woman with children who need her. A cold-hearted, calculating communist. They begin to weigh their prejudices, to argue among themselves over what to do with you, what you deserve. If they could persuade you to be the mother they want us all to be, self-sacrificing to the end, they would let you live. No woman, they believe, really has principles. Surely, for your sons, you will abandon what are, after all, only ideas, make it easy on everyone, turn penitent, agree to go quietly into oblivion.

This is when judgment turns to hate. You will not recant. The lawyers for the prosecution point out that you have been a forceful wife, a pushy, opinionated woman, and now you have proved yourself everything despicable. You will not turn your back on integrity to save your life for motherhood. You presume, they snarl, that your vision of justice is more important than the needs of your growing boys. They tell each other you are a bad wife and mother, and they sentence you to die.

I hear you, Ethel, your heart pounding as you refuse their tainted mercy, telling yourself that you know what you are giving your sons. They will take away the suppers, the hugs, the years of watching them grow, take away your presence by their beds at night and your face in the morning, but this they will not take. As they lead you away to your death, as they strap you into that evil chair, as they put their hands to the switch that will convulse you with electric current, you keep breathing, and with each breath, return the truth of yourself to your sons, your judges, the world.

1953: 105th and Fifth Avenue—New York

On a street corner in Manhattan something has washed up from tumult of a river once blue and sparkling. A shell that no longer echoes the sea, a broken branch, a poet with a mouth full of silence. An anonymous woman, unclaimed at the morgue, buried with the homeless and unnamed of this city.

Don't profane my death with tears, she had written. After a month of searching, friends and relatives will recognize the still face of Julia de Burgos in the police photograph and take her body from Potter's Island to Puerto Rico. She never wanted the flag-draped coffin, the obituaries, and the gravestone. Don't bury me, she had said, in the innocent earth, but leave me free. She imagined herself feeding the fragile worms, tangling perhaps in the roots of blooming orange trees, turning into earth of the earth she loved. I hear her speak of it from the nameless grave: *With what savage joy my bones will begin to open windows through my dark flesh as I give myself fiercely and freely to the elements and break my chains alone.*

1953: Dime Capitán

> *"La canción es una brújula. Si me pierdo me pongo a cantar."* — ROY BROWN

> *"He told me his wife went crazy.*
> *I asked him how he did it."* — MARY MACKEY

When I was a captive child, they took over my hands and made them do their will. Then they came to me and showed me my fingerprints on the crime, saying look what you have chosen to do. You caused this pain. This pain, they said, is who you are. But my hands were stolen, I say now. The fingerprints were mine. The crime was yours.

In this year of 1953, with Julia buried in a nameless pauper's grave, with Ethel's electric death burning fearfully across the newspaper headlines, the two Sylvias are still breathing life into words, but their ends are being manufactured in the women's magazine advice columns, in the shimmering masochism of the movies, in the deadly domesticity of 1950s wifehood. Sylvia Rexach is thirty-two and croons sweet melancholy music on the radio, singing, "Dime capitán, tu que conoces las aguas de este mar ... Tell me, Captain, you who know the waters of this sea, after the storm passes, what will be left upon the calm? An immense emptiness in my arms? Or perhaps a heart broken in pieces?" But the captains have no answers for her pain. They see only the white-capped surfaces where they pleasure-cruise. They have no interest in the deeper waters below. "Soy la arena que la ola nunca toca . . ." sings Sylvia. "I'm the sand that the wave never touches . . ."

Sylvia Plath is twenty-one and hanging to life by a thread from inside the echoing bell jar of her despair. Having attempted suicide, she is receiving shock treatment, electrical jolts to her brain to burn away unpleasantness. She writes of the revenge of the mushrooms, soft-fisted silent invaders pushing up against the weight of the earth. She writes bitter, brilliant poems like shards of glass. In the aftermath of Europe's devastation, she steals meta-phors of more visible anguish, calling men Nazis, calling herself Jewish, putting her head in an oven. She has only ten years left be-fore that grim London winter death. The tropical Sylvia has eight and will die in Santurce at the end of hurricane season, saying there are no more roses in this garden.

Literary men will write about these women's sadness and sui-cide as if it were the greatest poetic achievement of their lives, a glorious celebration of woman's inevitable suffering, an accom-plishment that merely living women must strive to emulate. They will poke among the lyrics looking for evidence that nothing could have been done to save them.

Their fingerprints are everywhere, but I proclaim that these women did not die by their own hands, that their fingers were in captivity, that death was prepared for them by others. That they fell in a brutal decade, murdered in the gender wars, unable to imagine there was solace to be found in the collective rage of women if they could have only waited five or six years, that they were not alone, that there could have been another ending to the song.

1954: Freedom Songs

The simmering begins to bubble and the bubbling to boil. Island racism is more intimate. Puerto Ricans aren't used to segregation, to "white only," to being refused service in restaurants because they are dark. Puerto Rican families listen to the radio and some watch on television, as Black students integrate southern schools through a gauntlet of police dogs and truncheons, and ugly crowds turned violent with threatened privilege. Black and brown soldiers grown accustomed to dignity overseas defy the white owners of lunch counters and bars, refusing to go away. Poor and dark mothers and fathers demand room for their children in the schools of their choice and, for once, the courts back them.

The papers in Puerto Rico report that immigrants contracted by the government to work in the States are angry about Jim Crow. In Chicago, women sent as domestic workers are promised good contracts, reasonable hours, and days off, but find themselves underpaid, on call twenty-four hours a day, and virtual slaves without passage home. In Florida workers in the fruit fields protest that they can't spend their money where they please. Illinois steelworkers are sent to sleep in unheated barracks in winter. Muttering turns to rumbling and breaks at last into defiant song: *Ain't gonna let nobody turn me around* merges into *No nos moverán* and from Mississippi to the barrio ordinary women find themselves capable of more than they knew, as neighbors talking in halls become tenant unions, church women take up picket signs, and la vecina que no habla inglés mouths the unfamiliar words, We shall overcome.

৯MILK THISTLE

Milk Thistle teaches guerrilla warfare. Adaptogen milagrosa, Milk Thistle works with what is here, the yellow layers of toxins, the charcoal grit, the green bile slow as crude oil pooling in the liver's reservoirs, waiting to learn to flow. Milk Thistle says take what you are and use it.

She's a junkyard artist, crafting beauty out of the broken. She's a magician, melting scar tissue into silk. She's a miner, fingering greasy lumps of river clay for emeralds. She can enter the damaged cells of your life and recreate your liver from a memory of health. She can pass her hands over this torn and stained tapestry of memory and show us beauty, make the threads gleam with the promise of something precious gained.

She will not flinch from anything you have done to keep yourself alive. Give it to me, she will say. I will make it into something new. She will show you your courage, hammered to a dappled sheen by use. She will remind you that you took yourself over and over to the edge of what you knew. She will remind you that the world placed limits on your powers. That you were not omnipotent. That some of the choices you made were not choices. Use what you are, she says again and again, insistent. You are every step of your journey, you are everything that has touched you, you are organic and unexpected. Use what you are.

1954: Transition

I am leaving the comfort and constriction of my mother's womb. This is the turbulent passageway of birth. Ancestors crowd around me, giving me advice, shouting last minute instructions about life on earth. I am being pressed, squeezed, strangled with the old things that once nourished me, shedding my skin of watery membrane, pushing through an endless place of panic toward something bright.

Are you with me? We are being pushed forward into power we do not think we know how to use. We are strangling on the old comforts, the contradictory messages, feeling skins that once held us in a moist embrace rip away, leaving our tender surfaces exposed, nerves tingling. We are erupting into our lives, uncertain what we must do there, listening for whatever inside us says yes.

I am being born into the lunch hour of a February day in the year nineteen hundred and fifty-four, into the heart of a century both grim and dazzling. I burst into a room so filled with sound and light that I am temporarily made deaf, my pupils tight against the blaze of sun. Shaken by the world that rushes in on me, at last my ears open and the first sound I hear is water trickling into a metal basin.

Are you here? We are being cut off from the old sources of certainty, watching them shrivel into shreds of rag. We do not bury the birth cord under the house to keep us from wandering. We carry it under our hearts as warning and direction, as company in dark. The noise around us is tremendous. Sometimes we have no idea what we are listening to. Sometimes there is the gift of quiet, and we hear the thin fall of water from a hidden spring. We are messy, we are covered with blood. We want to bathe in that water, but we cannot always find it.

I am being born on an autumn afternoon in nineteen sixty-four in the tangerine grove of Don Bernardo and Doña Luisa where Tita and I have been stealing tangerines. We hold our skirts full of fruit gathered in one hand and, with the other, each tries to hold the strands of barbed wire apart so we can pass through. We can hear that we have been discovered and Don Bernardo is growling threats. Tita is on the outside and I am still in the green shade, heart pounding, my cotton clothing catching on the barbs. "Hurry!" I whisper, frantically, and Tita, still clutching her skirt full of harvest, pulls the strands wider, and pulls me through, and we run, breathless and laughing, up the hill to eat tangerines in the sun.

We pull each other through. We steal sweetness and feed each other segments of our lives, sections of orange flesh bursting with what we are learning how to name. We tell each other stories, lift the strands of wire apart, whispering, "Hurry, you will be captured." We clutch the gathering in our skirts and don't surrender them even when we have to run. We make sunlit moments of laughter.

I am being born, and giving birth, on a scalding hot morning in July of nineteen eighty-eight. I expected to do this and that other sweet and sustaining thing, but birth is raw and unexpected. My mind steps into a blaze of light and I am convulsing on the floor, being whisked to a hospital, wake up strapped and wired to everything in the room. And I rise, plant my naked feet on the slick linoleum floor and my palms on the walls, and summon up power, more naked and unashamed than I have ever known.

We are all laboring. We plan every safeguard for our passage and all of them are useless. We cannot know until we know, what it is we need. We learn that listening to our hungers, each other's and our own, is the only preparation. There is no way to stop it once we begin. We strain and struggle and ask if we can go home now, change our minds. We bear down on possibility and are startled at what we find that we can do.

I am being born on a late summer day in nineteen ninety-six, pushing myself forward through the narrow opening carrying all these voices I have called to me, wrapped in my skirts. Carrying my own voice, leaving behind skins that only hamper me now. I am in transition, pushing myself out of myself. I have left behind the garments of shame. The camouflage of fear. I have taken my hands back from my tormentors. I have stolen as many of our names as I could carry from the orchards of the hacendados. My head is crowning. Can you see me coming? Are you with me?

Our voices pour like waters breaking, gushing from our vientres. Like the tough and nourishing roots of dandelions shoving stalks upward through cracks in pavement, we push our stubborn heads through the small spaces of windows barely ajar. We find our way into rooms that were always reserved for others and pick up everything we can use. Our loudness echoes off the walls. We pull each other past the sharp teeth of danger, lift each other's faces into the light. We break the membrane over our mouths and begin to breathe on our own. We are pushing into history, we are coming out of the corners, we are gathering our spirits, we are taking up the challenge, we are living in this heartbeat, we are deciding, (are you ready?) venga lo que venga, to be born.

Aché

LA BOTÁNICA (SOURCES)

Welcome to la botánica, where every ingredient used in *Remedios* is to be found somewhere on a shelf or in a box in the storage room in the back. If you want to know exactly what spice I use to season a particular story, want to put in a special order for additional names and dates, want to track an especially juicy bit of historical gossip to the person who heard the person who heard the one who was actually there, then follow me. (The names of suppliers are in the back, in the alphabetical bibliography.) Step carefully over those boxes of candles, the case of oils and incense, and duck your head so you don't get twigs in your hair from that big bunch of medicine I hung from the water pipe to dry. This way to the storeroom.

In the cupboard marked "las viejas" I have everything I gathered about the "Bisabuelas" and the "Abuelas," but first let me show you this shoe box marked "Yerba Buena" that's propped up on top.

YERBA BRUJA

YERBA BRUJA
There are many places to find out more about what was going on in Europe, Western Asia, and North Africa just before Columbus.

Some of the general works I drew on for this piece were *Lost Tribes and Promised Lands* by Ronald Sanders, *Europe and the People Without History* by Eric Wolf, and *Africa in History* by Basil Davidson.

REVISION

This piece came from reading one history book too many in which women appeared only in the footnotes. It draws from many sources, including Enriqueta Vila Vilar's *Historia de Puerto Rico, 1600–1650*; Angel Lopez Cantos's *Historia de Puerto Rico, 1650–1700*; Fernando Picó's *Historia General de Puerto Rico*; and *La esclavitud urbana en San Juan* by Mariano Negrón Portillo and Raúl Mayo Santiago.

BISABUELAS

So . . . on to the cupboard of Las Viejas. When you open the left door, there are shelves of old bones and red earth, leaves and stones. There are beautifully painted bowls and curved knives with stained blades, clusters of dried dates and a red and gold ear of corn, a digging stick and one for walking. This is the abode of the bisabuelas, the oldest ones.

"Gingko" is an herb that's good for your brain. It helps restore memory, increase concentration, and prevent strokes, *and* it's been around since dinosaurs. Who better to witness la primera madre? References for all the herb pieces are at the end of this guided tour.

"First Mother" came to me after I saw a documentary about her on *Nova* and demanded I put her in this book right at the beginning, since Africa is where everything started. I also read a somewhat confusing book called *The Hominid Gang* by Delta Willis that talks about all the científicos who are trying to figure out where we came from.

WOMEN OF YAMS

Everything in this section except the herb pieces and "Colors" came from Basil Davidson's *Africa in History*. "Colors" came from my imagination. "Wild Yam" is a powerful herb that has natural progesterone in it and is very nourishing to the stressed out. Related varieties of yams are a big part of the West African diet, which may contribute to their high incidence of twins. "Banana Peel" I learned about from my naturopath, Valerie Long. We tried it on my daughter's warts and they vanished.

WOMEN OF BREAD

"The Deer Mother," "The Peaceful Land," "Pig Mother," and "Mare's Milk" all came from Marija Gimbutas's groundbreaking archaeological work on ancient Europe *The Civilization of the Goddess*. "Deserts" comes from Davidson's *Africa in History*. "Cutting" is taken from *The Hosken Report: Genital and Sexual Mutilation of Females* by Fran Hosken. "Moriviví" and "Scars" came from my own life. I also drew ideas for the latter piece from Nancy Jay's fascinating work on the origins of sacrifice, *Throughout Your Generations Forever*.

WOMEN OF YUCA

"Pikimachay," "Potatoes," "Rainforest," "Corn," "Temples," and "City Girls" came from *The Atlas of Ancient America* and from *Atlas of the North American Indian*. "Turtle Women, Women of Trees" drew from José Juan Arrom's *Mitología y artes prehispánicas de las Antillas* and Mercedes Lopez Baralt's *El mito taíno: Levi-Strauss en las antillas*. "Tobacco" came from my personal experience with ritual.

ABUELAS

On the right side of the cabinet are shelves full of richly carved boxes, rolls of patterned cloth, a curve of ivory, the whiff of pepper. There are bundles of the bright feathers of tropical birds and letters in fading ink, lamps fragrant with oil, and pieces of charred cloth. Welcome to the home of the abuelas.

West African Women

All of the pieces in this section began with Basil Davidson's *Africa in History*. For "Not All Tribes Build Upward Toward the Sky" I was also inspired by Ifi Amadiume's work *Afrikan Matriarchal Foundations: The Igbo Case*. In "People, Pepper, Ivory, Gold" I wrote from many years of reading about early European-African relations, in addition to the details in Davidson's work. "Market Women" was also based on information in *African Women*, edited by Hay and Stichter, and from *The Black Women Cross-Culturally*, edited by Filomina Chioma Steady.

American Women

"Mayas" came from reading too many articles that uncritically celebrated Mayan temples and kings, and from Clive Ponting's excellent and comprehensive book *A Green History of the World*. "Against the Knife" sprang from a short section on the Toltecs in *Atlas of the North American Indian*. The information in "Caciques" that class hierarchy and patriarchy were intensifying in the Caribbean before the Spanish arrived comes from the works of Francisco Moscoso, including *Tribu y clases en el Caribe antiguo* and an earlier article, "Tributo y formación de clases en la sociedad de los taínos de las Antillas." I was also inspired by reading about the historical connections between the sacrifice of widows and the rise of patriarchy and class hierarchy in India, in Anand A. Yang's article "Whose Sati? Widow Burning in Early 19th Century India" and a similar connection among Mayans in *Women's Responses to Colonialist Domination: The Reproduction of Pre-Conquest Cultures in the Domestic Sphere*, a paper given by June Nash at a conference on *Rediscovering the Americas: Women in the Building of the New World,* held at SUNY Albany in November 1992.

"Bone and Hair and Shard" was born from my sorrow as I sorted through the fragmentary knowledge of archaeology for stories to tell that would link us to ancestors we know so little of. Names of peoples and details about their cultures come from the two atlases I used, *Atlas of Ancient America* by Benson, Snow, and Coe, and *Atlas of North American Indians* by Carl Waldman.

MEDITERRANEAN WOMEN

All the stories in "Arabian Nights" came from Leila Ahmed's *Women and Gender in Islam*, a rich and informative book looking at a broad span of time and geography with a very clear gaze. I learned about the agricultural cycles of work in medieval Spain in "Bread, Oil, Wine" from *El trabajo de las mujeres en la Edad Media hispana,* an extremely useful collection of articles that also gave me the material for "Juderías" and "Working Santiago de Compostela," and from *Butler's Lives of the Saints*. I also read *Santiago de Compostela: In the Age of Great Pilgrimages* by Marilyn Stokstad.

The "Poets of al-Andalus" I discovered in *Diwan de las poetisas de al-Andalus* by Teresa Garulo. To write "Fire at the Gates," I learned about the other side of the Crusades by reading Amin Maalouf's *The Crusades Through Arab Eyes*, a fascinating collection of medieval Arab accounts of the Crusades, put into context with short essays by Maalouf. "Olive Oil" is used to lubricate childbirth and make all kinds of salves and ointments. Olive oil can carry medicinal properties of herbs into hard-to-reach corners of our bodies. From this knowledge I dreamed up a personality for her. "Pomegranates" are a symbol of fertility and joy in Jewish tradition. I belong to a Jewish feminist earth-based spiritual community called Pardes Rimmonim, or Orchard of Pomegranates, and this piece was inspired in part by my friends there.

PREMONITIONS

"1478: Unfortunate Isles" was picked up from the works of Francisco Morales Padrón, especially *Canarias en America*, and from the chapter entitled "The Fortunate Isles" in *Ecological Imperialism: The Biological Expansion of Europe, 900–1900* by Alfred Crosby. "1482: Elmina Castle" came out of Basil Davidson's book and many readings and films over the years about the horrors of the slave forts on Africa's west coast. "1487: Malleus Maleficarum" was taken from *Witchcraze* by Ann Barstow and from the film *The Burning Time*. "1490: Stolen Women" came from years of reading and had many sources, including "The Traffic in Women" by Gayle Rubin, which appears in *Towards an Anthropology of Women*, edited by Rayna Reiter. "Bad Dreams: The Prophets" was inspired by widespread stories of indigenous premonitions about the coming of the Europeans to the Americas, some of which appear in Eduardo Galeano's *Genesis*. "Guabancex Stirs the Pot" is my own fantasy, based on tidbits in Arrom's *Arte y mitología prehispanica de las Antillas.* "Calendars" involved some encyclopedia research and a strong personal revulsion to using A.D., B.C., B.C.E. and C.E. as equally Eurocentric Christian-based measurements of time. "Discovery" was made from my own experiences intertwined with details of the history of the Spanish invasion taken from an artist's edition of Oviedo's chronicles called *The Conquest of Puerto Rico* and illustrated by Jack and Irene Delano.

HURACÁN, 1492–1599

Oh, this cupboard over here is all helter-skelter. Open these intricately carved doors and you'll find such a pile of broken pottery and weapons, unfinished weavings and gilt-edged manuscripts, a jumble of medicines and disasters, broken hearts and wild moments of possibility, and more blood and suffering than you'd ever want to see. To go into this box, you need to start out with this bottle of "Bitters" or you'll never be able to stand it. "Penetration" is a bloody cloth on the bottom shelf, but it has stained the wood. It was taken from my body and from the histories of all wars and conquests and from Ricardo Herren's *Conquista erotica de las Indias*. This old iron key, this "Lamento sefardita," comes from many stories of the departure of the Jews from Spain, which I have gleaned from books, family stories of Sephardic friends, and films about Sephardim and conversos, including sections of Cecil Roth's *Doña Gracia*. "Romero," or Rosemary, is an herb used for memory and clearheadedness.

When I wrote "1493 to 1511: Leyendas—Puerto Rico" I was inspired first by an article written by Beth Brant, called "Grandmothers of a New World," which included a very different perspective on Pocahontas than the "Indian maiden" of popular culture mythology. I was also inspired by Chicana feminist revisions of the story of Malinche, including the Marina poems of Lucha Corpi and in conversations over the years. Women like Malinche, Pocahontas, and Guanina have been stripped of their dignity, intelligence, and common sense in both the stories of conquest and many of the machista stories of resistance. They were neither naive damsels dazzled by the new boys in town, nor unprincipled traitors looking for advantage in the beds of conquerors, but savvy and powerful women negotiating their way through extreme difficulties. The characters of Agueybana and his followers were drawn from the behavior of real live guys I've encountered—you know who you are and so do my sisters.

I ran across "La Marcaida," Cortés's first wife in several biographies of Cortés and then followed up with *Un crimen de Hernán Cortés: La muerte de doña Catalina Xuarez Marcaida* by Alfonso Toro. The "Manikongo Affonso" appears in Davidson's *Africa in History.* The information in "1515: Toa" came from three main sources: Jalil Sued Badillo's *La mujer indígena en su sociedad* and his article "Las cacicas indoantillanas," and from *Documentos de la real hacienda de Puerto Rico*, compiled by Aurelio Tanodi.

"Piñones" is my putting a woman's voice to the story of the Piñon family in Sued Badillo and Angel Lopez Cantos's book *Puerto Rico Negro.* Marilyn Waring's book *If Women Counted: A New Feminist Economics* provided me with profound insights into the value of women's unpaid labor, how it upholds and makes profitable the work of men and how it is erased from our awareness. "1515: Shopping" also came from *Puerto Rico Negro* and comes from an actual list of purchases made by the Piñones in 1515.

"Plátano" comes from general readings in food history, including *Food* by Waverley Root and a note in one of the many general histories of Puerto Rico that I read, stating that a priest introduced plátano to Puerto Rico through the port at the Toa River in 1515. "Naborías" comes once again from Sued Badillo's works on indigenous women, from a list of women branded as slaves by Ponce de León.

There are many different accounts of the smallpox epidemics that swept the Americas. "The Speckled Death" is taken from several of them, including those in Carl Sauer's *The Early Spanish Main,* Alfred Colby's *Ecological Imperialism*, and *Dangerous Memories: Invasion and Resistance Since 1492* by the Chicago Religious Task Force on Central America. "Alegría" came out of my need to lighten things up a little in a century full of bad news and remember what keeps people going.

"Snakeskin," my version of the Malinche story, is taken from years of discussions with my Chicana sisters; from the poems of Lucha Corpi; Jerome Adams's *Latin American Heroes*; *Doña Marina Malintzin nació en el antiguio reino de Xalisco*, an old book by Gabriel Agraz Garcia de Alba located at the Bancroft library in Berkeley; and from my own invaded, colonized, rebellious, and many-tongued mestiza psyche.

"Conejo's Brothel" was brewed up from an entry in Federico Ribes Tovar's *Historia cronologica de Puerto Rico* about the opening of this brothel in San Juan, Verena Stolcke's article "Conquered Women" about how church and state tried to control sexuality and racial intermixture, information on the regulation of prostitution in Europe from Anderson and Zinsser's *A History of Their Own*, and Cynthia Enloe's work on prostitution and its role in maintaining military prowess in *Bananas, Beaches, and Bases: Making Feminist Sense of International Politics*.

I was inspired to write "Slave Mothers" after reading Jack Forbes's book *Africans and Native Americans*, which spoke of the enslavement of American peoples, and details in Sued Badillo's work about women from the Lesser Antilles who were slaves in Puerto Rico. "Limpieza" came from Verena Stolcke, Forbes's book, and James Blaut's excellent book *The Colonizer's Model of the World*. I wrote "Conversas at the Stake" after reading a chapter by Jaime Contreras in Betsy Perry and Anne Cruz's book *Culture and Control in Counter-Reformation Spain*, entitled "Aldermen and Judaizers: Cryptojudaism, Counter-Reformation, and Local Power." "Calendula" is an herb that is miraculous for healing burns, and I thought we could all use some at this point.

"Jigonsaseh" leaped out at me from the pages of a special edition of *Northeast Indian Quarterly* entitled *Indian Roots of Ameri-*

can Democracy. Her story was told by Peter Jemison, site director of the Historical Site at Gonandagan, where Jigonsaseh lived. "Indiera" was born of a few lines scattered here and there in Iñigo Abbad's *Historia geográfica, civil y natural de la isla de San Juan Bautista de Puerto Rico*, written at the end of the 1700s, and *Las encomiendas y esclavitud de los indios de Puerto Rico* by Eugenio Fernandez Mendez.

"Doña Gracia" came to me in Cecil Roth's biography of the same name, which details her life story in the context of the whole history of the expulsion of Spanish and Portuguese Jews and the new communities that were formed in the Low Countries and around the Mediterranean. "Teresa de Avila Counts Demons" was inspired by reading Alison Weber's piece "St. Teresa, Demonologist," in the Perry/Cruz anthology *Culture and Control in Counter-Reformation Spain*. "Flames" was taken from accounts in *Heterodoxia e inquisicion en Santo Domingo* by Carlos Deive and other general works on the Inquisition in the Americas.

What a tangle of silk threads and acrid smoke, captivity, invasion, overwhelming loss and unbridled greed, hope and despair. Close the carved cupboard gently on this century. It still has the power to leap out and fill our nostrils five hundred years later, and nothing in here has been resolved! Those ashes still smoulder.

JENJIBRE

This plain wooden chest over here, smelling of dried ginger, this is the one to look into next. Ginger gives courage, and there's plenty of it to be found here. "Catalina Steals Away," "S/he," and "Veracruz" are all taken from the life of Catalina Erauso. I first read about her in *Españolas en indias: mujeres-soldado, adelantadas y gobernadoras* by Carmen Pumar Martinez. It was only a short entry, but it intrigued me. I also read about her in more depth in Elizabeth Perry's *Gender and Disorder in Early Modern Seville* and finally in the newest edition of her autobiography, edited by Michele and Gabriel Stepto, *Lieutenant Nun: Memoir of a Basque Transvestite in the New World*.

The twin works by Enriqueta Vila Vilar and Angel Lopez Cantos, *Historia de Puerto Rico, 1600–1650* and *Historia de Puerto Rico, 1650–1700*, respectively, provided background information on this whole century and details that I used to write "Caribes," "Wild West," "Gingerbread," "Ana de Mendoza," "Playa Boqueron," "The House of Peace," and "Decree." *Los caribes* by Sued Badillo also contributed to the first of these pieces. "Wild West" and "Playa Boqueron" were enriched by reading *Los holandeses en el Caribe* by Cornelio Goslinga, Arturo Morales Carrión's *Puerto Rico and the Non-Hispanic Caribbean: A Study in the Decline of Spanish Exclusivism*, and an M.A. thesis by Hector Feliciano Ramos, "El contrabando ingles en el Caribe y el Golfo de Mexico 1748–1778."

"A Seed Falls in Pernambuco" and "The Death of Palmares" were taken from accounts of the escaped slave kingdom of Palmares in Richard Price's *Maroon Societies*. The versions of Queen Nzinga's story that I used for both "Nzinga's Stool" and "Nzinga, the Warrior Queen," came from David Sweetman's excellent little book *Women Leaders in African History*, with background, once more, from Basil Davidson. "Manahatta" and "Stuyvesant" came from the *Atlas of North American Indians* and *The Historical Atlas of New York*. I got "The Weavers of Dean" from *In Contempt of All Authority: Rural Artisans and Riot in the West of England, 1586–1660* by Buchanan Sharp, about bread riots and other uprisings among English weavers. "I Believe It Is No Sin" was taken from an inspiring paper presented by Allyson Poska at the Berkshire Women's History Conference in June of 1996, entitled *Sexuality and Moral Power in Early Modern Spain.* I found "Paula de Eguiluz" hidden in the pages of *Hetrodoxia e inquisicion en Santo Domingo* by Carlos Deive. "Llantén," or plantain, is a very common roadside herb used to treat cancer and heal wounds. "News of Sor Juana" came from *Feminist Perspectives on Sor Juana*, edited by Stephanie Merrim, and from *Reply to Sor Filotea*, by Sor Juana herself.

"The Weavers of Tayasal" came from a brief mention of the "final" defeat of the Mayans at Tayasal in the *Atlas of Ancient America* and from hearing June Nash's paper *Women's Responses to Colonialist Domination: The Reproduction of Pre-Conquest Cultures in the Domestic Sphere.* As for "Jenjibre," I drank many cups of ginger tea as I wrote this book and can testify to how invigorating it is.

PARTERAS

This small trunk is made of pine and ausubo, mahogany and capa prieto, cut rough and planed smooth. It is fastened with an iron clasp, and the wood has burn marks here and there. Welcome to the eighteenth century.

"The Forests Sail East" is taken from Clive Ponting's *A Green History of the World.* "White Pine" was prescribed by my naturopath in the form of the potent bioflavonoid pycnogynol. I also learned about White Pine's effectiveness for coughs and colds from Ida Wright, with whom I took a medicinal plants tutorial in college in the early 1970s. "The Country of Women" is based on a story told to my brother Ricardo by Pedro Matos, a community elder in Utuado. "Beatrice of Kongo" comes from David Sweetman's *Women Leaders in African History.* "Cangrejos" is from entries for 1714 and 1772 in *Historia cronológica de Puerto Rico* by Federico Ribes Tovar. "Cecilia Ortiz" was my ancestor. I learned about her in the parochial archives of Toa Alta. "Nannytown" is based on accounts of Nanny of the Windward Maroons of Jamaica in Richard Price's *Maroon Societies* and in Lucille Mathurin's *The Rebel Woman in the British West Indies During Slavery.* "The First Cafeto" is drawn from Luis Pumareda O'Neill's *La industria cafetalera de Puerto Rico, 1736–1969*. Fernando Pico's *Amargo café*, and Guillermo Baralt's *Yauco, O las minas de oro cafetaleras, 1756–1898*. "Many-Headed Hydra" was taken from an article called "The Many-Headed Hydra: Sailors, Slaves, and the Atlantic Working Class in the Eighteenth Century," by Marcus Rediker and Peter Linebaugh in *Gone to Croatan: Origins of North American Dropout Culture,* edited by Ron Sakolsky and James Koehnline. "Escapees" recounts the story of a slave escape found in Neville Hall's *Slave Society in the Danish West Indies.* Information for "The Song of the Forest" was taken from a doctoral dissertation by Juan Gonzalez Mendoza, "The Parrish of San German de Auxerre in Puerto Rico, 1765–1850: Patterns of Settlement and Development." "If Iñigo Had a Sister" is fiction, based on Fray Iñigo Abbad y Lasierra's *Historia geográfica, civil y natural de la isla de San Juan Bautista de Puerto Rico* and inspired by Virginia Woolf's essay "A Room of One's Own," in which she explores the life of Shakespeare's fictitious sister. The names and dates in "Párbulos" are taken from the parish records of Yauco for 1786 and from conversations with my father, Richard Levins, about causes of death among the poor. The account of the Le Jeune Case that I used in "Reverse Slavery" came from *The Black Jacobins* by C. L. R. James.

I learned about the medicinal and poisonous properties of "Anamú" from a book on Afro-Brazilian herb lore by Maria Thereza L. de Arruda Camargo, called *Plantas medicinais e de rituais afro-brasileiros,* and from María Dolores Hajosy Benedetti's work *Hasta los baños te curan: Remedios caseros y mucho más de Puerto Rico.*

LAZOS

"Melao," or Molasses, is produced by boiling down sugarcane juice and is rich in iron. The apprehension of slaveholders and the excitement of slaves in response to the Haitian Revolution are well-known. "News from Haiti" was based on mention of these reactions in Guillermo Baralt's *Esclavos rebeldes: Conspiraciones y sublevaciones en Puerto Rico (1795–1873)* and Benjamín Nistal Moret's *Esclavos prófugos y cimarrones: Puerto Rico 1770–1870*. The names and biographical details about the "War Widows" came from "La Inmigración de Mujeres Españolas a Puerto Rico en el Periodo Colonial Español" by Rosa Santiago Marazzi. "Yerba Buena" is a common name for many varieties of mint.

"Maestra Cordero" comes from Jack Delano's book *In Search of Maestro Cordero* and from a biographical sheet in the vertical files of the Sala Luisa Capetillo at the University of Puerto Rico in Cayey. "We Treated Them Well" was drawn from conversations with my family, from the birth and marriage registers in the parish archives of Toa Alta, and from a number of works on slave resistance in Puerto Rico, especially Guillermo Baralt's *Esclavos rebeldes: Conspiraciones y sublevaciones en Puerto Rico (1795–1873)* and Benjamín Nistal Moret's *Esclavos prófugos y cimarrones: Puerto Rico 1770–1870*.

"Runaways" refers to laws passed in 1824 punishing those who gave shelter to runaway slaves or to "free" women living separately from husbands, fathers, or other male guardians.

"Flora Tristan Reads in Bed," "Voyages," and "Some Lives Burn Like Quick Flame" all deal with the life of French-Peruvian feminist Flora Tristán. The main sources for information about her were *Flora Tristán, Utopian Feminist: Her Travel Diaries and Personal Crusade*, by Doris and Paul Beik; *The Feminism of Flora Tristan* by Maire Cross and Tim Gray; and Magda Portal's *Flora Tristan, precursora*.

"Maria Bibiana Writes" was drawn entirely from *Los silencios de María Bibiana Benitez* by María Arrillaga. A few details of "Maria Barbanera's" life were in the parish registers of Toa Alta and Naranjito. Some of the ways in which women bought freedom are also in *La esclavitud urbana en San Juan* by Mariano Negrón Portillo and Raúl Mayo Santiago. "Autos de Anti-Fe" is taken from Jaime Vicens Vives's *Approaches to the History of Spain*.

"Yellow Dock" is a remedy for anemia. Information on the impact of anemia on women's health, particularly women in the coffee regions, came from two master's theses: Evelyn Echevarría Echevarría's "La muerte nuestra de cada día: Pobreza y mortandad en Aguada, 1912–1942," and Rafael Lebrón Rivera's "Detengamos el jinete de la muerte: La plaga blanca ante un pueblo enfermo: La lucha por controlar la tuberculosis en Puerto Rico, 1900–1940."

"Campos de soledad" was drawn from the introduction of *The Defiant Muse: Hispanic Feminist Poems from the Middle Ages to the Present*, by Kate and Angel Flores, and from an interview with my great-uncle Florencio Moure about his great-grandparents who were from Ferrol, Galicia.

Background for "Francisca Brignoni" came from *El grito de Lares: sus causas y sus hombres* by Olga Jimenez de Wagenheim. Francisca Brignoni is mentioned briefly in one of the many accounts of the Lares uprising.

"The Freedwomen Contract Themselves" came from a footnote in *La esclavitud urbana en San Juan* by Mariano Negrón Portillo and Raúl Mayo Santiago.

"Tortures" was originally about the human rights work of Lola Rodriguez de Tió until I heard a speaker on the radio deliver an inspiring talk about Ida B. Wells. Unfortunately, the speaker was not identified before I had to turn off the radio. I then consulted *The Memphis Diary of Ida B. Wells*, *Lynching and the Excuse for It*, and *Crusade for Justice: The Autobiography of Ida B. Wells*.

"Damas" is taken from Yamila Azize's *Luchas de la mujer en*

Puerto Rico, 1898–1919; Maria L. Angelis's *Mujeres puertorrique-ñas*; and *Mujeres de Puerto Rico, desde el periodo de colonización hasta el primer tercio del Siglo 20* by Angela Negrón Muñoz. "Char-cas, or the True Story of Café au Lait," comes from information found in Guillermo Baralt's *Yauco, O las minas de oro cafetaleras, 1756–1898*; Laird W. Bergad's *Coffee and the Growth of Agrarian Capitalism in Nineteenth-Century Puerto Rico; Amargo café* by Fer-nando Picó; *La industria cafetalera de Puerto Rico, 1736–1969*, by Luis Pumareda O'Neill; and Cafetal adentro: una historia de los trabajadores agrícolas en el Puerto Rico del siglo 19 by Fernando Picó.

"Mercedes a caballo" is taken from an interview with my great-uncle Florencio Moure and from *Periodismo patriotico de Evaristo Izcoa Díaz* by Victor M. Gil de Rubio. "Luisa in Love" comes from Norma Valle Ferrer's *Luisa Capetillo: Historia de una mujer proscrita*. "Guabancex Again" is my own summary of the tempes-tuous turn of the century.

AGUACERO

"Ghost Dancing" was taken primarily from Arthur Amchan's bi-ography of Nelson Miles, *The Most Famous Soldier in America*, and Carl Waldman's *Atlas of North American Indians*. I also con-sulted *Yellowstone Command: Colonel Nelson A. Miles and the Great Sioux War, 1876–1877*, by Jerome A. Greene; George Wil-liam Baird's limited edition work, *A report to the citizens, concern-ing certain late disturbances on the western frontier involving Sitting Bull, Crazy Horse, Chief Joseph and Geronimo, opposed in the field by forces under the command of General Nelson A. (Bear-Coat) Miles*; and *Harper's Pictorial History of the War with Spain*, with an introduction by Major General Nelson A. Miles.

"Civilization" came from the account of the partition of Africa in Davidson's *Africa in History*. "The Death Train" was extracted from the doctoral dissertation of Ron Arroyo, who conducted oral history interviews with Hawaiian Puerto Ricans and generously shared his work with me. "Postcards of Colonialism" was based on a talk and slide show given by Kelvin Santiago at the Berkshire Conference on Women and History in 1993 entitled *"Just Like a Woman": The Spanish-American War and the Construction of Puerto Rico as Feminized Space* and on stereographs from the collection of the Library of Congress. "La otra Aurora" is based on interviews with various members of my mother's family. "Ruda" is an abortant and is also worn behind the ear or placed over a doorway for protection against bad luck and enemies.

"Lessons" is taken from two works by Lydia Milagros Gonzalez, "Tras el mundillo de la aguja" and *Una puntada en el tiempo: La industria de la aguja en Puerto Rico (1900–1929)*. "Opiniones" is a personal response to the life of Luisa Capetillo, based on her biography *Luisa Capetillo: Historia de una mujer proscrita*, by Norma Valle Ferrer, and a selection of her writing, *Amor y anarquía: Los escritos de Luisa Capetillo*, edited by Julio Ramos.

I first read of the death of "Delmira" in Eduardo Galeano's *Century of Wind*. I also read *Pasion y gloria de Delmira Agustini; su vida y su obra* and *Genio y figura de Delmira Agustini*, both by Clara Silva, and *Delmira Agustini* by Ofelia M. B. Benvenuto. "War Effort," "Lavanderas," and "Vida Alegre" were all taken from a master's thesis by José F. Monroig, *Con novedad en la retaguardia puertorriquena: Trabajo, mujeres e iglesias durante la primera guerra mundial*. "Maguey" was once used to treat the sores and other symptoms caused by syphilis. Renée Samson Flood's book *Lost Bird of Wounded Knee: Spirit of the Lakota* was the source for "Lost Bird." "Harlem" comes from family stories and *This Was Harlem, 1900–1950*, by Jervis Anderson. I found information for "Tuberculosis" in Rafael Lebrón Rivera's master's thesis, *Detengamos el jinete de la muerte: La plaga blanca ante un pueblo enfermo:*

La lucha por controlar la tuberculosis en Puerto Rico, 1900–1940.
"Mullein" was used to treat tuberculosis before antibiotics were
available. "Pasodoble" came from an interview with my grandmother, Aurora Moure Díaz.

   "Journey" and "Jane Speed Bookstore" came from interviews
with my parents, from photographs of Jane Speed's bookstore
given to me by Marge Franz, and from Robin Kelley's *Hammer
and Hoe: Alabama Communists During the Great Depression.*
"Hechos desconocidos" was based on a video of the same title by
Yamila Azize and Luis Alberto Aviles, their article "Los hechos desconocidos: Participación de la mujer en las Profesiones de Salud
en Puerto Rico (1898–1930)," and interviews with my grandmother, Aurora Moure Díaz.

DERRUMBE

"El Barrio" came from interviews with my abuela. "Tiempo
muerto" was taken from *La muerte nuestra de cada día: Pobreza y
mortandad en Aguada, 1912–1942*, a master's thesis by Evelyn
Echevarría Echevarría. "Malanga" comes from a childhood
among undernourished neighbors. "Pura Belpré" was based on
information in her papers at the Center for Puerto Rican Studies.
"Needleworkers" comes mostly from family stories. "Bread upon
the Waters" was taken from both the autobiography and a biography of Rose Pesotta. The first is *Bread upon the Waters*, published
in 1944. The second is *The Gentle General: Rose Pesotta, Anarchist
and Labor Organizer* by Elaine Leeder.

   "Julia in Naranjito," "Julia Drinks a River of Sorrow," and
"105th and Fifth Avenue" were taken mostly from literary and
biographical information about Julia de Burgos in *Julia de Burgos*,
edited by Manuel de la Puebla, and *Cronologia de Julia de Burgos*
by Edgar Martinez Masdeu. "Naranja" is good for stomach prob-

lems, and the crushed leaves are helpful for carsickness and other forms of nausea. "Madre patria" is a personal opinion. "Wartime at the PO" was based on a conversation I had with a woman I met on an airplane who had served as a censor during World War II and on information from Altagracia Ortiz's "The Lives of Pioneras: Bibliographic and Research Sources on Puerto Rican Women in the United States."

"The Ghetto Comes to the Barrio" is taken from interviews with my father, Richard Levins, about his aunt Eva Levins, who lived next door to Puerto Rican communist journalist Jesús Colón, and about his own memories of hearing about the Warsaw Ghetto Uprising, from a column by Jesús Colón entitled "The Jewish People and Us," which appears in *The Way It Was and Other Writings*, edited by Edna Acosta-Belén and Virginia Sanchez Korrol, and from my mother's memories of her relationships with Jewish neighbors in New York in the 1930s and 40s. "Nuestra guerra" also comes from my mother's memories of growing up in New York City during the war and from my father's memories of returning soldiers' responses to racism.

"Threads" was put together from *Memorias de Rosa Collazo*, edited by her daughter Lydia Collazo Cortés; from Ruth Reynold's papers at the Center for Puerto Rican Studies at Hunter College; from a paper presented by Blanca Vasquez at the Puerto Rican Studies Association conference of September 1996, entitled *Ruth Reynolds: A North American in the Nationalist Movement*; and from interviews with my parents, Rosario Morales and Richard Levins, about the life of Jane Speed de Andreu. "Stories" also came from interviews with my parents.

"No nascas" is based on information from the film *La operacion*, from discussions among reproductive rights activists, and from personal experience. "The Bad Mother" is loosely based on a panel chaired by Marge Franz at the 1993 Berkshire Conference on Women and History, entitled *Red Girls, Bad Girls*. I believe the information that Ethel Rosenberg's sentencing was partially based on a perception that her political commitments made her a bad wife and mother emerged during open discussion, but it may also have been contained in a paper entitled *The Bride of Stalin: Gender and Anti-Communism During the Cold War*, whose author I neglected to note at the time and have as yet been unable to trace.

"Dime Capitán" was taken from liner notes on an album of Silvia Rexach's music and Janet Malcolm's biography of Sylvia Plath, *The Silent Woman: Sylvia Plath and Ted Hughes*. "Freedom Songs" comes from interviews with my father. "Milk Thistle" is an adaptogen, an herb that helps the body adapt to stress, and is a very potent detoxifier for the liver. "Transition" is autobiographical.

GLOSSARY OF SELECTED WORDS

aguacero heavy downpour

ají sweet and hot Puerto Rican pepper

algarrobo tropical tree

asopao de almejas asopao: a rice stew made with chicken or seafood; almejas: clams

ausubo tropical hardwood tree

bacalaitos codfish fritters made from dry salt cod or bacalao

basta ya "enough already"

bisabuela great-grandmother

bohio palm thatched house made by the Arawak people, later used for small rural houses

Boriken Arawak name for the island of Puerto Rico

budín pudding

cacica or cacique Arawak leaders (women were cacicas, men caciques); different levels of cacique had different degrees of political power

cafetal Coffee "grove" or planting

canela cinnamon

capa prieto tropical hardwood tree

capitanes pobladores title given to landed citizens who were granted permission to found a new town

colmado grocery store

comida criolla "creole food," or traditional Puerto Rican cuisine.

criolla creole, meaning, during the Spanish colonial period, something pertaining to Puerto Rico or the other colonies as opposed to Spain; those born in Puerto Rico; native

derrumbe mud slide

encomienda system of forced labor set up by the Spanish in America

este vaise i aquel vaise "this one goes and that one goes and all of them, all of them go . . . "

finca farm

gente folks, people

guayacán tropical medicinal tree; the bark was used for syphilis

guineo banana

guingambo okra and also stews or gumbos made with it

hechos desconocidos "unknown facts"; also the title of a 1929 book on health care in Puerto Rico.

jengibre ginger

jíbara indigenous word now used to mean poor country people, especially from the mountains; sometimes derogatory, as in "hick," and sometimes a term of pride.

jubileo pension

la cancion es una brujula "Song is a compass. When I get lost I start singing . . ."

lucha struggle

manikongos rulers among the people of Kongo

manzanillo chamomile

mofongo dish made of fried green plantain and salt pork

naborías laboring class in Arawak society

ninfa nymph

no nascas do not be born

pa'lante "forward!" (a political slogan equivalent to "onward!")

palo mora tropical hardwood tree

parcela, parcelita a parcel of land, a small plot

pasodoble the two-step

pimienta black pepper

plátano plantain

sancocho a stew made with root vegetables and meat

sunnis rulers of the state of Songhai in West Africa

tipos types, characters

tostones fried plantain

vida alegre literally "the happy life," used to mean prostitution

vientre belly

viudas de vivos e mortos widows of the living and the dead

MEDICINE CABINET

I have studied herbal medicine for many years and accumulated knowledge from many sources, but those listed below are some of the books I consulted for this work.

Benedetti, María Dolores Hajosy. *Hasta los baños te curan: Remedios caseros y mucho más de Puerto Rico.* Maplewood, New Jersey: Waterfront Press, 1991.

Camargo, Maria Thereza L. de Arruda. *Plantas medicinais e de rituais afro-brasileiros.* Sao Paulo: ALMED, 1988.

Coon, Nelson. *Using Plants for Healing.* Emmaus, Penna.: Rodale Press, 1963.

Heinerman, John. *Science of Herbal Medicine: Pharmacological, Medical, Historical, Anthropological.* Orem, Utah: Bi-World Publishers, 1979.

Hutchens, Alma R. *Indian Herbology of North America: The Definitive Guide to Native Medicinal Plants and Their Uses.* Boston: Shambhala, 1991.

Lad, Vasant, and David Frawley. *The Yoga of Herbs.* Santa Fe: Lotus Press, 1986.

Lust, John. *The Herb Book.* New York: Bantam, 1974.

Moore, Michael. *Medicinal Plants of the Desert and Canyon West.* Santa Fe: Museum of New Mexico Press, 1989.

Pompa, Gerónimo. *Medicamentos indígenas.* Panama: Editorial America, S.A.

Tierra, Michael. *The Way of Herbs.* Santa Cruz: Unity Press, 1980.

Tierra, Michael. *Planetary Herbology.* Santa Fe: Lotus Press, 1988.

INDEX OF HISTORICAL PERSONS

FRAY IÑIGO ABBAD Y LASIERRA
A Spanish monk who traveled in Puerto Rico in the 1770s and wrote *Historia geográfica, civil y natural de la isla de San Juan Bautista de Puerto Rico.*

RAMON EMETERIO BETANCES
Betances was a mulatto doctor from Mayagüez who became one of the principal leaders of the Lares uprising of 1868.

MARIANA BRACETTI
Bracetti was a leader of one of the underground cells that took part in the 1868 uprising against Spain. She was called "Brazo de Oro" or "Golden Arm" and sewed the flag for the revolutionary movement.

CASTAÑER AND PIETRI
Castañer and Pietri were major landholders in the coffee region of Western Puerto Rico in the late nineteenth and early twentieth century.

ROSA COLLAZO
A nationalist activist and the wife of Oscar Collazo who attempted to assassinate President Truman in 1950.

Maestro Rafael Cordero

The younger brother of Celestina Cordero, Rafael was a cigar maker and ran a school for boys of many class and "race" backgrounds. He is portrayed in a famous painting, surrounded by his pupils.

Manolo El Leñero

Manuel Rojas, a Venezuelan immigrant to Puerto Rico, was one of the leaders of the 1868 uprising against Spain. He was called "El Leñero" or "The Woodcutter."

Luis Ferré

The Ferrés are a wealthy family from Ponce. Luis Ferré was governor of Puerto Rico in the 1970s.

Dolores "Lolita" Lebron

Lolita Lebron led three male Puerto Rican Nationalists in an attack on the U.S. Congress on March 1, 1954. She spent twenty-five years in prison and is a heroic figure to the Puerto Rican independence movement.

Pedro Matos

A respected community elder in Utuado, Puerto Rico.

Luis Muñoz Rivera

Muñoz Rivera was an autonomist politician at the end of the nineteenth century. His son Luis Muñoz Marín was the first elected governor of Puerto Rico.

Mansa Musa

Ruler of Mali starting in 1312.

Don Pedro

Pedro Albizu Campos was the leader of the Puerto Rican Nationalist Movement and was active from the 1920s until his death in the 1960s. A fiery speaker and popular leader, he spent many years in prison.

Saladin

Salah-al-Din Yusuf ibn Ayyub, Egyptian sultan who defeated the crusaders in 1187 and went on to take Jerusalem.

Sundiata

Sundiata expanded and consolidated the new state of Mali through the conquest of much of Ghana in 1240.